FUNDAMENTALS OF ACCOUNTING

BASIC ACCOUNTING PRINCIPLES SIMPLIFIED FOR ACCOUNTING STUDENTS

Donatila Agtarap-San Juan

AuthorHouse™
1663 Liberty Drive, Suite 200
Bloomington, IN 47403
www.authorhouse.com
Phone: 1-800-839-8640

©2007 Donatila Agtarap-San Juan. All rights reserved.

No part of this book may be reproduced, stored in a retrieval system, or transmitted by any means without the written permission of the author.

First published by AuthorHouse 9/19/2007

ISBN: 978-1-4343-2299-9 (sc)

Library of Congress Control Number: 2007904825

Printed in the United States of America
Bloomington, Indiana

This book is printed on acid-free paper.

FUNDAMENTALS OF ACCOUNTING

*BASIC ACCOUNTING PRINCIPLES
SIMPLIFIED FOR ACCOUNTING STUDENTS*

DONATILA AGTARAP-SAN JUAN

FOREWORD

I often hear my students say "I don't like accounting. It is hard". Sometimes they approach me and tell me "It is not you, but I really can not understand accounting. While I am inside the classroom listening to you, I understand the lesson but if I study on my own, I am lost. I can not remember what you discussed in class". These are not unusual comments I get from my accounting students. I try to explain to them that I do not disagree with what they say, but as we progress in the study of accounting, they will find out that accounting is not as hard as they think and that in due time, they can develop an interest in accounting.

I have adopted a teaching approach whereby I try to present accounting in very simple terms, using examples that students can relate to, which will enable them to understand the concept by connecting to the example. At the same time I teach accounting in what I call the step-by-step method. I start with the concept, followed by examples and illustrative problems. Assignments are always given to test if students understand the concepts and apply them through problem solving.

I observed that students have an inherent dislike for subjects that require the application of concepts learned. Accounting is involved with learning concepts and applying the concepts in problem solving. To complicate matters, in the application of concepts, numbers and mathematics, another "disliked" subject is oftentimes used.

I teach accounting in addition to other business subjects, like management and marketing. Because students have a notion that accounting is difficult, they develop a mental block in understanding accounting concepts which then makes it difficult for the faculty to teach accounting. So accounting is not only difficult to learn but it is also difficult to teach.

I believe that anything can be learned and learning is a life-long process. Our capacity to learn is limitless. As I analyze the situation of the accounting student, I decided that I can do something to present accounting in a student-friendly and simplified format. I decided to write a basic accounting textbook that will discuss what accounting is all about and walk the student through the steps in the accounting process. As the accounting process is discussed, the connection of the different steps is emphasized. In this book, eight business entities engaged in services that are familiar to students are used in the chapter problems so that the student can relate to the relationship of one accounting process to another. Ordinary day to day words are used to discuss the various accounting concepts and principles.

The objective of the book is to simplify accounting to enable the students acquire a strong basic foundation of accounting knowledge. The study of accounting is progressive; a student must know the basic accounting concepts before he can understand more advanced accounting concepts. A student who has a weak foundation in accounting concepts will have difficulty learning more advanced accounting courses. Oftentimes, I encounter students enrolled in higher accounting courses who have very weak basic accounting know how. These students are the ones who eventually drop out from their accounting courses. I am challenged to inspire students that they can learn accounting; but I feel that I have to do my part. By writing a textbook that I know is simple but comprehensive enough to be understood, I hope I can reach more students, not only the ones I teach.

To the accounting students, I dedicate this book to you and I hope that I am able to inspire you to pursue an accounting career. I know you can do it!!

FUNDAMENTALS OF ACCOUNTING
BASIC ACCOUNTING PRINCIPLES
SIMPLIFIED FOR ACCOUNTING STUDENTS

TABLE OF CONTENTS

PART I   **INTRODUCTION TO THE ACCOUNTING PROCESS**

CHAPTER 01   **THE ACCOUNTING PROFESSION**

- Accounting definition
- Accountability of the accountant
- Bookkeeping, accounting and auditing
- Users of financial information
- Generally accepted accounting principles (GAAPS)
  - Going concern
  - Conservatism
  - Separate business entity
  - Consistency
  - Full disclosure
  - Materiality
  - Matching of costs and revenues
  - Monetary measurement
  - Stable currency
  - Objectivity
  - Realization
- Career opportunities for accountants
  - Management accountant
  - Certified Public Accountant (CPA)
  - Internal auditor
- Review Questions
- Self-assessment Examination
- Problems

02   **THE ACCOUNTING EQUATIONS**

- Basic accounting equation
- Expanded accounting equation
- Accounting elements
  - Assets
  - Liabilities
  - Capital
  - Revenues
  - Expenses
  - Drawing
- Classification of assets

Classification of liabilities
Importance of understanding accounting elements
Preparation of expanded accounting equation chart
Review Questions
Self-assessment Examination
Problems

PART II   THE ACCOUNTING PROCESS

CHAPTER 03   ANALYZING TRANSACTIONS

Business transaction
Types of business transactions
Analyzing and its importance
Separate business entity concept
Rules of debit and credit
Normal balance of account
Double entry accounting system
Chart of accounts
Transaction analysis chart
T account as an analysis tool
Posting, footing and balancing T account
Review Questions
Self-assessment Examination
Problems

04   THE BOOKS OF ACCOUNTS

Accounting cycle and accounting period
Calendar year and fiscal year
Accounting process – input, processing and output
Steps in the accounting process
Books of accounts
The general journal
Journalizing
Parts of a general journal entry
Rules in journalizing
Special combination journals
Types of accounting entries
The general ledger
Rules in posting to the general ledger
Review Questions
Self-assessment Examination
Exercises
Problems

05 THE TRIAL BALANCE

The summarizing process
Types of trial balance
    Trial balance
    Adjusted trial balance
    Post-closing trial balance
Review Questions
Self-assessment Examination
Problems

06 THE ADJUSTING ENTRIES

Definition of adjusting entries
Purpose of adjusting entries
Matching of costs and revenues
Cost recovery principle
Expressed/explicit vs. implied/implicit transactions
Cash basis and accrual basis accounting
Types of adjusting entries
Accounting for prepaid expenses
    Asset method
    Expense method
Accrual of expenses and payables
Accrual of revenues and receivables
Accounting for unearned revenues
    Liability method
    Revenue method
Long-term assets
Types of long-term assets
Depreciation expense using the straight line method
    Historical cost
    Salvage value
    Depreciable cost
    Useful life
    Accumulated depreciation (allowance for depreciation)
    Book value
Accounts receivable
Bad debts expense
    Direct write-off and allowance method
        Allowance method using the percentage of sales
Review Questions
Self-assessment Examination
Problems

07 THE WORKSHEET

The worksheet as an accounting tool
Worksheet money columns
    Trial balance
    Adjustments
    Adjusted trial balance
    Income statement
    Balance sheet
Preparing the worksheet
Review Questions
Self-assessment Examination
Problems

08 THE FINANCIAL STATEMENTS

Accounting reports
Formal and informal accounting reports
Financial statements
    Income statement
        Single-step income statement
        Multiple-step income statement
    Equity statement
        Statement of owner's equity
        Statement of partners' equity
        Statement of stockholders' equity
    Balance sheet
        Account form balance sheet
        Report form balance sheet
    Statement of cash flows
        Direct method and indirect method
        Operating activities
        Financing activities
        Investing activities
Review Questions
Self-assessment Examination
Exercises
Problems

09 THE CLOSING ENTRIES and THE POST CLOSING TRIAL BALANCE

Definition of closing entries
Purpose of closing entries
Nominal or temporary accounts

Real or permanent accounts
Types of closing entries
Income and expense summary account
Post-closing/after closing trial balance
Review Questions
Self-assessment Examination
Problems

10 THE REVERSING ENTRIES

Definition of reversing entries
Purpose of reversing entries
Types of reversing entries
    Prepaid expenses using the expense method
    Unearned revenues using the revenue method
    Accrued revenues and receivables
    Accrued expenses and payables
Review Questions
Self-assessment Examination
Exercises
Problems

PART III FINANCIAL STATEMENTS INTERPRETATION

CHAPTER 11 FINANCIAL STATEMENTS ANALYSIS

Assessing company performance
Qualitative evaluation
    Company reputation
    Business ethics practices
    Corporate responsibility projects
    Competitive advantage
Sources of financial information
    Internal sources
    External sources
Quantitative evaluation
    Trend analysis
    Vertical analysis
    Horizontal analysis
    Component percentages
    Financial ratios
        Short term liquidity ratios
            Working capital
            Current ratio
            Acid test/quick ratio

    Accounts receivable turnover ratio
    Days sales in receivable
    Inventory turnover ratio
    Days sales in inventory
    Cash-to-cash operating cycle
   Long-term solvency ratios
    Total debts to total assets ratio
    Total debts to total equity ratio
    Interest coverage ratio
   Profitability ratios
    Gross profit ratio
    Return on equity
    Return on sales
    Return on assets
    Asset turnover ratio
  Evaluation of financial ratios
   Historical evaluation
   Benchmarks or rule of thumb
   Comparison with competitors' performance
Review Questions
Self-assessment Examination
Problems

CHAPTER 01 THE ACCOUNTING PROFESSION

LEARNING OBJECTIVES

L01 Define accounting. Describe some of the functions involved in accounting.

L02 Explain why accounting is called the language of business.

L03 Discuss the professional code of ethics of accountants.

L04 Identify and describe professional bodies that issue pronouncements on accounting principles and standards.

L05 Differentiate bookkeeping, accounting and auditing.

L06 Identify the users of financial information and the financial information needs of each user.

L07 Define generally accepted accounting principles. Identify and describe the GAAPs.

L08 Differentiate a management accountant from a public accountant.

L09 Differentiate an internal auditor from an external auditor.

L10 Discuss the career opportunities for accountants.

CHAPTER 01 THE ACCOUNTING PROFESSION

ACCOUNTING DEFINED

Accounting is the art of collecting, analyzing, recording and posting, summarizing and reporting financial transactions in a significant and orderly manner to provide useful information essential to decision making. Accounting also includes the function of interpreting the significance of the relationships of information reflected in the financial statements. Financial statements are the financial reports produced in the accounting process and consist of the income statement, balance sheet, equity statement and the statement of cash flows. Note that accounting is interested in transactions that are financial in nature, meaning only transactions measurable in terms of money are the subject matter of any accounting activity. If a business entity celebrates its 10th anniversary, this is a milestone for the business; however, this event is not considered an accounting transaction. On the other hand, if the business spent money to celebrate its anniversary, then the amount of money spent will be properly reflected in the accounting records. Accounting also makes sure that reporting of financial transactions is done in a significant manner. Generally accepted accounting principles (GAAPs) are uniformly and consistently applied in the recording of transactions and in the preparation of financial statements, so that users of financial information will not be misled when they use the information reflected in the financial statements.

Accounting is oftentimes referred to as the **language of business.** The financial statements are used to communicate the results of the operations and financial strength of a business entity. By evaluating the information reflected in audited financial statements, the users of financial information are able to make a judgment on the financial strength and viability of a business entity. By making a comparison of the financial statements of a business entity from year to year, a knowledgeable financial professional will be able to measure the profitability, direction and financial condition of a business entity. By making a comparison of the financial performance of a business entity with its competitors over a specific period of time, then one can measure the competitive financial strength of a business entity. Note that when people want to make a judgment related to a business entity, very often they do not communicate directly with the personnel of the business entity. They usually analyze the financial statements before making a financial decision concerning the business entity. The financial statements then serve as the communication medium by which the financial health of a business entity is measured.

THE ACCOUNTING PROFESSION

The accounting profession is a responsible and accountable profession. Accountants adhere to very high standard of professional ethics and professional conduct. Compared with other professions, members of the accounting profession, specifically the certified public accountant (CPA) are accountable to every person who relied on the financial statements in making a decision using the information contained in such statement, regardless of the fact that these parties did not engage his services directly in the first place. A medical doctor is only accountable to the patients that he treats. His accountability and responsibility is limited to the patients who engaged his services. In the same manner, a lawyer is only accountable to the clients that he represents. He is obligated to defend his clients alone, and his services are limited to the clients who come to him for legal services. What about the CPA? The scope of the CPA's responsibility **seems to be unlimited**. Firstly, he is accountable to the business entity that engaged his professional services. When a CPA expresses an opinion on the financial statements of a business entity, the financial statements become **audited financial statements** and oftentimes the external users of the financial statements require audited financial statements when they evaluate the financial health of a business entity. In addition to his clients, the CPA is **accountable to the general public,** which means **anybody who relied on the audited financial statements in making business decisions.** If the decision maker feels that he was misled in making a decision using the audited financial statements and he feels that the CPA did not exercise due professional care and diligence in the performance of the audit, he can sue the CPA, even though he did not engage the professional services of the CPA, he simply used the audited financial statements in his decision making. The word **public** in the title **Certified Public Accountant** carries a lot of responsibility and accountability on the part of the CPA. That is why the CPA adheres to generally accepted auditing standards when he audits the financial records and when he expresses an opinion on the financial statements of a business entity. It must be noted though that the financial records and the financial statements are owned by the business entity and the representations are done by the business entity.

Because of the enormous responsibility and accountability of the CPA, in practically all countries, a national professional organization establishes principles, rules and procedures that guide accountants in the performance of their professional responsibilities. In the United States, the American Institute of Certified Public Accountants (AICPA) is the national governing membership body that oversees this responsibility. The AICPA establishes ethical and auditing standards to be adhered to by CPAs in the performance of audit. It also conducts and administers the licensing examination for CPAs, which is essential before an accountant can discharge the function of a CPA (which is to issue an auditor's report). Under the AICPA umbrella, there are two separate bodies that issue pronouncements about accounting standards, the Financial Accounting Standards Board (FASB) and the Government Accounting Standards Board (GASB). The FASB issues pronouncements on accounting principles from 1974 to the present. From 1959 to 1973, the predecessor of FASB, the Accounting Principles Board (APB) of the AICPA, through its various accounting technical committees issued pronouncements on accounting principles. The GASB issues pronouncements about accounting principles and accounting standards concerning the accounting in the government sector.

Many business entities operate internationally, and this is now more predominantly practiced during the 21st century. With globalization and the advancement in information technology and telecommunications, the world is now the marketplace for many businesses. These business changes offer challenges to the accounting profession, as more and more people all over the world will now be relying on the financial statements in making business decisions. As a consequence, it is not unusual for professional associations of accountants and auditors from all over the world to be consulting each other on various accounting and auditing principles, standards and procedures. For instance, Japanese accountants through its equivalent of AICPA may come to consult with AICPA committee members with respect to specific accounting issues. International conferences and various professional fora are conducted by the members of the accounting profession to consult with each other, communicate and discuss various accounting and auditing concerns that will benefit the international accounting and auditing profession. The International Accounting Standards Committee (IASC) was formed in 1973 as an independent private sector organization that aims to synchronize accounting principles, rules, procedures, covenants and practices for financial reporting throughout the world. As of June 2006, 146 professional accounting organizations from 106 member countries are represented in the IASC.

BOOKKEEPING, ACCOUNTING and AUDITING

Many people are confused about bookkeeping, accounting and auditing. Oftentimes, a layman thinks that these three are synonymous with one another. **Bookkeeping** is the recording phase of the accounting process. It involves recording accounting journal entries in the general journal and posting these general journal entries in the general ledger. The general journal and the general ledger are the two books of accounts; hence the person who keeps and maintains these books is called the **bookkeeper**. Bookkeeping is only one of the steps involved in the accounting process. As you can see later, there are other activities involved in accounting, in addition to bookkeeping. Therefore, accounting covers a wider scope of activities compared with bookkeeping. **Auditing (sometimes referred to as public accounting)** involves the application of generally accepted auditing standards, methods, testing and procedures in order to determine that business entities adhere to generally accepted accounting principles in the preparation of their financial statements. The auditor, specifically, the **certified public accountant (CPA)** after conducting a thorough audit, issues an audit report whereby he expresses an opinion whether the financial statements present fairly the results of operation and financial condition of the business in accordance with generally accepted accounting principles (GAAPs) that are consistently applied. The CPA therefore must be very well versed in the application of GAAPs. In terms of scope of accounting knowledge, among the three (bookkeeper, accountant, auditor), the CPA/auditor is seen as the one with the broadest accounting know how and expertise. The minimum educational attainment for an accountant is a four year baccalaureate degree major in accounting, whereas the CPA must pass the licensing examination in addition to the completion of a baccalaureate degree in accounting.

USERS OF FINANCIAL INFORMATION

Users of financial information can be classified into **external users** and **internal users.** **External users** of financial information are those who are not part of the operation of the business entity such as the **creditors, investors, government, labor unions and the**

general public. Creditors are outside parties who extend credit or provide loans to the business entity. Banks, financial institutions and trade suppliers are examples of creditors. Creditors use the financial statements of business entity in order to evaluate the credit worthiness of the business; to be assured that the business will be able to pay its maturing financial obligations on time. When a business entity applies for a loan, the banks want to make sure that the interest and principal payments will be paid as they become due. Suppliers want to make sure that they will be paid on time when they extend trade credits to customers. Suppliers do not want to have a build up of bad debts or uncollectible accounts receivables. **Investors** are outside parties who invest money into the business with the hope that they will earn money for their investments. The stockholders of a publicly traded corporation usually evaluate the dividend payment history and the market value of the stock of the corporation, in addition to the overall environment where the business operates before buying the stock of a particular corporation. The information used in the evaluation made by potential investor stockholders is obtained from the financial statements of the corporation. The **government** is a user of the financial information because taxes collected are based on the financial statements that the business entity files with government agencies, such as the Internal Revenue Service (IRS). **Labor unions** are interested in the financial condition of a business in order to assess if the business can afford improvements in wages and fringe benefits that it will propose during labor-management bargaining negotiations. It is impractical for labor unions to ask for wage and benefit improvements that the business entity can not afford. The **general public** is a user of the financial information. Sometimes, law suits are filed against business entities and the financial statements can show the financial capability of the business to pay the amount of damages and legal claims filed against it.

Internal users of financial information are those who are part of the operation of the business. **Management** uses various financial reports, in addition to the financial statements in order to evaluate its operational performance and to address specific and potential areas in its operations that require management action. At the same time, management wants to see if its strategic plans can be supported financially by the business. Some expansion programs, for instance, penetrating the international market, opening new plants, rehabilitating old plant facilities, etc. require a big amount of financial resources and management must be able to make a decision based on the financial information available. Management also makes decisions with respect to salary and benefits improvements, negotiations with labor unions and therefore it must be knowledgeable about its financial ability and capability to satisfy many of its commitments. A well-informed management team is in a better position to make sound decisions in all aspect of the business operations. **Employees** are also internal users of financial information. Employees want to work for business entities that will not go bankrupt. Employees do not want to be casualties of retrenchment programs resulting from cost reduction measures implemented by businesses. At the same time, some companies have pension plans that invest in its own stocks and when employees opt to invest in the stock of its employer, employees want to make sure that they will not lose their nest egg. Therefore, employee-investors must be aware of the financial viability of their employer, because if something wrong happens financially, they will be doubly hit. Unfortunately, this is what happened to many employees of Enron. Before the collapse of

Enron in 2002, it was one of the best performing stocks in the stock market. Many employees thought they have a secured nest egg at retirement. Many long time employees of Enron lost their life time savings when the market value of Enron stocks plummeted as soon as its corporate scandals were exposed.

The **board of directors** is a group of individuals who are elected by stockholders. Directors are tasked with policy making responsibilities and together with the top management make important decisions with respect to the strategic directions of the company. Some directors are also members of top management. Sometimes, corporations have outside directors. **Outside directors** are not involved with the operations of the business. It is oftentimes a subject of debate whether to classify the board directors as external users or internal users of financial information. Since directors are privy into the affairs of the business tasked with policy making decisions, it is therefore more appropriate to classify them as internal users rather than external users of financial information.

GENERALLY ACCEPTED ACCOUNTING PRINCIPLES (GAAPs)

As mentioned earlier, the FASB issues pronouncements on generally accepted accounting principles. It is essential that certain principles are followed by accountants in order to maintain the integrity, reliability and fairness of financial statements. Financial statements of companies are evaluated by various users from year to year. At the same time financial statements of various companies are evaluated by professionals when they make decisions pertaining to these companies. In order to enhance the comparability of financial statements it is essential that they are prepared following the generally accepted accounting principles, rules and procedures. For purposes of this book, accounting principles, accounting concepts and accounting assumptions are used synonymously. These are accounting practices that are used as the framework that guides the recording of financial transactions and the preparation of financial statements to preserve their reliability, integrity and comparability. These are adopted in order to protect all users of financial information and provide them with reliable information useful in decision making.

The principle of **going concern** stipulates that the business entity will continue its normal operations and will not terminate its business operations. Can you imagine if this principle is not applied in the recording of business transactions and in the preparation of financial statements? The user of the financial statements will always have a doubt as to the continuous existence of the business. If this is the case, then potential investors will not be investing in a business that will be terminating its operations because they do not want to lose their investment. How are creditors affected, if at the back of their minds, they doubt the continued existence of their debtor? Creditors will stop lending to businesses that have the threat of stopping its operations, because these businesses will not be able to settle their financial obligations. What about the employees of the business? Of course employees do not want to work for companies that will be closing down its operations. The principle of **conservatism** provides that if there is a choice among several alternative courses of action, the accountant must select the one that will result in the least favorable effect on the results of operations and financial conditions. In other words, if there is a choice between two equally acceptable accounting methods or procedures, the alternative that will result in lower net income or less favorable effect on balance sheet items must be used. The principle of conservatism prevents companies from manipulating financial transactions to reflect more favorable outcome. It protects the users of financial statements who rely on the financial statements with respect to the representations of the business about its financial health. The principle of **separate business entity** states that the business entity has a personality separate and distinct from its owners. All business transactions are analyzed and recorded from the point of view of the business, not from the point of view of the owner. The assets of the business are not the assets of the owner. The owner can not use the asset of the business to pay for his personal expenses and treat his personal expenses as expenses of the business. If the owner is given the opportunity to raid the coffers of the business to pay for his personal expenses, the operating funds of the business might be exhausted which might eventually result in bankruptcy. Again, this principle is followed to protect the various users of financial information. The principle of **consistency** states that accounting principles, rules, methods and procedures must be applied in the same manner from year to year in order to enhance the comparability and maintain the integrity of financial statements. Do you think that financial statements will be reliable if business can simply use accounting principles, methods, rules and procedures as they please, changing from one method to another that will produce better results in its favor? If this is allowed, naturally businesses will switch to accounting practice that will be favorable to them from year to year. It will be very difficult to make evaluations of financial statements from year to year if they are prepared in inconsistent manner. For instance, if the business used the straight line method of depreciation, it must follow this method consistently from year to year. Or if the allowance method is used in accounting for bad debts expense, it must stick to the allowance method every year. However, changes in accounting principles, methods, rules and procedures are allowed if the change will produce a fairer presentation of the financial statements. If an accounting change was made, proper disclosure must be made in the financial statements and the effect in prior period financial statements must be disclosed. The principle of **full disclosure** provides that accounting information and other relevant information must be identified and explained in the financial statements so that the financial statements will provide better information and will not be misleading to the users of the financial information. Disclosures are shown in the financial statements either as footnotes accompanying the financial statements or shown in the body of the financial statements as a parenthetical note after the affected accounts. Some information that need to be disclosed are non-recurring items that are material in amount, subsequent events that occurred after the balance sheet date but before the publication of the audited financial statements (for instance, if a fire gutted the factory of the business and the effect is material, the financial impact of the fire must be disclosed), changes in accounting principles, rules, methods and procedures, etc. Disclosures are made in order to provide information to users of financial statements so that they are guided properly when they make decisions relying on the representations made in the financial statements. The principle of **materiality** is closely related to the full disclosure principle. According to the principle of materiality, businesses are obligated to disclose in their financial statements significant or material information that might affect the judgment of a reasonably informed person in making a decision that might be influenced by knowing or not knowing the material information. In actual practice, some companies establish specific cut off amounts for specific accounts to define material amounts. Of course what constitutes as material amount for one company maybe immaterial or insignificant for another company, because of the differences in company size, operational territories, market environment, etc. For example, ABC Company has outstanding accounts receivable of $100,000 as of December 31, 2005. It determined that its major customer XYZ Company filed for bankruptcy on January 10, 2006. ABC Company has outstanding receivable of $70,000 from XYZ Company. Since the $70,000 receivable from XYZ is substantial relative to the total receivable of ABC Company (70% of the total) and there is very little chance that it is collectible since XYZ Company is already bankrupt, the amount is considered material and should be disclosed in the financial statements as uncollectible. However, if the total receivable of ABC Company is $10,000,000, then the $70,000 uncollectible account from XYZ is considered immaterial and therefore need not be disclosed in the financial statements. The principle of **matching of costs and revenues** provides that revenues must be recorded in the same accounting period or over the same periods as expenses, costs or expenditures are spent or will provide the benefits, to earn the revenues. For instance, the business bought a long-term asset delivery van for $25,000 in 2005. It is estimated that the van will be used to deliver products over a five-year period. It is not correct to record $25,000 as expense in 2005 because the van will be useful for 5 years. The correct accounting treatment is to record in 2005 the purchase of the delivery van as an asset. During the period 2005-2009, it is necessary to record **depreciation expense** to match the expense against the revenues that will be generated with the use of the delivery van. The principle of **monetary measurement** means that money is the most appropriate unit of measure used in recording financial transactions and reporting financial statements. Related to the monetary measurement principle is the principle of **stable currency** which states that the purchasing power of the currency used in the recording of transactions and in the preparation of the financial statements is not subject to major fluctuations in value. Therefore, users of the financial statements are confident that the monetary values expressed in the financial statements will maintain its integrity since the currency is stable and not subject to major devaluation. If users are not assured of the stability of the currency used, there will be a lot of fears about the reliability of the representations made in the financial statements. At the same time, there maybe a lot of speculations made about the economic stability of the country using an unstable currency. Of course situations may arise when the currency of a particular country is subject to major fluctuations and the accounting procedures for these situations are appropriately discussed in advanced accounting courses. The principle of **objectivity** provides that financial information reflected in the accounting records and in the financial statements is unbiased and verifiable by objective and fair validation of documentary evidence. Before transactions are recorded, source documents (invoices, official receipts, checks, etc.) which are always verifiable, are used as the basis for recording the entries in the books of accounts. For example, if a business buys computer equipment for $5,000 and issued check 0001 to pay for the computer; the documentary evidence used as the basis in recording the cash purchase of the computer are the sales invoice of the supplier and the check issued for the payment. Businesses can not invent or manufacture journal entries in their books of accounts simply because they wanted to do so without verifiable evidences of these transactions. The **realization** principle identifies that changes in assets, liabilities, revenues, costs, capital and expenses should not be recognized until the change is definitely certain and that the change is measurable in monetary terms to justify the recognition in the books of accounts. Therefore, income realization must happen before income recognition. For instance, the point of sale is considered to be the appropriate time to recognize income. Businesses do not record the sale until it is definitely certain that it has occurred; inquiries from prospective customers are not recognized as sales. The principles of conservatism and objectivity support income realization.

CAREER OPPORTUNITIES FOR ACCOUNTANTS

Career opportunities for accountants can be grouped into two classifications, based on the clientele that they serve. Private accountants are those who provide services to companies who engaged their services only; while public accountants, generally called the CPA or the external auditor are engaged by companies and are also accountable and responsible to external users of financial information.

Private accountants are commonly referred to as **management accountants**. Management accountants are usually employees of companies. The functions performed by management accountants may include general accounting, subsidiary ledger accounting, cost accounting, budgeting, financial planning and forecasting, tax planning, tax accounting, management advisory services, etc. The **chief financial officer (CFO)** is the highest ranked financial position in a business organization and he has the primary responsibility of managing effectively and efficiently the financial affairs of the business. **General accountants** perform the activities included in the accounting process from analyzing of business transactions to the preparation and interpretation of financial statements. **Subsidiary ledger accountants** maintain individual subsidiary ledger records of major general ledger accounts such as accounts receivable, accounts payable, fixed asset accounts, etc. Accountants who keep track of product costs and who establish standard costs for direct materials, direct labor and overhead in a manufacturing concern are called **cost accountants**. **Budget accountants** analyze a company's budget by analyzing variances between actual amounts spent and budgeted amounts and identifying the causes for these variances. **Financial planning and forecasting** are functions that include predicting future financial results and financial condition based on assumptions of the different variables such as interest rates, inflation rate, sales growth, sales volume, pricing considerations and other prevailing situation existing in the environment that the business operates. **Tax accountants** provide tax planning and tax preparation services to help clients obey taxation laws, pay the correct minimum taxes and educate them about taxation issues with the end in view of assisting them maximize their wealth and net worth through tax compliance. Accountants also are tasked to render **management advisory services** to provide advice and inputs in areas that require critical decisions by top management. All the above functions are done by a management accountant. A **certified management accountant (CMA)** is a management accountant duly certified by the Institute of Management Accountant that he passed the certification examination, obtained the required educational and professional experience in accounting practice in the private sector.

An auditor can be classified as either external auditor (CPA) or internal auditor. The **internal auditor** is an employee of the business entity and his functions include strengthening the internal controls, safeguarding business assets, security and risk management and making sure that company policies are being followed. The internal auditor plays a very important role because many companies fail because internal controls are so weak that wrongdoings are easily committed for long periods of time without being detected. If companies do not safeguard their assets, in due time many of them collapse as there are no more assets to back up the operations of the business. In the present age of information technology, when many business operations are dependent on computer and telecommunication technology, businesses and customers are so concerned about the security risks that computer facilities and files are exposed to. A relatively new opportunity is available to internal auditors in the area of information technology. Oftentimes internal auditors are consulted by software systems analysts and designers to provide input on how to tighten security controls in computerized systems. A **certified internal auditor (CIA)** is a person who successfully passed the certification examination administered by the Institute of Internal Auditor. An information systems auditor is a person who applies his information systems knowledge in the overall business process with emphasis on internal controls, risk and security management and safeguarding company assets. A **certified information systems auditor (CISA)** is an information systems auditor who successfully passed the examination administered by the Information Systems Audit and Control Association (ISACA), an organization present in more than 100 countries with the objective of conducting research and development and providing guidelines in the governance, control and assurance of information, computer and telecommunication technology and further the knowledge of the information system auditing as a profession. As mentioned earlier, the **external auditor** otherwise known as the **CPA** is a professional who passed the licensing examination administered by the American Institute of CPAs (AICPA). The CPA is a person who examines the financial records of the business and issues an auditors report where he expresses an opinion on the financial statements of the business. Once an **auditor's report** accompanies the financial statements, they become **audited financial statements.** Users of financial statements rely on the audited financial statements and base their decisions on the representations made in the financial statements. If the stocks of a corporation are traded in the stock exchanges, such as the New York Stock exchange, it is mandatory that the audited financial statements be filed with the Securities and Exchange Commission (SEC).

The unfortunate corporate scandals in recent years that caused the major collapse of businesses resulted in tighter SEC filing requirements. The United States Congress passed the **Sarbanes-Oxley (SOX) Act of 2002** that amended securities and other laws in order to prevent corporations from committing massive financial irregularities and fraud to protect the investing public. The SOX act changed corporate governance particularly in the areas of directors and officers' responsibilities, regulation of public accounting firms, reporting requirements and enforcement. The SOX Act applies to US and non-US corporations that have equity and debt securities registered with the SEC under the Securities Act of 1934. As an aftermath of corporate scandals, **forensic accountants** are being used during the prosecution and trials of corporate crimes.

So many career opportunities are available to accountants and the significant roles that they play in the business world continue to expand and become indispensable as businesses give a lot of importance to the different functions that accountants perform.

CHAPTER 01   THE ACCOUNTING PROFESSION

REVIEW QUESTIONS

1. What is accounting? Identify the various functions included in accounting.

2. Why is accounting called the language of business?

3. Identify the effects of globalization in the accounting profession.

4. Why are generally accepted accounting principles adopted?

5. Identify and describe the generally accepted accounting principles.

6. What is the Sarbanes-Oxley Act of 2002?

7. Differentiate bookkeeping, accounting and auditing.

8. Why is the scope of the CPA's responsibility considered to be unlimited?

9. What are some professional bodies that are tasked to issue pronouncements on GAAPs?

10. Who are the internal users of financial information? What are their financial information needs?

11. Who are the external users of financial information? What are their financial information needs?

12. Identify and describe the career opportunities for management accountants.

13. Identify and describe the career opportunities for auditors.

14. What are audited financial statements?

15. Identify some institutions that administer certification examinations for accountants.

CHAPTER 01 THE ACCOUNTING PROFESSION

REVIEW EXAMINATION

TRUE OR FALSE: *WRITE TRUE or FALSE IN THE BLANK BEFORE EACH ITEM.*

_____ 01. Accounting is the art of collecting, analyzing, recording and posting, summarizing and reporting financial transactions in a significant manner in order to provide useful information essential to decision making.

_____ 02. Accounting is interested in transactions that are financial in nature, meaning only transactions measurable in terms of money are the subject matter of any accounting activity.

_____ 03. Bookkeeping is oftentimes referred to as the language of business.

_____ 04. The financial statements are used to communicate the results of the business operations and financial strength of a business entity.

_____ 05. When people want to make a judgment related to a business entity, very often they communicate directly with the personnel of the business entity.

_____ 06. The accounting profession is a responsible and accountable profession.

_____ 07. The scope of the CPA's responsibility seems to be very limited.

_____ 08. The CPA is not accountable to the general public, which means anybody who relied on the audited financial statements in making business decisions.

_____ 09. With globalization and the advancement in information technology and telecommunications, the world is now the marketplace for many businesses.

_____ 10. Auditing is the recording phase of the accounting process.

_____ 11. Labor unions are outside parties who extend credit or provide loans to the business entity.

_____ 12. The board of directors are interested in the financial condition of a business in order to assess if the business will be able to afford wages and fringe benefits that it will propose during labor management bargaining negotiations.

_____ 13. External users of financial information are those who are part of the operation of the business.

_____ 14. The board of directors is a group of individuals who are elected by stockholders.

_____ 15. The separate entity principle stipulates that the business entity will continue its normal operations and will not terminate its business operations

_____ 16. The principle of consistency states that accounting principles, rules, methods and procedures must be applied in the same manner from year to year in order to enhance the comparability and maintain the integrity of financial statements.

_____ 17. Public accountants are commonly referred to as management accountants.

_____ 18. Budget accountants analyze a company's budget by analyzing variances between actual amounts spent and budgeted amounts and identifying the causes for these variances.

_____ 19. The internal auditor is an employee of the business entity and his functions include strengthening the internal controls, safeguarding business assets, security and risk management and making sure that company policies are being followed.

_____ 20. The United States Congress passed the Securities Act of 2002 that amended securities and other laws in order to prevent corporations from committing massive financial irregularities and fraud to protect the investing public.

FILL IN THE BLANK: *WRITE THE CORRECT ANSWER IN THE SPACE PROVIDED.*

01. _____ is the art of collecting, analyzing, recording and posting, summarizing and reporting financial transactions in a significant manner in order to provide useful information essential to decision making.

02. Financial statements are the financial reports produced in the accounting process and consist of the _____, _____, _____ and the _____.

03. Accounting is oftentimes referred to as the _____.

04. By evaluating the information reflected in audited financial statements, _____ of financial information are able to make a judgment on the financial strength and viability of a business entity.

05. The _____ serve as the communication medium by which the financial health of a business entity is measured.

06. When a CPA expresses an opinion on the financial statements of a business entity, the financial statements become _____ financial statements.

07. In the United States, the _____ is the national governing membership body that oversees that ethical and auditing standards are adhered to by CPAs in the performance of audit.

08. The _____ issues pronouncements on accounting principles from 1974 to the present.

09. The _____ issues pronouncements about accounting principles and accounting standards concerning the accounting in the government sector.

10. The _____ was formed in 1973 as an independent private sector organization that aims to synchronize accounting principles, rules, procedures, covenants and practices for financial reporting throughout the world.

11. _____ involves the application of generally accepted auditing standards, methods, testing and procedures in order to determine that business entities adhere to generally accepted accounting principles in the preparation of their financial statements.

12. _____ are outside parties who invest money into the business with the hope that they will earn money for their investments.

13. The _____ is a user of the financial information because the taxes collected are based on the financial statements that the business entity files with government agencies, such as the Internal Revenue Service (IRS).

14. It is oftentimes a subject of debate whether to classify the_____ as external users or internal users of financial information.

15. It is essential that generally accepted accounting principles are followed by accountants in order to maintain the _____, _____ and _____ of financial statements.

16. The principle of _____ stipulates that the business entity will continue its normal operations and will not terminate its business operations.

17. The principle of _____ provides that if there is a choice among several alternative courses of action, the accountant must select the one that will result in the least favorable effect on the results of operations and financial conditions.

18. The principle of _____ states that the business entity has a personality separate and distinct from its owners.

19. All business transactions are analyzed and recorded from the point of view of the _____, not from the point of view of the owner.

20. The principle of _____ states that accounting principles, rules, methods and procedures must be applied in the same manner from year to year in order to enhance the comparability and maintain the integrity of financial statements.

21. The principle of _____ provides that accounting information and other relevant information must be identified and explained in the financial statements so that the financial statements will provide better information and will not be misleading to the users of the financial information.

22. According to the principle of _____, businesses are obligated to disclose in their financial statements significant or material information that might affect the judgment of a reasonably informed person in making a decision that might be influenced by knowing or not knowing the material information.

23. The principle of _____ provides that revenues must be recorded in the same accounting period or over the same periods as expenses, costs or expenditures are spent or will provide the benefits, to earn the revenues.

24. The principle of _____ means that that money is the most appropriate unit of measure used in recording financial transactions and reporting financial statements.

25. The principle of stable currency which states that the purchasing power of the currency used in the recording of transactions and in the preparation of the financial statements is not subject to _____.

26. The principle of objectivity provides that financial information reflected in the accounting records and in the financial statements is unbiased and verifiable by objective and fair validation of _____.

27. The chief financial officer (CFO) is the highest ranked financial position in a business organization and he has the primary responsibility of managing effectively and efficiently the _____ affairs of the business.

28. _____ accountants keep track of product costs and establish standard costs for direct materials, direct labor and overhead in a manufacturing concern.

29. Financial _____ and _____ are functions that include predicting future financial results and financial condition based on assumptions of the different variables such as interest rates, inflation rate, sales growth, sales volume, pricing considerations and other prevailing situation existing in the environment that the business operates.

Fundamentals of Accounting

30. A certified management accountant (CMA) is a management accountant duly certified by the _____ that he passed the certification examination, obtained the required educational and professional experience in accounting practice in the private sector.

31. The internal auditor is an employee of the business entity and his functions include strengthening the _____, safeguarding _____, _____ and _____ management and making sure that _____ are being followed.

32. A certified internal auditor (CIA) is a person who successfully passed the certification examination administered by the _____.

33. A _____ is an information systems auditor who successfully passed the examination administered by the Information Systems Audit and Control Association (ISACA).

34. The CPA is a person who examines the financial records of the business and issues an auditors report where he expresses an _____ on the financial statements of the business.

35. If the stocks of a corporation are traded in the stock exchanges, such as the New York Stock exchange, it is mandatory that the audited financial statements must be filed with the _____.

36. The United States Congress passed the _____ that amended securities and other laws in order to prevent corporations from committing massive financial irregularities and fraud to protect the investing public.

37. As an aftermath of corporate scandals, _____ are being used during the prosecution and trials of corporate crimes.

38. Oftentimes internal auditors are consulted by software systems analysts and designers to provide input on how to tighten _____ in computerized systems.

39. An auditor can be classified as either _____ auditor or _____ auditor.

40. _____ maintain individual subsidiary ledger records of major general ledger accounts such as accounts receivable, accounts payable, fixed asset accounts, etc.

CHAPTER 02   THE ACCOUNTING EQUATIONS

LEARNING OBJECTIVES

L01   Differentiate the basic accounting equation from the expanded accounting equation.

L02   Define accounting elements. Identify and describe each accounting element.

L03   Define assets. Identify and describe the types of assets.

L03   Define liabilities. Identify and describe the types of liabilities.

L04   Discuss the importance of understanding the accounting elements.

L05   Define the expanded accounting equation chart and discuss how it helps in understanding the accounting equation.

CHAPTER 02 THE ACCOUNTING EQUATIONS

THE ACCOUNTING EQUATIONS

The **basic accounting equation** is expressed as $A = L + OE$. A stands for assets, L stands for liabilities and OE stands for owner's equity. The basic accounting equation serves as the foundation in analyzing business transactions. However, only the **three basic accounting elements** are expressed in the basic accounting equation. To make it easier for accounting students to analyze accounting transactions, the expanded accounting equation is introduced.

The **expanded accounting equation** is expressed as $A = L + (C - D) + (R - E)$. In addition to the basic accounting elements, assets and liabilities, the third basic accounting element, the owner/s' equity is expanded to include C for capital, R for revenues, E for expenses and D for drawing (for sole proprietorship and partnership) or dividends (for corporation).

THE ACCOUNTING ELEMENTS

The expanded accounting equation contains all the **six accounting elements**, namely, **assets, liabilities, capital, revenues, expenses and drawing**. It is therefore a lot easier to analyze transactions using the expanded accounting equation because all the accounting elements are represented in the expanded accounting equation. The basic accounting equation, in a way, "hides" capital, revenues, expenses and drawing in one basic accounting element, the owner's equity.

Assets are (1) anything that the business owns such as cash, land, building, car, office equipment, computer, etc. (2) rights that are convertible into cash or another form of asset such as accounts receivable (the business has a right to collect the receivable from customer if it performs a service or sells merchandise and the customer did not pay cash at the time of purchase), patents (rights granted to inventor of products or technology), copyrights (rights granted to authors, musicians, composers, singers, painters, artists, sculptors, etc.); (3) prepaid expenses such as when the business makes a payment for car insurance covering a period of one year or makes advanced payment for one-year rent.

Assets are classified into current assets, long-term assets, temporary investments and long-term investments.

Current assets are cash and non-cash assets that will be converted into cash or will be consumed, used or expired within one year or one operating cycle whichever is longer. Cash, accounts receivable, merchandise inventory, supplies, prepaid expenses such as prepaid insurance, office supplies, notes receivable collectible in one year are examples of current assets. **Cash** includes bills, coins, checks and money orders still in the possession of the business and not yet deposited; and money in the bank that are readily available for use. **Accounts receivable** pertains to outstanding accounts collectible from customers for products sold or services rendered on account. **Merchandise inventory** are goods on hand that are intended to be sold to customers. **Prepaid expenses** are expenses paid in advance that will be used, consumed or expired within one year or one operating cycle, whichever is longer.

Long-term assets are assets that are useful to the business for more than one year or one operating cycle, whichever is longer. Long-term assets are also known as (1) plant assets; (2) fixed assets; (3) property, plant and equipment and (4) long-lived assets. Long-term assets are classified into tangible assets, intangible assets and natural resources or wasting assets. **Tangible assets** are long-term assets with physical substance (sensitive to the senses), such as land, building, car, computer, office furniture and fixtures, etc. **Intangible assets** are long-term assets that have no physical substance. These are basically rights that have monetary values such as copyrights, patents, goodwill and trademarks. **Natural resources or wasting assets** are long-term assets that are exhaustible or depletable, once consumed they are not replaceable such as mineral deposits, marble deposits, oil deposits, coal deposits, etc.

Temporary investments and long-term investments are topics appropriately covered in advanced accounting courses and will not be discussed in this book.

Liabilities are the debts (indebtedness, loans or payables) of business, anything that it owes. Businesses often incur liabilities in the course of its operations. Sometimes businesses decide not to pay cash when they buy assets or incur expenses. When this happens, it gives rise to a liability. Liabilities are classified based on their maturity period; **current liabilities** mature within one year or one operating cycle whichever is longer, whereas **long-term liabilities** have maturity dates beyond one year or one operating cycle whichever is longer.

Some commonly known liabilities are:

Accounts Payable	current liability that results when business does not pay cash when asset is purchased or expense is incurred
Notes Payable	liability that results when the business issues a promissory note to serve as evidence of its indebtedness
Mortgage Payable	liability that results when the business gets a mortgage backed up by a real estate property as collateral; this is usually a long-term liability
Wages Payable	current liability for unpaid wages for services already done by employees
Interest Payable	unpaid interest on outstanding loans or liabilities

Unearned Revenue   current liability for advanced collection of revenue for products not yet delivered or services not yet rendered

Owner's Equity is the claim of the owner/s in the assets of the business. There are two parties who have legal rights to the assets of the business; the owners and the creditors. The creditors' claims are represented by the liabilities while the claims of the owner/s are represented by the owner/s equity. In the expanded accounting equation, owner/s' equity is expressed as (C - D) + (R - E)

Capital is the balance of the original investment of the owner/s increased by the cumulative owner/s' additional investments and net income and decreased by the cumulative net losses and owner/s' drawings or withdrawals (dividends for corporations). After the closing process (discussed in chapter 9) when revenues, expenses and drawing or dividends are ultimately closed to capital (retained earnings for corporations), the balance of the capital account is the amount of the owner/s' claim in the assets of the business.

Revenues represent the total amount of products or services billed to customers. At the time of sale, the customers can pay for the product or service through cash payment or payment on account or on credit. If payment is on account, the transaction gives rise to accounts receivable. If the customer, instead of making cash payment issued a promissory note, then it gives rise to notes receivable.

Expenses are the costs and charges that the business incurs to earn the revenues. The most common expenses are rent expense, utilities expense, wages expense, transportation expense, supplies expense, delivery expense, travel expense, gasoline expense, telephone expense, taxes and licenses expense, depreciation expense, insurance expense, miscellaneous expense, interest expense, etc. In the income statement, expenses are deducted from revenues to arrive at the results of operations, which can either be a net income or net loss. If expenses are less than revenues, then the business operations result in net income. If expenses are greater than revenues, then the business suffers a net loss for the period.

Drawing represents the withdrawal of cash or other assets by the owner from the business, for his own personal use. The equivalent of drawing in a corporation is **dividends** which represent the return that stockholders earn from investments in corporation. Drawing and dividends effectively reduce capital.

IMPORTANCE OF UNDERSTANDING THE ACCOUNTING ELEMENTS

The pillar of the basic foundation of accounting knowledge rests on a very good understanding of the accounting elements.

It is very important to know all the six accounting elements because the rules of debit and credit which are used in the analysis of transactions, recording in the general journal, posting in the general ledger are based on the accounting element

affected by the transaction. Likewise, in the preparation of financial statements, the accounting elements also dictate the financial information shown in each particular financial statement.

In analyzing transactions, recording in the general journal and posting to the general ledger, the rules of debits and credits are used to identify the necessary action (debit or credit) to the affected accounts. The **rules of debits and credits are based on the affected accounting elements**. In the preparation of financial statements, again, items shown in each financial statement are also based on the accounting elements, meaning, **accounting elements are exclusively shown in specific financial statements, except for ending capital that is reported in both the equity statement and the balance sheet**. Remember this as the analyzing, posting and reporting processes are discussed in later chapters.

EFFECT OF TRANSACTIONS ON THE ACCOUNTING ELEMENTS

Let us use the transactions of Efficient Services for the month of December 2005 in understanding the expanded accounting equation.

DATE	TRANSACTION ANALYSIS
Dec 01 2005	Received $150,000 investment from Clark Kent to start Efficient Services. Issued official receipt (OR) 001.
	The receipt of $150,000 increased the asset cash and increased the capital of Clark Kent in Efficient Services by the same amount.
02	Issued check (CK) 001 for office supplies, $3,000
	The purchase of office supplies increased the asset office supplies by $3,000 and the payment of $3,000 resulted in a decrease in asset cash.
03	Bought computer equipment from Best Buy, $15,000. Issued CK 002 for $3,000 down payment. Balance is on account.
	The purchase of computer increased the asset computer for the purchase price of $15,000. The asset cash is decreased by the $3,000 down payment while the liability accounts payable increased by $12,000.

06	Bought delivery van from A-J Car Dealership, $25,000. Issued CK 003 for $2,000 down payment. Balance is on account.
	The purchase of delivery van increased the asset delivery van for the purchase price of $25,000. The asset cash is decreased by the $2,000 down payment and the liability accounts payable is increased by balance of $23,000 ($25,000 minus $2,000).
07	Paid rent for one year, $3,000. Issued CK 004.
	The payment of rent $3,000 decreased the asset cash and increased the asset prepaid rent by the same amount.
08	Performed services for cash, $5,000. Issued OR 002 and service invoice (SI) 001.
	By performing a service paid in cash, revenues increased by $5,000 and asset cash increased by the same amount.
09	Performed services, $10,000. Issued OR 003 for the $4,000 down payment and SI 002 for the full amount. Balance is on account.
	By performing a service, revenues increased by $10,000. Asset cash is increased by the $4,000 down payment and asset accounts receivable is increased by the $6,000 balance ($10,000 minus $4,000).
13	Obtained bank loan, $50,000. Issued promissory note (PN) 001.
	The proceeds of the bank loan, $50,000 increased the asset cash while the liability loans payable is increased by the same amount.
14	Paid $300 for van maintenance expense. Issued CK 005.
	The payment of van maintenance expenses decreased the asset cash by $300 and increased van maintenance expense by the same amount.
15	Paid wages, $3,000. Issued CK 007. CK 006 was voided.
	The payment of wages decreased the asset cash by $3,000 and increased wages expense by the same amount.

16	Performed services, $20,000. Issued OR 004 for the $4,000 down payment and SI 003 for the full amount. Balance is on account.
	By performing a service, revenues increased by $20,000. Asset cash is increased by the $4,000 down payment while another asset, accounts receivable increased by $16,000 ($20,000 minus $4,000).
17	Issued OR 005 for $6,000 collected from customers (see Dec 10).
	The collection from customers increased the asset cash by $6,000 and decreased the asset accounts receivable by the same amount.
18	Issued CK 008 as payment for telephone expense, $400.
	The payment of telephone expense decreased the asset cash by $400 and increased telephone expense by the same amount.
19	Issued CK 009 as payment for electric bill, $600.
	The payment of electricity decreased the asset cash by $600 and increased electricity expense by the same amount.
20	Issued CK 010 partial payment to Best Buy, $6,000 (see Dec 03).
	The partial payment to Best Buy decreased the asset cash by $6,000 and decreased the liability accounts payable by the same amount.
21	Issued CK 011 payment to A-J Dealership, $5,000 (see Dec 06).
	The partial payment to A-J Dealership decreased the asset cash by $5,000 and decreased the liability accounts payable by the same amount.
22	Issued CK 012 to Clark Kent for cash withdrawal, $4,000.
	Clark Kent's withdrawal of $4,000 decreased the asset cash and increased drawing by the same amount.
23	Collected $2,000 from customers on account. Issued OR 007.
	The $2,000 collections from customers' accounts increased the asset cash and decreased the asset accounts receivable by the same amount.

28   Paid entertainment expense, $400. Issued CK 013.

      The payment of entertainment expense decreased the asset cash by $400 and increased entertainment expense by the same amount.

30   Paid wages, $5,000. Issued CK 014.

      The payment of wages decreased the asset cash by $5,000 and increased wages expense by the same amount.

PREPARING THE EXPANDED ACCOUNTING EQUATION CHART

In preparing the expanded accounting equation chart, the balance of all the accounting elements (assets, liabilities, capital, revenues, expenses and drawing) must be computed after every transaction. This is to be assured that the equality of the expanded accounting equation is maintained at all times. The transaction amount is simply written in the appropriate column of the affected accounting element. The balance is computed by adding the transaction amount to the preceding balance to reflect an increase or by subtracting the transaction amount from the preceding balance to reflect a decrease. To start a new page, the last balance in the preceding page must be copied or **brought forward** to the new page.

For example, the transaction on December 1 is recorded in the expanded accounting equation chart as an increase in asset and an increase in capital. Since both are increases, the amounts are simply added to the assets and capital columns in the chart to get the balance. The transaction on December 3 for the purchase of computer from Best Buy is shown as an increase in asset computer for the total purchase price, a decrease in asset cash for the down payment and an increase in liability, accounts payable for the balance.

EFFICIENT SERVICES
EXPANDED ACCOUNTING EQUATION CHART
MONTH OF DECEMBER 2005

Page 1

ASSETS = LIABILITIES + CAPITAL + REVENUES − EXPENSES − DRAWING

DATE	DESCRIPTION	ASSETS	=	LIABILITIES	+	CAPITAL	+	REVENUES
December								
01	Initial investment	150,000	=			150,000		
	BALANCE	150,000	=			150,000		
02	Bought office supplies	+ 3,000						
	Paid cash	− 3,000						
	BALANCE	150,000	=			150,000		
03	Bought computer	+15,000						
	Paid down payment	− 3,000						
	Balance on account			12,000				
	BALANCE	162,000	=	12,000	+	150,000		
06	Bought delivery van	+25,000						
	Paid down payment	− 2,000						
	Balance on account			23,000				
	BALANCE	185,000	=	35,000	+	150,000		
07	Paid cash for one year rent	−3,000						
	Prepaid Rent	+3,000						
	BALANCE	185,000	=	35,000	+	150,000		
08	Performed cash services	+ 5,000						+ 5,000
	BALANCE	190,000	=	35,000	+	150,000		5,000
09	Performed services							+ 10,000
	Received down payment	+ 4,000						
	Balance on account	+ 6,000						
	BALANCE	200,000	=	35,000	+	150,000		+15,000
13	Obtained bank loan	+50,000		50,000				
	BALANCE	250,000	=	85,000	+	150,000		+15,000

EFFICIENT SERVICES
EXPANDED ACCOUNTING EQUATION CHART
MONTH OF DECEMBER 2005

Page 2

DATE	DESCRIPTION	ASSETS	=	LIABILITIES	+	CAPITAL	+	REVENUES	−	EXPENSES	−	DRAWING
December												
14	BALANCE FORWARD	250,000	=	85,000	+	150,000	+	15,000				
	Paid van maintenance	− 300							−	300		
	BALANCE	249,700	=	85,000	+	150,000	+	15,000	−	300		
15	Paid wages	− 3,000							−	3,000		
	BALANCE	246,700	=	85,000	+	150,000	+	15,000	−	3,300		
16	Performed services	+ 4,000						20,000				
	Balance on account	+16,000										
	BALANCE	266,700	=	85,000	+	150,000	+	35,000	−	3,300		
17	Cash collection	+ 6,000										
	Receivable reduced	− 6,000										
	BALANCE	266,700	=	85,000	+	150,000	+	35,000	−	3,300		
18	Paid telephone expense	− 400							−	400		
	BALANCE	266,300	=	85,000	+	150,000	+	35,000	−	3,700		
19	Paid electricity expense	− 600							−	600		
	BALANCE	265,700	=	85,000	+	150,000	+	35,000	−	4,300		
20	Paid account	− 6,000		− 6,000								
	BALANCE	259,700	=	79,000	+	150,000	+	35,000	−	4,300		
21	Paid account	− 5,000		− 5,000								
	BALANCE	254,700	=	74,000	+	150,000	+	35,000	−	4,300		

EFFICIENT SERVICES
EXPANDED ACCOUNTING EQUATION CHART
MONTH OF DECEMBER 2005

Page 3

DATE December	DESCRIPTION	ASSETS	=	LIABILITIES	+	CAPITAL	+	REVENUES	−	EXPENSES	−	DRAWING
22	BALANCE FORWARD	254,700	=	74,000	+	150,000		+35,000		−4,300		
	Owner withdrawal	− 4,000										− 4,000
23	BALANCE	250,700	=	74,000	+	150,000		+35,000		− 4,300		− 4,000
	Cash collection	+ 2,000										
	Receivable reduced	− 2,000										
28	BALANCE	250,700	=	74,000	+	150,000		+35,000		− 4,300		− 4,000
	Paid entertainment expense	− 400									− 400	
30	BALANCE	250,300	=	74,000	+	150,000		+35,000		− 4,700		− 4,000
	Paid wages	− 5,000									− 5,000	
	BALANCE	245,300	=	74,000	+	150,000		+35,000		− 9,700		− 4,000

IMPORTANT: Note that the equality of the expanded accounting equation is maintained after every transaction. This is reflected in the amount shown in the BALANCE line after every transaction.

CHAPTER 02   THE ACCOUNTING EQUATIONS

REVIEW QUESTIONS

1. What is the basic accounting equation?

2. Why is there a need for the expanded accounting equation?

3. Why is it important to understand the accounting elements?

4. What are the accounting elements?

5. What are assets? Identify, describe and give examples of the types of assets.

6. What are liabilities? Identify, describe and give examples of the types of liabilities.

7. What is the accounting element capital?

8. What are revenues?

9. What are expenses? Give examples of expenses.

10. What is drawing?

11. How does the expanded accounting equation chart assist in understanding the accounting equation?

CHAPTER 02 THE ACCOUNTING EQUATIONS

REVIEW EXAMINATION

TRUE or FALSE: *WRITE TRUE or FALSE IN THE SPACE PROVIDED.*

_____ 01. The basic accounting equation is expressed as A = L + OE.

_____ 02. Only the three basic accounting elements are expressed in the expanded accounting equation.

_____ 03. The expanded accounting equation is expressed as A = L + (C-D) + (R-E)

_____ 04. The basic accounting equation contains all the six accounting elements.

_____ 05. The expanded accounting equation, in a way, "hides" capital, revenues, expenses and drawing in one basic accounting element, the owner's equity.

_____ 06. Assets are anything that the business owns.

_____ 07. Current assets are cash and non-cash assets that will be converted into cash within one year or one operating cycle whichever is longer.

_____ 08. Cash, accounts receivable, merchandise inventory, supplies, prepaid expenses such as prepaid insurance, office supplies, notes receivable collectible in one year are examples of long-term assets.

_____ 09. Long-term assets are assets that are useful to the business for more than one year or one operating cycle, whichever is longer.

_____ 10. Intangible assets are long-term assets with physical substance.

_____ 11. Natural resources or wasting assets are long-term assets that are exhaustible, such as mineral deposits, marble deposits, oil deposits and coal deposits.

_____ 12. Liabilities are the debts of business, anything that it owes.

_____ 13. Liabilities are classified based on their maturity period.

_____ 14. Long term liabilities mature within one year or one operating cycle whichever is longer.

_____ 15. Accounts Payable results when the business issues a promissory note to serve as evidence of its indebtedness.

_____ 16. Interest Payable represents the unpaid interest due on outstanding loans.

_____ 17. Owner's Equity is the claim of the creditors in the assets of the business

_____ 18. In the expanded accounting equation, owner/s' equity is expressed as (C - D) + (R - E)

_____ 19. Expenses represent the total amount of products or services billed to customers.

_____ 20. Revenues are the costs and charges that the business incurs.

_____ 21. If expenses are more than revenues, then the business operations result in net income.

_____ 22. Drawing represents the withdrawal of cash or other assets by the owner from the business, for his own personal use.

_____ 23. The pillar of the basic foundation of accounting knowledge rests on a very good understanding of the accounting elements.

_____ 24. It is very important to know all the six accounting elements because the rules of debit and credit which are used in the analysis of transactions, recording in the general journal, posting in the general ledger are based on the accounting element affected by the transaction.

_____ 25. In preparing the expanded accounting equation chart, the balance of all the accounting elements (assets, liabilities, capital, revenues, expenses and drawing) is not computed after every transaction.

FILL IN THE BLANK: *WRITE THE CORRECT ANSWER IN THE SPACE PROVIDED.*

01. In preparing the expanded accounting equation chart, the _____ of all the accounting elements (assets, liabilities, capital, revenues, expenses and drawing) must be computed after every transaction.

02. _____ represents the withdrawal of cash or other assets by the owner from the business, for his own personal use.

03. _____ are the costs and charges that the business incurs to earn the revenues.

04. Revenues represent the total amount of products or services billed to _____.

05. Tangible assets are long-term assets with _____ substance.

06. _____ assets are assets that are useful to the business for more than one year or one operating cycle, whichever is longer.

07. Cash, accounts receivable, merchandise inventory, supplies, prepaid expenses, office supplies, notes receivable collectible in one year are examples of _____ assets.

08. The _____ accounting equation, in a way, "hides" capital, revenues, expenses and drawing in one basic accounting element, the owner's equity.

09. The _____ accounting equation is expressed as A = L + (C - D) + (R - E)

10. The _____ accounting equation is expressed as A= L + OE.

11. In the preparation of financial statements, the _____ dictate the financial information shown in each particular financial statement.

12. _____ are the creditors' claims in the assets of the business while the owner/s claims are shown as _____.

13. _____ are current liabilities for advanced collection of revenue for products not yet delivered or services not yet rendered.

14. _____ are long-term assets that are basically rights that have monetary values such as copyrights, patents, goodwill and trademarks.

15. Assets are classified into _____, _____, _____ and _____.

16. It is easier to analyze transactions using the _____ because all the accounting elements are represented.

17. Only the three basic accounting elements, _____, _____ and _____ are expressed in the basic accounting equation.

18. The third basic accounting element, the _____ is expanded to include C for capital, R for revenues, E for expenses and D for drawing.

19. _____ are rights granted to inventor of products or technology.

20. _____ arises when the business sells a product or performs a service and receives no cash payment from the customer when the service is performed or when the product is sold.

PROBLEMS

REMINDER: STUDY THE CHART OF ACCOUNTS. WHEN WORKING ON EACH TRANSACTION, CLASSIFY THE ACCOUNTS AFFECTED WHETHER THEY BELONG TO ASSETS, LIABILITIES, CAPITAL REVENUES, EXPENSES OR DRAWING. THE CHART OF ACCOUNTS WILL GUIDE YOU IN DETERMINING THE ACCOUNTING ELEMENTS. THERE ARE ALWAYS TWO OR MORE ACCOUNTS AFFECTED IN EACH TRANSACTION. THE EQUALITY OF THE EXPANDED ACCOUNTING EQUATION, $A = L + (C - D) + (R - E)$ MUST BE MAINTAINED AT ALL TIMES.

Problem 01   GLOBAL DELIVERY SERVICES

Mr. Juan del Mundo decided to start Global Delivery Services to provide delivery services to existing businesses in the community. Oftentimes, business owners need to make deliveries, however, it is not practical for them to employ full time driver and assistant and maintain delivery trucks. Mr. del Mundo feels confident that he can help these businessmen by providing them efficient, fast and reliable delivery services. The chart of accounts for Global Delivery Services is shown below:

CHART OF ACCOUNTS

Code	Account Title	Code	Account Title
ASSETS		**REVENUES**	
101	Cash	501	Delivery Fees
103	Accounts Receivable		
103.1	Allowance for Bad Debts	**EXPENSES**	
105	Office Supplies		
107	Prepaid Insurance	600	Bad Debts Expense
109	Prepaid Rent	601	Rent Expense
110	Notes Receivable	602	Wages Expense
112	Interest Receivable	603	Telephone Expense
126	Truck	604	Electricity Expense
126.1	Accumulated Depreciation – Truck	605	Transportation Expense
127	Computer Equipment	606	Gasoline Expense
127.1	Accumulated Depreciation - Computer Equipment	607	Office Supplies Expense
		608	Advertising Expense
128	Furniture	611	Depreciation Expense – Truck
128.1	Accumulated Depreciation – Furniture	612	Depreciation Expense – Computer Equipment
		613	Depreciation Expense – Furniture
		616	Truck Maintenance Expense

LIABILITIES

201 Accounts Payable
203 Notes Payable
205 Interest Payable
207 Wages Payable
211 Loans Payable

CAPITAL

301 Juan del Mundo, Capital

DRAWING

401 Juan del Mundo, Drawing

617 Insurance Expense
618 Taxes and Licenses Expense
699 Miscellaneous Expenses

OTHER REVENUES

703 Interest Revenues

OTHER EXPENSES

801 Interest Expense

The transactions of Global Delivery Services for the month of June, 2006 are shown below:

June 01 Juan del Mundo invested $150,000 cash and a delivery truck worth $20,000 to start Global Delivery Services. Official receipt (OR) 1001 was issued.

02 Paid NY ALL Insurance with check (CK) 1001 for one year auto insurance, $2,400.

02 Bought office supplies, $1,500. Issued CK1002 for the $500 down payment and a 90 day 6% promissory note (PN) 1001 for the balance.

03 Issued CK 1003 for one year advanced rent, $12,000.

04 Bought office furniture, $2,400. Issued CK 1004.

08 Delivered packages for Gourmet Food Supplies on account, $5,000. Issued service invoice (SI)1001.

09 Issued CK 1005 for computer equipment bought, $5,000.

11 Issued OR1002 to Gourmet Food Supplies for collection on account, $2,000 for services rendered on June 08.

12 Made deliveries for Fresh Produce on account, $7,000. Issued SI 1002.

15	Issued OR 1003 for balance of account collected from Gourmet Food Supplies, $3,000.
16	Paid wages, $2,500. CK 1006 was cashed at the bank for payment of the employees' payroll.
17	Issued CK 1007 to pay for electricity bill, $200.
19	Issued CK 1008 to pay for gasoline bill received from Honest Gasoline Station, $500.
22	Issued CK 1009 to pay for telephone bill, $185.
23	Juan del Mundo withdrew $1,000 for personal use. Issued CK 1010.
24	Collected $5,000 from Fresh Produce. Issued OR 1004.
25	Performed delivery services for Delectable Delights, $8,000. Issued SI 1003 and OR1005 for the $2,000 received as down payment, balance on account.
30	Paid wages, $3,500. Cashed CK 1011 at the bank for payroll money.
30	Collected $3,000 from Delectable Delights. Issued OR 1006.

REQUIRED: Analyze the transactions of Global Delivery Services.
Identify the accounting elements affected in each transaction.
Prepare the expanded accounting equation chart.

GLOBAL DELIVERY SERVICES
EXPANDED ACCOUNTING EQUATION CHART
FOR THE MONTH ENDED
ASSETS=LIABILITIES+CAPITAL+REVENUES-EXPENSES-DRAWING

PAGE 1

DATE	DESCRIPTION	ASSETS	LIABILITIES	CAPITAL	REVENUES	EXPENSES	DRAWING

GLOBAL DELIVERY SERVICES
EXPANDED ACCOUNTING EQUATION CHART
FOR THE MONTH ENDED
ASSETS=LIABILITIES+CAPITAL+REVENUES-EXPENSES-DRAWING

PAGE 2

DATE	DESCRIPTION	ASSETS	LIABILITIES	CAPITAL	REVENUES	EXPENSES	DRAWING
	BALANCE FORWARD						

GLOBAL DELIVERY SERVICES
EXPANDED ACCOUNTING EQUATION CHART
FOR THE MONTH ENDED _____
ASSETS=LIABILITIES+CAPITAL+REVENUES-EXPENSES-DRAWING

PAGE 3

DATE	DESCRIPTION	ASSETS	LIABILITIES	CAPITAL	REVENUES	EXPENSES	DRAWING
	BALANCE FORWARD						

Problem 02 Garden Landscaping & Pool Services

Garden Landscaping & Pool Services (GLPS) is a family operated business located in Long Island, a suburb of New York City. GLPS maintains the yard of customers by mowing lawn, trimming bushes, cutting trees and fertilizing and taking care of plants and trees. During winter months, customers can also call them to plow snow. GLPS also provides swimming pool services such as cleaning, opening and closing pools.

The chart of accounts and trial balance as of November 30, 2005 (reflecting transactions from January 2005) are shown below:

CHART OF ACCOUNTS

Code	Account Title
ASSETS	
101	Cash
103	Accounts Receivable
103.1	Allowance for Bad Debts
105	Office Supplies
106	Pool and Garden Supplies
107	Prepaid Insurance
109	Prepaid Rent
110	Notes Receivable
112	Interest Receivable
126	Truck
126.1	Accumulated Depreciation – Truck
127	Computer Equipment
127.1	Accumulated Depreciation - Computer Equipment
128	Furniture
128.1	Accumulated Depreciation – Furniture
140	Pool & Yard Equipment
140.1	Accumulated Depreciation - Pool & Yard Equipment

Code	Account Title
REVENUES	
501	Service Fees
EXPENSES	
600	Bad Debts Expense
601	Rent Expense
602	Wages Expense
603	Telephone Expense
604	Electricity Expense
605	Transportation Expense
606	Gasoline Expense
607	Office Supplies Expense
608	Advertising Expense
609	Pool & Garden Supplies Expense
611	Depreciation Expense – Truck
612	Depreciation Expense – Computer Equipment
613	Depreciation Expense – Furniture
614	Depreciation Expense – Pool & Yard Equipment
616	Truck Maintenance Expense
617	Insurance Expense
618	Taxes and Licenses Expense

619	Pool & Yard Equipment Maintenance Expense
699	Miscellaneous Expenses

LIABILITIES
201   Accounts Payable
203   Notes Payable
205   Interest Payable
207   Wages Payable
220   Unearned Service Fees

OTHER REVENUES
703   Interest Revenues

CAPITAL
301   John Flowers, Capital

OTHER EXPENSES
801   Interest Expense

DRAWING
401   John Flowers, Drawing

GARDEN LANDSCAPING & POOL SERVICES
TRIAL BALANCE
NOVEMBER 30, 2005

	DEBIT	CREDIT
Cash	287,700	
Accounts Receivable	45,000	
Allowance for Bad Debts		2,000
Pool and Garden Supplies	10,000	
Office Supplies	3,000	
Prepaid Insurance	3,600	
Prepaid Rent	12,000	
Truck	25,000	
Accumulated Depreciation – Truck		4,000
Computer Equipment	5,000	
Accumulated Depreciation – Computer Equipment		1,000
Pool & Yard Equipment	22,000	
Accumulated Depreciation – Pool & Yard Equipment		2,000
Accounts Payable		8,300
John Flowers, Capital		136,350
John Flowers, Drawing	12,000	
Service Fees		358,000
Wages Expense	55,000	
Telephone Expense	1,650	
Electricity Expense	2,200	
Gasoline Expense	12,000	
Miscellaneous Expenses	15,500	
	511,650	511,650

Transactions for December 2005 are shown below:

Dec 01   In preparation for snow storm, bought salt from HIJ Hardware, $300 on account. HIJ issued sales invoice 9785.

      03   Issued check 9002 for office supplies bought last month from XYZ Printers, $1,500.

      04   Performed snow plowing services, $8,000; received $4,000 cash and balance on account. Issued official receipt numbers 4801-4875 for cash received and service invoices 2772-2846 for the whole amount.

      07   Paid printer for advertising flyers, with check 9003, $300.

      12   Performed tree cutting services, $4,000. Issued service invoice 2847 and official receipt 4876 for cash collected.

      14   Performed bush trimming services, $4,000 on account. Issued service invoice 2848.

      15   Cashed check 9004 to pay workers' wages, $3,500.

      18   Performed tree cutting services, $2,500. Issued service invoice 2849 and official receipt 4877.

      19   Performed snow plowing services, $12,000. Issued official receipts 4878 to 4948 for $9,800 cash collected. Balance of $2,200 on account. Issued service invoices 2850-2927 for the whole amount.

      22   Collected $4,000 for bush trimming done on December 14. Issued official receipts 4949-4961.

      23   Collected $5,000 for snow plowing services done on December 04 and December 19. Issued official receipts 4962-5002.

      27   Paid electricity bill with check 9005, $125.

      28   Paid telephone bill with check 9006, $100.

      29   Collected $38,000 from outstanding customers accounts for previous services rendered. Issued official receipts 5003-5028.

      30   John Flowers cashed check 9007 for personal use, $5,000.

      30   Cashed check 9008 to pay workers' wages and incentives, $7,500.

REQUIRED: Analyze the transactions of Garden Landscaping & Pool Services. Identify the accounting elements affected in each transaction. Prepare the expanded accounting equation chart.

REMINDER: Since this is a business that is already operating, classify the accounts in the trial balance into assets, liabilities, capital, revenues, expenses and drawing and compute the total for each accounting element. In computing the total assets, subtract the accumulated depreciation amounts from the gross amount of the asset accounts; subtract allowance for bad debts from accounts receivable. These totals shall be the balance forward for the first line of page 1 (trial balance line) of the expanded accounting equation chart.

GARDEN LANDSCAPING & POOL SERVICES
EXPANDED ACCOUNTING EQUATION CHART
FOR THE TWELVE MONTHS ENDED _____
ASSETS=LIABILITIES+CAPITAL+REVENUES-EXPENSES-DRAWING

PAGE 1

DATE	DESCRIPTION	ASSETS	LIABILITIES	CAPITAL	REVENUES	EXPENSES	DRAWING
	TRIAL BALANCE						

GARDEN LANDSCAPING & POOL SERVICES
EXPANDED ACCOUNTING EQUATION CHART
FOR THE TWELVE MONTHS ENDED
ASSETS=LIABILITIES+CAPITAL+REVENUES-EXPENSES-DRAWING

PAGE 2

DATE	DESCRIPTION	ASSETS	LIABILITIES	CAPITAL	REVENUES	EXPENSES	DRAWING
	BALANCE FORWARD						

GARDEN LANDSCAPING & POOL SERVICES
EXPANDED ACCOUNTING EQUATION CHART
FOR THE TWELVE MONTHS ENDED
ASSETS=LIABILITIES+CAPITAL+REVENUES-EXPENSES-DRAWING

PAGE 3

DATE	DESCRIPTION	ASSETS	LIABILITIES	CAPITAL	REVENUES	EXPENSES	DRAWING
	BALANCE FORWARD						

Problem 03 GRADE A PLUS TUTORIAL SERVICES

Charles Teach, a retired college professor decided to provide tutorial and test preparation services to students. He hired 3 instructors and offered his services through flyers and advertisements in some free daily newspapers circulated near colleges and universities. Charles Teach was an excellent professor and he inspired so many students to achieve for the highest grade possible. A plus (A+) is his grade goal for students who avail of his services and this is the inspiration behind the business name of his company. Intercity Colleges outsourced its Academic Resource Center to Grade A Plus Tutorial Services (GAPTS) for a flat monthly fee of $28,000. GAPTS also accepts walk-in students from other schools.

The chart of accounts and transactions for the month of October, 2005 are shown below:

CHART OF ACCOUNTS

Code	Account Title	Code	Account Title
ASSETS		**REVENUES**	
101	Cash	501	Tutorial Fees
103	Accounts Receivable		
103.1	Allowance for Bad Debts	**EXPENSES**	
105	Office Supplies		
107	Prepaid Insurance	600	Bad Debts Expense
109	Prepaid Rent	601	Rent Expense
110	Notes Receivable	602	Wages Expense
112	Interest Receivable	603	Telephone Expense
126	Car	604	Electricity Expense
126.1	Accumulated Depreciation – Car	605	Transportation Expense
127	Computer Equipment	606	Gasoline Expense
127.1	Accumulated Depreciation - Computer Equipment	607	Office Supplies Expense
		608	Advertising Expense
128	Furniture	611	Depreciation Expense – Car
128.1	Accumulated Depreciation – Furniture	612	Depreciation Expense – Computer Equipment
		613	Depreciation Expense – Furniture
		616	Car Maintenance Expense
		617	Insurance Expense
		618	Taxes and Licenses Expense
		699	Miscellaneous Expenses

LIABILITIES

201 Accounts Payable
203 Notes Payable
205 Interest Payable
207 Wages Payable

CAPITAL

301 Charles Teach, Capital

DRAWING

401 Charles Teach, Drawing

OTHER REVENUES

703 Interest Revenues

OTHER EXPENSES

801 Interest Expense

Transactions for October, 2005 are shown below:

Oct 01 Charles Teach invested $50,000 cash and a brand new car, $20,000 to start Grade A Plus Tutorial Services. Issued official receipt 0001.

02 Paid one year advanced car insurance, $1,800 with check 1001.

03 Bought computer equipment on account, $12,000. Best Computer Staples issued sales invoice 5467.

04 Bought tables and chairs, $10,000. Paid $2,000 down payment with check 1002 and balance of $8,000 on account. Best Computer Staples issued sales invoice 5498.

05 Paid TGIF Printers with check 1003 for advertising flyers, $380.

06 Bought office supplies, $500, on account. Received sales invoice 7635.

07 Billed Intercity Colleges for one week tutorial services, $7,000. Issued service invoice 0001.

08 Performed tutorial services to walk-in students, $3,000. Issued official receipts 0002-0049 and service invoices 0002-0050.

10 Charles Teach made an additional cash investment, $10,000. Issued official receipt 0050.

14 Issued official receipt 0051 to Intercity Colleges for cash collected $7,000 for bill dated October 07.

15 Paid tutors' wages, $6,000. Issued checks 1004 to 1006.

17	Issued service invoice 0051 to Intercity Colleges for one week tutorial services, $7,000.
18	Issued check 1007 to Best Computer Staples as payment for purchases on October 3 and 4, $10,000.
25	Performed tutorial services to walk-in students, $2,000. Issued official receipts 0052-0072 and service invoices 0052-0072.
26	Issued official receipt 0073 to Intercity Colleges for bill on October 17, $7,000.
26	Issued service invoice 0073 to Intercity Colleges $7,000.
29	Issued check 1008 to pay electricity bill, $200.
30	Issued check 1009 to pay gasoline bill from Honest Gas Station, $450.
30	Issued check 1010 to pay telephone bill, $180.
30	Paid tutors' wages, $6,000. Issued checks 1011-1013.
30	Issued official receipt 0074 to Intercity Colleges $7,000, (October 26 bill).
30	Issued service invoice 0074 to Intercity Colleges, $7,000.
31	Charles Teach cashed check 1014 for his personal use, $3,000.

REQUIRED: Analyze the transactions of Grade A Plus Tutorial Services. Identify the accounting elements affected in each transaction. Prepare the expanded accounting equation chart.

GRADE A PLUS TUTORIAL SERVICES
EXPANDED ACCOUNTING EQUATION CHART
FOR THE MONTH ENDED _____
ASSETS=LIABILITIES+CAPITAL+REVENUES-EXPENSES-DRAWING

PAGE 1

DATE	DESCRIPTION	ASSETS	LIABILITIES	CAPITAL	REVENUES	EXPENSES	DRAWING

GRADE A PLUS TUTORIAL SERVICES
EXPANDED ACCOUNTING EQUATION CHART
FOR THE MONTH ENDED _____
ASSETS=LIABILITIES+CAPITAL+REVENUES-EXPENSES-DRAWING

PAGE 2

DATE	DESCRIPTION	ASSETS	LIABILITIES	CAPITAL	REVENUES	EXPENSES	DRAWING
	BALANCE FORWARD						

GRADE A PLUS TUTORIAL SERVICES
EXPANDED ACCOUNTING EQUATION CHART
FOR THE MONTH ENDED
ASSETS=LIABILITIES+CAPITAL+REVENUES-EXPENSES-DRAWING

PAGE 3

DATE	DESCRIPTION	ASSETS	LIABILITIES	CAPITAL	REVENUES	EXPENSES	DRAWING
	BALANCE FORWARD						

Problem 04   Jolie Kids Day Care Services

Carey Jolie used to work for a big corporation but she was laid off when her company decided to downsize because of continued financial losses. Carey Jolie wanted to have more job security and never again become a victim of corporate decisions, so she decided to put up her own business. She noticed that there are many working mothers in her neighborhood who need to send their pre-school children to day care centers. She made a feasibility study and attended seminars about child care providers and when she felt that she was ready, she used her separation pay settlement to start the Jolie Kids Day Care Services.

The chart of accounts and transactions for September, 2005 are shown below:

CHART OF ACCOUNTS

Code	Account Title	Code	Account Title
ASSETS		**REVENUES**	
101	Cash	501	Day Care Fees
103	Accounts Receivable		
103.1	Allowance for Bad Debts	**EXPENSES**	
105	Day Care Supplies		
107	Prepaid Insurance	600	Bad Debts Expense
109	Prepaid Rent	601	Rent Expense
110	Notes Receivable	602	Wages Expense
112	Interest Receivable	603	Telephone Expense
126	Van	604	Electricity Expense
126.1	Accumulated Depreciation – Van	605	Transportation Expense
127	Computer Equipment	606	Gasoline Expense
127.1	Accumulated Depreciation - Computer Equipment	607	Day Care Supplies Expense
		608	Advertising Expense
128	Furniture	611	Depreciation Expense – Van
128.1	Accumulated Depreciation – Furniture	612	Depreciation Expense – Computer Equipment
		613	Depreciation Expense – Furniture
		616	Van Maintenance Expense
		617	Insurance Expense
		618	Taxes and Licenses Expense
		699	Miscellaneous Expenses
LIABILITIES			
		OTHER REVENUES	
201	Accounts Payable		
203	Notes Payable		
205	Interest Payable		
205	Wages Payable	703	Interest Revenues

Fundamentals of Accounting

CAPITAL

301   Carey Jolie, Capital

DRAWING

401   Carey Jolie, Drawing

OTHER EXPENSES

801   Interest Expense

Transactions for September 2005 are shown below:

Sept 01   Carey Jolie invested $80,000 cash and her van worth $10,000 to start Jolie Kids Day Care Services (JKDCS). Issued official receipt 0001.

01   Paid one year advanced rent for September 01, 2005 to August 31, 2006, $12,000. Issued check 0001.

02   Bought tables and chairs, $1,500, on account. Kids Toys & Stuff issued sales invoice 6677.

03   Issued check 0002 to Better Printers for advertising flyers, $500.

04   Issued check 0003 to Day Care Suppliers, $1,000 for various supplies.

05   Received $3,000 for day care services for 15 kids. Issued official receipts 0002-0016 and service invoices 0001-00015.

07   Cashed check 0004 to pay for weekly wages, $1,000.

09   Performed day care services on account, $1,000. Issued service invoices 0016-0020.

10   Performed day care services, $2,000. Received $500 cash and balance on account. Issued official receipt 0017 and service invoices 0021-0030.

12   Bought computer, $3,000 and issued promissory note 0001 payable in 90 days at 6% interest. Best Computer issued sales invoice 7789.

14   Cashed check 0005 to pay for weekly wages, $1,200.

17   Collected $1,000 for services rendered on Sept 09. Issued official receipts 0018-0022.

20   Issued check 0006 to Kids & Stuff, $500 for purchase on Sept 02.

21   Received $3,000 for day care services for 15 kids. Issued official receipts 0023-0037 and service invoices 0031-0044.

22	Cashed check 0007 to pay weekly wages, $1,200.
25	Collected balance of account for services done on Sept 10, $1,500. Issued official receipts 0038-0040.
28	Received $2,000 for day care services rendered. Issued official receipts 0041-0050 and service invoices 0045-0054.
29	Paid electricity bill with check 0008, $200.
29	Paid telephone bill with check 0009, $150.
30	Cashed check 0010 to pay weekly wages, $1,200.
30	Received $3,000 for day care services for 15 kids. Issued official receipts 0051-0065 and service invoices 0055-0069.
30	Issued check 0011 to Carey Jolie, $3,000. This is cash withdrawal for personal use.

REQUIRED: Analyze the transactions of Jolie Kids Day Care Services.
Identify the accounting elements affected in each transaction.
Prepare the expanded accounting equation chart.

JOLIE KIDS DAY CARE SERVICES
EXPANDED ACCOUNTING EQUATION CHART
FOR THE MONTH ENDED
ASSETS=LIABILITIES+CAPITAL+REVENUES-EXPENSES-DRAWING

PAGE 1

DATE	DESCRIPTION	ASSETS	LIABILITIES	CAPITAL	REVENUES	EXPENSES	DRAWING

JOLIE KIDS DAY CARE SERVICES
EXPANDED ACCOUNTING EQUATION CHART
FOR THE MONTH ENDED
ASSETS=LIABILITIES+CAPITAL+REVENUES-EXPENSES-DRAWING

PAGE 2

DATE	DESCRIPTION	ASSETS	LIABILITIES	CAPITAL	REVENUES	EXPENSES	DRAWING
	BALANCE FORWARD						

JOLIE KIDS DAY CARE SERVICES
EXPANDED ACCOUNTING EQUATION CHART
FOR THE MONTH ENDED
ASSETS=LIABILITIES+CAPITAL+REVENUES-EXPENSES-DRAWING

PAGE 3

DATE	DESCRIPTION	ASSETS	LIABILITIES	CAPITAL	REVENUES	EXPENSES	DRAWING
	BALANCE FORWARD						

Problem 05   JAMES DEANE TOURS

James Deane is interested in visiting historical sites and popular destinations. As an employee of a travel agency, he used to take care of the booking arrangements of his customers. He recently inherited a substantial amount of money. He decided to fulfill his dream of going to different places. James Deane Tours was set up to provide tour services to groups of people. He hired 2 full-time drivers and 2 driver assistants, and he decided to act as tour guide.

The chart of accounts and the transactions for June 2005 are shown below:

CHART OF ACCOUNTS

Code	Account Title	Code	Account Title
ASSETS		**REVENUES**	
101	Cash	501	Tour Service Fees
103	Accounts Receivable		
103.1	Allowance for Bad Debts	**EXPENSES**	
105	Office Supplies		
106	Video and DVD Supplies		
107	Prepaid Insurance	600	Bad Debts Expense
109	Prepaid Rent	601	Rent Expense
110	Notes Receivable	602	Wages Expense
112	Interest Receivable	603	Telephone Expense
126	Tour Bus	604	Electricity Expense
126.1	Accumulated Depreciation – Tour Bus	605	Transportation Expense
127	Computer Equipment	606	Gasoline Expense
127.1	Accumulated Depreciation - Computer Equipment	607	Office Supplies Expense
		608	Advertising Expense
128	Furniture	611	Depreciation Expense – Tour Bus
128.1	Accumulated Depreciation – Furniture		
129	Video & DVD Equipment	612	Depreciation Expense – Computer Equipment
129.1	Accumulated Depreciation - Video & DVD Equipment	613	Depreciation Expense – Furniture
		614	Depreciation Expense – Video & DVD Equipment
		615	Video and DVD Supplies Expense
		616	Bus Maintenance Expense
		617	Insurance Expense
		618	Taxes and Licenses Expense
		699	Miscellaneous Expenses

LIABILITIES

201   Accounts Payable
203   Notes Payable
205   Interest Payable
207   Wages Payable
211   Loans Payable

CAPITAL

301 James Deane, Capital

DRAWING

401   James Deane, Drawing

OTHER REVENUES

703   Interest Revenues

OTHER EXPENSES

801   Interest Expense

The transactions of James Deane Tours for June 2005 are shown below:

June 01   James Deane invested $300,000 to start James Deane Tours. Issued official receipt 0001.

01   Paid license and business permit with check 0001, $250.

02   Bought 2 tour busses from ABC Dealership, $100,000. Issued check 0002 for $20,000 down payment and promissory note 0001 payable in 120 days at 6% for the balance.

03   Paid one year auto insurance, $24,000 with check 0003.

04   Bought computer on account, $3000. Computer Store issued sales invoice 8888.

05   Bought video camera and DVD equipment, on account, $1800. Manhattan Photo issued sales invoice 99875.

07   Paid Manhattan Photo with check 0004 for various DVDs and video supplies, $500.

08   Paid one year advanced rent for parking spaces for busses, $2,400. Issued check 0005.

09   Provided tour services for Microcisco company picnic, $8,000. Issued official receipt 0002 for $4,000 down payment and service invoice 0001 for the whole amount. Balance of $4,000 is on account.

11   Provided tour services for the educational trip of Boro College, $7,000 on account. Issued service invoice 0002.

12   Collected $4,000 from Microcisco for services on June 09. Issued official receipt 0003.

14   Issued check 0006 to DEF Gas Station for gasoline purchases, $500.

15   Issued official receipt 0004 to Boro College for account collected, $7,000.

15   Cashed check 0007 for wages paid, $6,000.

17   Provided tour services for field trip of St. Anne's School, $9,000 on account. Issued service invoice 0003.

20   Issued check 0008 for bus maintenance charges, $500.

21   Issued check 0009 as payment for computer bought on June 04, $3,000.

22   Issued check 0010 as partial payment to Manhattan Photo, $800.

23   Provided transportation for out of state trip of N'Stones Band, $12,000. Received $7,000 down payment, balance on account. Issued service invoice 0004 for the total amount and official receipt 0005 for the down payment.

24   Paid DEF Gas Station for gasoline purchases, $800. Issued check 0011.

28   Paid telephone bill and mailed check 0012, $175.

29   Paid electricity bill and mailed check 0013, $250.

30   Owner cashed check 0014 for personal use, $2,000.

REQUIRED: Analyze the transactions of James Deane Tours.
Identify the accounting elements affected in each transaction.
Prepare the expanded accounting equation chart.

JAMES DEANE TOURS
EXPANDED ACCOUNTING EQUATION CHART
FOR THE MONTH ENDED
ASSETS=LIABILITIES+CAPITAL+REVENUES-EXPENSES-DRAWING

PAGE 1

DATE	DESCRIPTION	ASSETS	LIABILITIES	CAPITAL	REVENUES	EXPENSES	DRAWING

JAMES DEANE TOURS
EXPANDED ACCOUNTING EQUATION CHART
FOR THE MONTH ENDED
ASSETS=LIABILITIES+CAPITAL+REVENUES-EXPENSES-DRAWING

PAGE 2

DATE	DESCRIPTION	ASSETS	LIABILITIES	CAPITAL	REVENUES	EXPENSES	DRAWING
	BALANCE FORWARD						

JAMES DEANE TOURS
EXPANDED ACCOUNTING EQUATION CHART
FOR THE MONTH ENDED
ASSETS=LIABILITIES+CAPITAL+REVENUES-EXPENSES-DRAWING

PAGE 3

DATE	DESCRIPTION	ASSETS	LIABILITIES	CAPITAL	REVENUES	EXPENSES	DRAWING
	BALANCE FORWARD						

Problem 06   HAVE FUN DAY CAMP

Have Fun Day Camp is a family operated business owned by Wella Care. She used to be a nursery school teacher but she felt that she needed to care for her two young toddlers, so she started the day camp for kids ages 3 to 7. She was lucky to find a nice space with a big yard which she used as the playground for the kids during the summer. The children are given instructions in reading, math and writing. They are taught art and crafts skills. Have Fun Day Camp started operations in October 1, 2005. So far, Wella Care is happy with her new found pursuit as a young entrepreneur. She has five teacher assistants who help her run the day camp.

The chart of accounts and trial balance of Have Fun Day Camp as of November 30, 2005 are shown below:

CHART OF ACCOUNTS

Code	Account Title	Code	Account Title
ASSETS		**REVENUES**	
101	Cash	501	Day Camp Fees
103	Accounts Receivable		
103.1	Allowance for Bad Debts	**EXPENSES**	
105	School Supplies		
106	Toys & Crafts Supplies		
107	Prepaid Insurance	600	Bad Debts Expense
109	Prepaid Rent	601	Rent Expense
110	Notes Receivable	602	Wages Expense
112	Interest Receivable	603	Telephone Expense
126	Van	604	Electricity Expense
126.1	Accumulated Depreciation – Van	605	Transportation Expense
127	Computer Equipment	606	Gasoline Expense
127.1	Accumulated Depreciation - Computer Equipment	607	School Supplies Expense
		608	Advertising Expense
128	Furniture	609	Toys & Crafts Supplies Expense
128.1	Accumulated Depreciation - Furniture	611	Depreciation Expense – Van
129	Playground Equipment	612	Depreciation Expense – Computer Equipment
129.1	Accumulated Depreciation - Playground Equipment	613	Depreciation Expense – Furniture
		614	Depreciation Expense – Playground Equipment
		616	Van Maintenance Expense
		617	Insurance Expense
		618	Taxes and Licenses Expense

699 Miscellaneous Expenses

LIABILITIES

OTHER REVENUES

201 Accounts Payable
203 Notes Payable
204 Interest Payable
205 Wages Payable
220 Unearned Day Camp Fees

703 Interest Revenues

CAPITAL

OTHER EXPENSES

301 Wella Care, Capital

801 Interest Expense

DRAWING

401 Wella Care, Drawing

HAVE FUN DAY CAMP
Trial Balance
November 30, 2005

	DEBIT	CREDIT
Cash	98,900	
Accounts Receivable	1,200	
School Supplies	500	
Toys & Crafts Supplies	1,000	
Prepaid Insurance	1,000	
Prepaid Rent	20,000	
Van	25,000	
Playground Equipment	1,800	
Furniture	2,200	
Computer Equipment	12,000	
Accounts Payable		5,000
Notes Payable		10,000
Wella Care, Capital		100,000
Day Camp Fees		72,700
Rent Expense	4,000	
Insurance Expense	200	
Wages Expense	18,000	
Telephone Expense	400	
Electricity Expense	500	
Gasoline Expense	1,000	
	187,700	187,700

Transactions for December 2005 are shown below:

Dec 01 Issued official receipt 092 for $1,200 on customers account collected.

02 Bought computers from Office Buys on account, $8,000. Received purchase invoice 094.

04 Sent out service invoices 0100-0150 for services rendered, $10,000.

06 Cashed check 0023 to pay wages, $3,500.

07 Paid suppliers accounts and issued check 0024, $3,000.

09 Collected customers accounts for bills sent on Dec 04, $10,000. Issued official receipts 093-0145.

10 Paid ABC Printers for promotional flyers with check 0025, $500.

11 Paid electricity expense with check 0026, $180.

11 Sent out service invoices 0151-0190 for services rendered, $11,000.

12 Cashed check 0027 to pay for weekly wages, $3,500.

13 Paid ABC Catering with check 0028 for Time with Parents meeting, $300. This expense is charged to miscellaneous expenses.

16 Collected customers accounts for bills sent on Dec 11, $11,000. Issued official receipts 00146-00186.

18 Sent out service invoices 0191-0241 to parents, $13,000.

19 Received purchase invoice 7645 for school supplies bought from Office Buys on account, $1,300.

22 Issued check 0029 to Office Buys for partial payment of account, $2,000.

24 Paid ABC Catering with check 0030 for food served at Christmas Party, $500.

24 Collected customers accounts for bills sent on Dec 18, $11,000. Issued official receipts 00187-0235.

24 Cashed check 0031 to pay for wages, $7,000.

27	Sent out service invoices 0242-0282, $12,000.
30	Issued check 0032 to Wella Care for withdrawal for personal use, $3,000.

REQUIRED: Analyze the transactions of Have Fun Day Camp.
Identify the accounting elements affected in each transaction.
Prepare the expanded accounting equation chart.

REMINDER: Since this is a business that is already operating, classify the accounts in the trial balance into assets, liabilities, capital, revenues, expenses and drawing and compute the total for each accounting element. In computing total assets, subtract the accumulated depreciation amounts from the gross amount of the asset accounts; subtract allowance for bad debts from accounts receivable. These totals shall be the balance forward for the first line of page 1 (trial balance line) of the expanded accounting equation chart.

HAVE FUN DAY CAMP
EXPANDED ACCOUNTING EQUATION CHART
FOR THREE MONTHS ENDED
ASSETS=LIABILITIES+CAPITAL+REVENUES-EXPENSES-DRAWING

PAGE 1

DATE	DESCRIPTION	ASSETS	LIABILITIES	CAPITAL	REVENUES	EXPENSES	DRAWING
	TRIAL BALANCE						

HAVE FUN DAY CAMP
EXPANDED ACCOUNTING EQUATION CHART
FOR THREE MONTHS ENDED _____
ASSETS=LIABILITIES+CAPITAL+REVENUES-EXPENSES-DRAWING

PAGE 2

DATE	DESCRIPTION	ASSETS	LIABILITIES	CAPITAL	REVENUES	EXPENSES	DRAWING
	BALANCE FORWARD						

HAVE FUN DAY CAMP
EXPANDED ACCOUNTING EQUATION CHART
FOR THREE MONTHS ENDED
ASSETS=LIABILITIES+CAPITAL+REVENUES-EXPENSES-DRAWING

PAGE 3

DATE	DESCRIPTION	ASSETS	LIABILITIES	CAPITAL	REVENUES	EXPENSES	DRAWING
	BALANCE FORWARD						

Problem 07 Beautiful Hollywood

Daia Narra is an enterprising individual who has worked as a beautician in one of the well-known beauty salons in Hollywood, California. After saving enough money for capital she decided to set up her own beauty services business. Initially, she decided not to lease a place, because rent was expensive. She planned to do home service for which she could charge higher. Daia Narra offers hair cut and styling, manicure and pedicure, make-up and massage services. She hired 5 part time assistants who are on call whenever her clients require their services.

The chart of accounts and the transactions for March 2006 are shown below:

CHART OF ACCOUNTS

Code	Account Title
ASSETS	
101	Cash
103	Accounts Receivable
103.1	Allowance for Bad Debts
105	Office Supplies
106	Beauty Supplies
107	Prepaid Insurance
109	Prepaid Rent
110	Notes Receivable
112	Interest Receivable
126	Van
126.1	Accumulated Depreciation – Van
127	Computer Equipment
127.1	Accumulated Depreciation - Computer Equipment
128	Furniture
128.1	Accumulated Depreciation – Furniture
129	Beauty Parlor Equipment
129.1	Accumulated Depreciation - Beauty Parlor Equipment

Code	Account Title
REVENUES	
501	Service Fees
EXPENSES	
600	Bad Debts Expense
601	Rent Expense
602	Wages Expense
603	Telephone Expense
604	Electricity Expense
605	Gasoline Expense
606	Office Supplies Expense
607	Beauty Supplies Expense
608	Advertising Expense
611	Depreciation Expense – Van
612	Depreciation Expense – Computer Equipment
613	Depreciation Expense – Furniture
614	Depreciation Expense – Beauty Parlor Equipment
616	Van Maintenance Expense
617	Insurance Expense
618	Taxes and Licenses Expense
699	Miscellaneous Expenses

LIABILITIES

201   Accounts Payable
203   Notes Payable
205   Interest Payable
207   Wages Payable
211   Loans Payable

CAPITAL

301   Daia Narra, Capital

DRAWING

401   Daia Narra, Drawing

OTHER REVENUES

703   Interest Revenues

OTHER EXPENSES

801   Interest Expense

The transactions of Beautiful Hollywood for March 2006 are shown below:

Mar 01   Daia Narra invested $100,000 to start Beautiful Hollywood (BH). BH issued official receipt (OR) 0001.

02   Issued check (CK) 0001 to pay for business license and permits, $500.

03   Bought beauty supplies from Confidential Charm, on account, $1,500. Confidential Charm issued invoice 5489.

04   Issued CK 0002 to Print-with-us to pay for advertisement and flyers, $500; and office supplies, $800.

05   Bought beauty parlor equipment from Instant Make-over, $3,000. Issued CK 0003 for the $500 down payment and a 90 day 6% promissory note (PN) 0001 for the balance.

07   Performed beauty services for a bridal entourage, $5,000. Issued OR 0002 for the $2,000 down payment; balance on account. Issued service invoice (SI) 0001 for $5,000.

09   Performed hair and make-up services for models in a fashion show, $10,000. Issued SI 0002 and OR 0003 for the $5,000 down payment; balance due in 10 days.

15   Bought van, $15,000. Paid Holly Dealership $3,000 with CK0004, balance on account. Received invoice 7842 from Holly Dealership.

15	Paid one year insurance on van with CK 0005, $1,800.
16	Cashed CK 0006 to pay beauticians' wages, $3,000.
17	Collected balance of account for services done on March 7. Issued OR 0004 for $3,000.
18	Daia Narra cashed check 007, $1,000, for her personal use.
21	Performed hair and make up services for junior and senior students at Brentwood High School, $4,500. Issued SI 0003-33 and OR 0005–35.
25	Issued CK 0008 as partial payment to Confidential Charm for beauty supplies bought on March 3, $1,000.
28	Collected balance of account for fashion show services done on March 9, $5,000. Issued OR 0036.
29	Bought beauty supplies from Beverly Hills Supplies, $700, on account. Beverly Hills issued invoice 39867.
30	Cashed CK 0009 to pay beauticians' wages, $3,000.
30	Issued CK 0010 to Corner Gas Station for gasoline purchases, $570.
31	Issued CK 0011 to Daia Narra for personal use, $2,000.
31	Issued and mailed CK 0012 to pay telephone bill, $150.

REQUIRED: Analyze the transactions of Beautiful Hollywood.
Identify the accounting elements affected in each transaction.
Prepare the expanded accounting equation chart.

BEAUTIFUL HOLLYWOOD
EXPANDED ACCOUNTING EQUATION CHART
FOR THE MONTH ENDED _____
ASSETS=LIABILITIES+CAPITAL+REVENUES-EXPENSES-DRAWING

PAGE 1

DATE	DESCRIPTION	ASSETS	LIABILITIES	CAPITAL	REVENUES	EXPENSES	DRAWING

BEAUTIFUL HOLLYWOOD
EXPANDED ACCOUNTING EQUATION CHART
FOR THE MONTH ENDED
ASSETS=LIABILITIES+CAPITAL+REVENUES-EXPENSES-DRAWING

PAGE 2

DATE	DESCRIPTION	ASSETS	LIABILITIES	CAPITAL	REVENUES	EXPENSES	DRAWING
	BALANCE FORWARD						

BEAUTIFUL HOLLYWOOD
EXPANDED ACCOUNTING EQUATION CHART
FOR THE MONTH ENDED
ASSETS=LIABILITIES+CAPITAL+REVENUES-EXPENSES-DRAWING

PAGE 3

DATE	DESCRIPTION	ASSETS	LIABILITIES	CAPITAL	REVENUES	EXPENSES	DRAWING
	BALANCE FORWARD						

Problem 08   Reliable Security Management Services

After the tragedy of September 11, 2001, security concerns became an important issue for many companies. Reli Able decided to start a security management services company. He used to head the facilities security management department of a major financial institution in Wall Street. With his experience and business contacts, he felt that he is now ready to become an entrepreneur. It has been a life long dream for him to head his own business. On May 1, 2002, Reli Able formed the Reliable Security Management Services.

The chart of accounts is shown below:

CHART OF ACCOUNTS

Code   Account Title

ASSETS

Code	Account Title
101	Cash
103	Accounts Receivable
103.1	Allowance for Bad Debts
105	Office Supplies
107	Prepaid Insurance
109	Prepaid Rent
110	Notes Receivable
112	Interest Receivable
126	Van
126.1	Accumulated Depreciation – Van
127	Computer Equipment
127.1	Accumulated Depreciation - Computer Equipment
128	Security Services Equipment
128.1	Accumulated Depreciation - Security Services Equipment
129	Furniture
129.1	Accumulated Depreciation - Furniture
130	Surveillance Equipment
130.1	Accumulated Depreciation - Surveillance Equipment

Code   Account Title

REVENUES

Code	Account Title
501	Security Service Fees

EXPENSES

Code	Account Title
600	Bad Debts Expense
601	Rent Expense
602	Wages Expense
603	Telephone Expense
604	Electricity Expense
605	Transportation Expense
606	Gasoline Expense
607	Office Supplies Expense
608	Advertising Expense
609	Depreciation Expense - Security Services Equipment
612	Depreciation Expense – Van
613	Depreciation Expense – Computer Equipment
614	Depreciation Expense - Furniture
615	Depreciation Expense - Surveillance Equipment
616	Van Maintenance Expense
617	Insurance Expense
618	Taxes and Licenses Expense
699	Miscellaneous Expenses

LIABILITIES

201 Accounts Payable
203 Notes Payable
205 Interest Payable
207 Wages Payable
211 Loans Payable

CAPITAL

301 Reli Able, Capital

DRAWING

401 Reli Able, Drawing

OTHER REVENUES

703 Interest Revenues

OTHER EXPENSES

801 Interest Expense

Transactions for May 2002 are shown below:

May 01   Reli Able invested $200,000 to start Reliable Security Management Services. Issued official receipt 0001.

01   Paid license and other business permits with check 0001, $500.

02   Bought security services equipment from A-1 Security Equipment, $20,000. Invoice 7778 was received. Issued check 0002 for $5,000 down payment and promissory note 0001 payable in 60 days at 3% for the balance.

03   Bought van from Ford-Bayside Dealership, $22,000. Issued check 0003 for the $3,000 down payment and balance on account. Ford-Bayside issued sales invoice 457890.

03   Paid one year auto insurance, $2,400 with check 0004.

04   Bought computer on account, $3000. Bayside Computer Store issued sales invoice 9985.

05   Bought surveillance equipment, on account, $1800. Manhattan Eye On You issued sales invoice 998752.

09   Paid Manhattan Eye On You with check 0005 to settle May 05 purchase.

09   Paid six months advanced rent for office space, $2,400. Issued check 0006.

09	Provided security services to visiting president of ABCD Company, $18,000. Issued official receipt 0002 and service invoice 0001.
10	Provided security services to famous actors for the premiere of a movie, $27,000. Issued official receipt 0003 for the $7,000 down payment and service invoice 0002 for the whole amount. Balance is on account.
12	Collected $14,000 for services on May 10. Issued official receipt 0004.
13	Issued check 0007 to THE Gas Station for gasoline purchases, $300.
16	Issued official receipt 0005 for balance collected for services on May 10 $6,000.
16	Cashed check 0008 for wages paid, $17,000.
16	Provided security services during the United Nations General Assembly meeting, $25,000, on account. Issued service invoice 0003.
20	Issued check 0009 to THE Gas Station for gasoline expenses, $500.
21	Issued check 0010 as payment for computer bought on May 04, $3,000.
22	Issued check 0011 as partial payment to Ford Bayside Dealership, $5,000.
22	Provided security services for the concert tour of Michael Spring Band, $29,000. Received $19,000 down payment, balance on account. Issued service invoice 0004 for the total amount and official receipt 0006 for the down payment.
23	Issued official receipt 0007 to UN General Assembly for services rendered on May 16, $25,000.
24	Paid THE Gas Station for van maintenance, $800. Issued check 0012.
25	Paid telephone bill and mailed check 0013, $255.
27	Paid electricity bill and mailed check 0014, $450.
30	Cashed check 0015 for wages paid, $22,000.
31	Owner cashed check 0016 for personal use, $8,000.
REQUIRED:	Analyze the transactions of Reliable Security Management Services. Identify the accounting elements affected in each transaction. Prepare the expanded accounting equation chart.

RELIABLE SECURITY MANAGEMENT SERVICES
EXPANDED ACCOUNTING EQUATION CHART
FOR THE MONTH ENDED
ASSETS=LIABILITIES+CAPITAL+REVENUES-EXPENSES-DRAWING

PAGE 1

DATE	DESCRIPTION	ASSETS	LIABILITIES	CAPITAL	REVENUES	EXPENSES	DRAWING

RELIABLE SECURITY MANAGEMENT SERVICES
EXPANDED ACCOUNTING EQUATION CHART
FOR THE MONTH ENDED
ASSETS=LIABILITIES+CAPITAL+REVENUES-EXPENSES-DRAWING

PAGE 2

DATE	DESCRIPTION	ASSETS	LIABILITIES	CAPITAL	REVENUES	EXPENSES	DRAWING
	BALANCE FORWARD						

RELIABLE SECURITY MANAGEMENT SERVICES
EXPANDED ACCOUNTING EQUATION CHART
FOR THE MONTH ENDED
ASSETS=LIABILITIES+CAPITAL+REVENUES-EXPENSES-DRAWING

PAGE 3

DATE	DESCRIPTION	ASSETS	LIABILITIES	CAPITAL	REVENUES	EXPENSES	DRAWING
	BALANCE FORWARD						

CHAPTER 03   ACCOUNTING PROCESS: ANALYZING TRANSACTIONS

LEARNING OBJECTIVES

L01   Define business transaction.

L02   Define the analyzing step and its importance in the accounting process.

L03   Explain the separate business entity concept.

L04   Explain the rules of debit and credit.

L05   Discuss the role of the rules of debit and credit in the accounting process.

L06   Define the normal balance of accounts

L07   Explain the double entry accounting system.

L08   Define and identify the purpose of the chart of accounts.

L09   Describe the transaction analysis chart and the T account. Discuss how they are used to facilitate the analysis of transaction.

L10   Explain the procedures used in using the T account.

CHAPTER 03 ACCOUNTING PROCESS: ANALYZING TRANSACTIONS

ANALYZING TRANSACTIONS

A **business transaction** is any event or happening measured in terms of money that has an affect on the financial condition or results of operations of a business entity. Each business transaction results in balanced effect to at least two accounts. For example, the purchase of computer for cash is a business transaction. This transaction increases the asset computer and decreases the asset cash. It has a balanced effect and in accounting this transaction is recorded as debit to asset computer because it is increased and a credit to asset cash because cash is decreased. On the other hand, if the computer is bought on account, instead of a decrease in asset cash, an increase in a liability, accounts payable is recognized. The increase in liability is recorded as a credit to accounts payable.

As business transactions happen, the effect (increase or decrease) of the transaction on the accounting elements are evaluated. **Analyzing** is the process of evaluating the effects of business transactions on the accounting elements. Analyzing is the first step in the accounting process. It is very important because if the analysis of transactions is incorrect, wrong journal entries will be recorded in the general journal and this error will be carried over to the financial statements. It is therefore imperative that the correct transaction analysis be made in order to arrive at accurate financial reports. Remember that these financial reports are the ones utilized by users of financial information in making decisions about the business.

SEPARATE ENTITY CONCEPT

According to the accounting principle of **separate business entity, the business entity is separate and distinct from its owners**. The business entity and its owners are two separate personalities, distinct and different from each other. **Transactions must be analyzed from the point of view of the business entity** and not from the point of view of the owners. Many accounting students get confused when they analyze business transactions because they make a wrong assumption that the business entity and the owners are one and the same. For example, when an owner invests cash in the business, from the point of view of the business entity, the asset cash of the business is increased and the capital of the owner in the business is also increased. On the other hand, from the point of view of the owner, the asset cash of the owner is decreased and his asset investment in the business is increased. For this transaction, the first set of analysis must be used, since it is the one based on the business entity's point of view. To avoid erroneous analysis, always bear in mind that transactions must be evaluated from the point of view of the business entity and that the owners and the business entity are separate and distinct from each other.

TYPES OF BUSINESS TRANSACTIONS

Transactions happen continuously and repetitiously as the business entity goes through its usual operations. Every day, business entities pay expenses, purchase assets, perform services, sell products, borrow money and incur liabilities, collect receivables, pay liabilities, allow owners to withdraw funds for personal use, etc. The same transactions happen throughout the life of the business and the same transactions are analyzed, recorded, reported and interpreted in the accounting process. Accounting is precise and specific. For a unique transaction, the same analysis is done, and the same general journal entry is made in the accounting records. For example, if the owner invested cash to start a business, the debit is always to asset cash and the credit is always to capital. For the same transaction, the general journal entry is always the same no matter how many times the same transaction occurs. To familiarize students in the accounting process, he will be presented with numerous problems to solve and practice the accounting knowledge and principles that he has learned. As he becomes adept in analyzing transactions, it will become easier for him to analyze, record, summarize, report and interpret financial information. The accounting student should not feel discouraged if initially he is somewhat confused and feels at a loss in analyzing transactions. As he progresses in his accounting course, he will become more familiar with the same transactions being presented to him and he will develop a more confident feeling as he eventually processes transactions accurately.

Some typical business transactions are summarized below:

Investment by the owner
- Cash investment (cash is received from the owner as investment in the business)
- Non-cash investment (non-cash assets such as equipment, furniture, tools, etc are invested by the owner)

Performance of service or sale of product
- For cash (cash is received from customer for services rendered or products sold)
- On account (cash is not received from customers when services are rendered or when products are sold; customer will pay at a later date)
- With down payment and balance on account (cash down payment is received from the customer and the remainder is to be paid at a later date)

Purchase of asset
- For cash (cash is paid to fully pay for asset bought)
- On account (no cash is paid at time of purchase of asset; payment to be made at a later date)
- With down payment and balance on account (cash down payment is made and the remainder is to be paid at a later date)

Collection of customer account (accounts receivable)
- For cash (cash is received from customer to fully settle account)
- With promissory note (customer's promissory note is issued to settle account)

Payment of supplier accounts (accounts payable)
- For cash (cash is paid to supplier/creditor to fully settle accounts payable)
- With promissory note (issuance of promissory note to settle accounts payable)

Payment of expense (cash is paid to pay expenses)

Withdrawal of assets, usually cash, for owner's personal use

Payment of dividends, for corporation

These transactions will be included in the illustrations and problems covered in succeeding chapters.

REVIEW OF EXPANDED ACCOUNTING EQUATION

In the process of analyzing transactions, the **rules of debit and credit** dictate the action to take, based on the effect of the transaction on the accounting elements. Let us review the expanded accounting equation, $A = L + (C-D) + (R-E)$. Do you remember what these letters stand for? These letters stand for the six accounting elements:

- A for Assets, anything that the business owns
- L for Liabilities, anything that the business owes
- C for Capital, the claim of the owner/s in the assets of the business
- R for Revenues, the amount charged by the business to its customers for services performed or products sold (effectively increases owner's equity)
- E for expenses, the amount spent by the business to earn the revenues (effectively decreases owner's equity)
- D for Drawing (for sole proprietorship and partnership) or Dividends (for corporation), owner's withdrawal of assets, usually cash for personal use (effectively decreases owner's equity)

Remember that capital, revenues, expenses and drawing/dividends are components of owner's equity.

RULES OF DEBIT and CREDIT

In accounting, **debit simply means the left side of the account** and **credit simply means the right side of the account. There should be no other meaning to be associated with debit and credit.** Many accounting students relate debit and credit to some other meanings, such as debit card, credit card, credit rating, credit bank account balance, debit bank account balance, etc. It is when students associate debit and credit to these meanings that they get confused when analyzing business transactions. Moreover, some students associate debit and credit to mathematical processes of addition and subtraction. Again, debit and credit should not be associated to any mathematical process, because the mathematical action to take depends on the effect of the transaction on the accounting elements. To avoid being confused, do not give any other meaning to debit other than the left side of the account, and to credit other than the right side of the account.

The **rules of debit and credit** identify the action to take (debit or credit) to specific accounts based on the effect (increase or decrease) of the transaction to the accounting elements. The rules of debit and credit are directly related to the expanded accounting equation. Both of them are based on the accounting elements. The expanded accounting equation is expressed as $A = L + C + R - E - D$. In algebra, the expanded accounting equation can also be expressed as $A + E + D = L + C + R$. The accounting elements on the left side of this derived equation, **assets, expenses and**

drawing/dividends follow the same debit and credit rule and the accounting elements on the right side of this derived equation, **liabilities, capital and revenues follow the same debit and credit rule. The debit and credit rule for the assets, expenses and drawing/dividends is the opposite of the debit and credit rule for liabilities, capital and revenues.**

The rules of debit and credit for each accounting elements are shown below:

ACTION (DEBIT OR CREDIT)	EFFECT ON ACCOUNTING ELEMENT
DEBIT	INCREASES in ASSETS
DEBIT	INCREASES in EXPENSES
DEBIT	INCREASES in DRAWING/DIVIDENDS
CREDIT	INCREASES in LIABILITIES
CREDIT	INCREASES in CAPITAL
CREDIT	INCREASES in REVENUES

You would notice that although there are six accounting elements, there are basically only TWO sets of rules for debits and credits. One set of rule for assets, expenses and drawing/dividends (left side of derived equation) and another set of rule, which is the opposite of the first rule for liabilities, capital and revenues (right side of derived equation).

Based on the above rules, can you fill in the action to take for *decreases in the accounting elements below*?

ACTION (DEBIT OR CREDIT)	EFFECT ON ACCOUNTING ELEMENT
_____	DECREASES in ASSETS
_____	DECRESASES in EXPENSES
_____	DECREASES in DRAWING/DIVIDENDS
_____	DECREASES in LIABILITIES
_____	DECREASES in CAPITAL
_____	DECREASES in REVENUES

If you answered CREDIT for the first 3 items for decreases in assets, expenses and drawing/dividends and DEBIT for the last 3 items for decreases in liabilities, capital and revenues, you are correct.

The following illustration summarizes the rules of debit and credit.

ASSETS, EXPENSES and DRAWING		LIABILITIES, CAPITAL and REVENUES	
DEBIT	CREDIT	DEBIT	CREDIT
INCREASES	DECREASES	DECREASES	INCREASES

NORMAL BALANCE OF ACCOUNTS

The **normal balance** of accounts is the **increased side** of the account. Going back to the rules of debit and credit, what is the increased side of assets, expenses and drawing/dividends? Isn't **debit the increased side of assets, expenses and drawing**? What is the increased side of liabilities, capital and revenues? **Credit is the increased side of liabilities, capital and revenues.** Therefore, **debit balance is the normal balance of assets, expenses and drawing/dividends and credit balance is the normal balance of liabilities, capital and revenues.** It is important to know the normal balance of accounts because this knowledge will be helpful in analyzing transactions, recording general journal entries, posting to the general ledger and preparing accounting reports.

THE DOUBLE ENTRY ACCOUNTING SYSTEM

According to the **double entry accounting system (also called the dual accounting system), a business transaction affects at least two accounts and the debit and credit amounts recorded for the affected accounts must be balanced.** For example, if the business paid $500 for rent, the two accounts affected are asset Cash and expense Rent Expense. Cash is decreased by $500 and Rent Expense is increased by $500. Therefore following the rules of debit and credit, to record this particular transaction, debit Rent Expense for $500 and credit Cash for $500. **A transaction can affect more than two accounts.** If the business bought a computer for $5,000 and paid a down payment of $1,000 and balance on account, there are three accounts affected. The asset Computer increased by $5,000; asset Cash decreased by $1,000 and liability Accounts Payable increased by $4,000. To record this transaction, the business need to debit Computer for $5,000, credit Cash for $1,000 and credit Accounts Payable for $4,000. Note that the debit amount ($5,000) is equal to the sum of the credit amounts ($1,000 + $4,000 = $5,000).

THE CHART OF ACCOUNTS

Business entities develop a **chart of accounts, a list of account titles with their corresponding account codes that the business will use in recording and posting in the books of accounts and in reporting in the financial statements. The purpose of the chart of accounts is to make sure that the same account title and account codes are used for the same transaction in order to have uniformity in recording the same transactions.** Since there are many internal and external users of financial information shown in the financial statements of the business, it is therefore important to use standardized account titles so that there is consistency in the recording of specific transactions and reporting the same in the financial statements. In recording transactions, the **account titles as shown exactly in the chart of accounts must be used.**

Account codes are assigned based on the accounting elements. The prefix or the first digit in the account code identifies the accounting element of the account and the next 2 or 3 digits (small businesses usually have fewer accounts than larger businesses, so small businesses usually have 3 digit account codes and large businesses have 4 digit account codes) **is the sequence or order number of the account in the accounting element. Businesses assign the sequence number in the order that the accounts are presented in the financial statements.**

Businesses usually assign the following account code prefixes:

1	Assets
2	Liabilities
3	Capital
4	Drawing
5	Revenues
6	Expenses
7	Other Revenues
8	Other Expenses

Note that the prefixes are arranged in accordance with the order that they are shown in the financial statements. Balance sheet accounts, such as assets, liabilities and owner's equity are assigned lower prefix numbers compared with the income statement accounts of revenues and expenses.

A typical chart of accounts for a service business is shown.

EFFICIENT SERVICES
CHART OF ACCOUNTS

Code	Account Title	Code	Account Title
ASSETS		**REVENUES**	
101	Cash	501	Revenues
103	Accounts Receivable		
103.1	Allowance for Bad Debts		
105	Office Supplies	**EXPENSES**	
107	Prepaid Insurance		
109	Prepaid Rent	601	Rent Expense
110	Notes Receivable	602	Wages Expense
112	Interest Receivable	603	Telephone Expense
120	Land	604	Electricity Expense
122	Building	605	Transportation Expense
122.1	Accumulated Depreciation – Building	606	Gasoline Expense
124	Car	607	Office Supplies Expense
124.1	Accumulated Depreciation – Car	608	Entertainment Expense
126	Delivery Van	609	Depreciation Expense - Building
126.1	Accumulated Depreciation – Delivery Van	610	Depreciation Expense - Car
127	Computer	611	Depreciation Expense – Delivery Van
127.1	Accumulated Depreciation – Computer	612	Depreciation Expense – Computer

128	Furniture	613	Depreciation Expense – Furniture
128.1	Accumulated Depreciation – Furniture	615	Van Maintenance Expense
		699	Miscellaneous Expenses

LIABILITIES

201	Accounts Payable
203	Notes Payable
205	Interest Payable
207	Wages Payable
209	Unearned Revenues
221	Loans Payable

OTHER REVENUES

701	Rental Revenues
703	Interest Revenues

OTHER EXPENSES

801	Interest Expense

CAPITAL

301 Clark Kent, Capital

DRAWING

401 Clark Kent, Drawing

DEVICES FOR ANALYZING TRANSACTIONS

Devices or tools are used to facilitate analyzing transactions. This book will discuss two of these, namely, the transaction analysis chart and the T account. The transaction analysis chart is a preliminary analysis of transactions and shows the following information:

Date of transaction
Accounting element (asset, liability, capital, revenues, expense, drawing or dividend)
Account title (as shown in the chart of accounts)
Effect (increase or decrease)
Action (debit or credit)
Debit amount
Credit amount

The heading of the transaction analysis chart shows the name of the business on the first line, the title of the report (transaction analysis chart) on the second line and the period covered on the third line. In processing each transaction, all debits must be written before the credits. A blank or space line separates each transaction. At the end of the report, total debit column must equal total credit column.

The supporting source documents mentioned in each transaction of Efficient Services will be used in later chapter on journalizing transactions in the general journal.

Let us use the transactions of Efficient Services in December 2005 to illustrate the preparation of the transaction analysis chart.

Dec	01 2005	Received $150,000 investment from Clark Kent to start Efficient Services. Issued official receipt (OR) 001.
	02	Issued check (CK) 001 for office supplies, $3000.
	03	Bought computer equipment from Best Buy, $15,000. Issued CK 002 for $3,000 down payment. Balance is on account.
	06	Bought delivery van from A-J Car Dealership, $25,000. Issued CK 003 for the $2,000 down payment. Balance is on account.
	07	Paid one year rent, $3,000. Issued CK 004.
	08	Performed services for cash, $5,000. Issued OR 002 and sales invoice (SI) 001.
	09	Performed services, $10,000. Issued OR 003 for the $4,000 down payment and SI 002 for the full amount. Balance is on account.
	13	Obtained bank loan, $50,000. Issued promissory note (PN) 001.
	14	Paid $300 for van maintenance. Issued CK 005.

15	Paid wages, $3,000. Issued CK 007. CK 006 was voided.
16	Performed services, $20,000. Issued OR 004 for the $4,000 down payment and SI 003 for the full amount. Balance is on account.
17	Issued OR 005 for $6,000 collected from customers (see on Dec 10).
18	Issued CK 008 as payment for telephone expense, $400.
19	Issued CK 009 as payment for electricity expense, $600.
20	Issued CK 010 partial payment to Best Buy, $6,000 (see Dec 03).
21	Issued CK 011 payment to A-J Dealership, $5,000 (see Dec 06).
22	Issued CK 012 to Clark Kent for cash withdrawal, $4,000.
23	Collected $2,000 from customers on account. Issued OR 007.
28	Paid entertainment expense, $400. Issued CK 013.
30	Paid wages, $5,000. Issued CK 014.

EFFICIENT SERVICES
Transaction Analysis Chart
For one month ended December 31, 2005

Date	Accounting Element	Account Title	Effect	Action	Debit Amount	Credit Amount
12-01	Asset	Cash	increase	debit	150,000	
	Capital	Cark Kent, Capital	increase	credit		150,000
12-02	Asset	Office Supplies	increase	debit	3,000	
	Asset	Cash	decrease	credit		3,000
12-03	Asset	Computer	increase	debit	15,000	
	Asset	Cash	decrease	credit		3,000
	Liability	Accounts Payable	increase	credit		12,000
12-06	Asset	Delivery Van	increase	debit	25,000	
	Asset	Cash	decrease	credit		2,000
	Liability	Accounts Payable	increase	credit		23,000
12-07	Asset	Prepaid Rent	increase	debit	3,000	
	Asset	Cash	decrease	credit		3,000
12-08	Asset	Cash	increase	debit	5,000	
	Revenue	Revenues	increase	credit		5,000
12-09	Asset	Cash	increase	debit	4,000	
	Asset	Accounts Receivable	increase	debit	6,000	
	Revenue	Revenues	increase	credit		10,000
12-13	Asset	Cash	increase	debit	50,000	
	Liability	Loans Payable	increase	credit		50,000
12-14	Expense	Van Maintenance Expense	increase	debit	300	
	Asset	Cash	decrease	credit		300
12-15	Expense	Wages Expense	increase	debit	3,000	
	Asset	Cash	decrease	credit		3,000
12-16	Asset	Cash	increase	debit	4,000	
	Asset	Accounts Receivable	increase	debit	16,000	
	Revenue	Revenues	increase	credit		20,000
12-17	Asset	Cash	increase	debit	6,000	
	Asset	Accounts Receivable	decrease	credit		6,000

EFFICIENT SERVICES
Transaction Analysis Chart
For one month ended December 31, 2005

Date	Accounting Element	Account Title	Effect	Action	Debit Amount	Credit Amount
12-18	Expense	Telephone Expense	increase	debit	400	
	Asset	Cash	decrease	credit		400
12-19	Expense	Electricity Expense	increase	debit	600	
	Asset	Cash	decrease	credit		600
12-20	Liability	Accounts Payable	decrease	debit	6,000	
	Asset	Cash	decrease	credit		6,000
12-21	Liability	Accounts Payable	decrease	debit	5,000	
	Asset	Cash	decrease	credit		5,000
12-22	Drawing	Clark Kent, Drawing	increase	debit	4,000	
	Asset	Cash	decrease	credit		4,000
12-23	Asset	Cash	increase	debit	2,000	
	Asset	Accounts Receivable	decrease	credit		2,000
12-28	Expense	Entertainment Expense	increase	debit	400	
	Asset	Cash	decrease	credit		400
12-30	Expense	Wages Expense	increase	debit	5,000	
	Asset	Cash	decrease	credit		5,000
				TOTAL	313,700	313,700

Note that for very transaction analyzed, at least one debit and one credit account are affected, that is, at least two accounts are affected. It is also possible that a transaction can affect three or more accounts (see 12-06; 12-09 and 12-16 transactions).

The total debit amount and the total credit amount for each transaction are equal.

THE T ACCOUNT

The **T account** is an accounting device that facilitates the analysis of transactions. It is called the T account because it is in the form of the letter T. A **T account has three parts, namely, the account title or account name, the debit side on the left side and the credit side on the right side. One T account is created for every account title.** A transaction affecting the particular account title is posted either in the debit side or the credit side of the T account. In posting transactions to the T account it is advisable to indicate the date on the left side of each posted amount. It is easier to trace errors later if the postings are cross referenced by date.

After all transactions are posted to the T account, the amounts on each side of the T account are totaled. **Footing** is the process of computing the total of each side of the T account by adding all the amounts on each side. Therefore since there are two sides to a T account, a **T account can have one or two footings, the debit footing and the credit footing. Footing is computed only if there are more than one amount posted on the side of the account, if there is only one amount posted, there is no need to compute the footing.** It is possible that a T account can have several amounts posted on one side and no amount posted or only one amount posted on the other side. In this case, compute the footing only on the side that has more than one amount posted. For instance if the account Revenues has several amounts posted on the credit side and no amount posted on the debit side, then the credit footing must be computed and no debit footing is computed. In this example, the account Revenues has only one footing, the credit footing. The account Cash is always an active account, meaning there are many transactions that affect the Cash account. Cash usually has many amounts posted on both the debit and credit sides. The debit footing and credit footing must be computed for accounts with more than one amount posted on both sides of the account. As earlier mentioned, there is no need to compute the footing if an account has only one amount posted on the side and the footing for that side is equal to that one amount posted.

Balancing is the process of computing the balance or net amount of an account by getting the difference between the debit footing and the credit footing. **There is no need to compute the balance if an account has only one footing, the footing is already the balance of the account. The balance of an account is computed by deducting the smaller footing from the larger footing and the resulting balance is placed on the side with the larger footing.**

The transactions of Efficient Services for the month of December, 2005 which were analyzed and processed using the Transaction Analysis Chart are used to illustrate posting to the T account, computing the debit and credit footings and the account balance.

One T account is created for each account title.

The information shown in Transaction Analysis Chart for the date, account title, debit amount and credit amount are used in posting the transactions to the T accounts.

Remember the steps in posting transactions to T account:

(1) Write the date and amount on the appropriate side (debit side or credit side)
(2) Compute the debit and credit footings, if needed
(3) Compute the account balance, if needed

The postings to the T accounts of Efficient Services are shown below:

CASH				ACCOUNTS PAYABLE			
12/01	150,000	12/02	3,000	12/20	6,000	12/03	12,000
12/08	5,000	12/03	3,000	12/21	5,000	12/06	23,000
12/09	4,000	12/06	2,000		11,000		35,000
12/13	50,000	12/07	3,000				-11,000
12/16	4,000	12/14	300			BAL	24,000
12/17	6,000	12/15	3,000				
12/23	2,000	12/18	400				
		12/19	600				
		12/20	6,000				
		12/21	5,000				
		12/22	4,000				
		12/28	400				
		12/30	5,000				
	221,000		35,700				
	-35,700						
BAL	185,300						

LOANS PAYABLE			
		12/13	50,000

CLARK KENT, CAPITAL			
		12/01	150,000

REVENUES			
		12/08	5,000
		12/09	10,000
		12/16	20,000
		BAL	35,000

COMPUTER			
12/03	15,000		

CLARK KENT, DRAWING			
12/22	4,000		

DELIVERY VAN			
12/06	25,000		

OFFICE SUPPLIES			
12/02	3,000		

ACCOUNTS RECEIVABLE			
12/09	6,000	12/17	6,000
12/16	16,000	12/23	2,000
	22,000		8,000
	-8,000		
BAL	14,000		

PREPAID RENT			
12/07	3,000		

VAN MAINTENANCE EXPENSE			
12/14	300		

WAGES EXPENSE			
12/15	3,000		
12/30	5,000		
BAL	8,000		

TELEPHONE EXPENSE			
12/18	400		

ENTERTAINMENT EXPENSE			
12/28	400		

ELECTRICITY EXPENSE			
12/19	600		

Note that no debit or credit footing was computed for the T accounts that have only one amount posted: Office Supplies, Prepaid Rent, Delivery Van, Computer, Loans Payable, Clark Kent, Capital, Clark Kent, Drawing, Van Maintenance Expense, Telephone Expense, Electricity Expense and Entertainment Expense. The balance of these accounts is the amount posted on the T account.

The balance of Revenues is equal to the credit footing, since there are no amounts posted on the debit side of the T account. The balance of Wages Expense is equal to the debit footing. Remember that the footing is equal to the sum of all the amounts posted on one side of the T account.

For accounts that have several amounts posted on both sides, the debit footing and credit footing are computed. The balance of these accounts is equal to the difference between the debit and credit footings. The resulting balance is reflected on the side with the larger footing. In the above T accounts, study the computation of the balance for Cash, Accounts Receivable and Accounts Payable.

The balances of the T accounts as of December 31, 2005 are summarized below:

ACCOUNT TITLE	DEBIT	CREDIT
Cash	185,300	
Accounts Receivable	14,000	
Office Supplies	3,000	
Prepaid Rent	3,000	
Computer	15,000	
Delivery Van	25,000	
Accounts Payable		24,000
Loans Payable		50,000
Clark Kent, Capital		150,000
Clark Kent, Drawing	4,000	
Revenues		35,000
Van Maintenance Expense	300	
Wages Expense	8,000	
Telephone Expense	400	
Entertainment Expense	400	
Electricity Expense	600	
Van Maintenance Expense	300	
	259,000	259,000

CHAPTER 03 ACCOUNTING PROCESS: ANALYZING TRANSACTIONS

REVIEW QUESTIONS

1. What is a business transaction? Identify the types of business transactions.

2. What is the analyzing process? Why is correct analysis of transactions very important?

3. Explain the separate business entity concept.

4. What are the two basic rules of debits and credits?

5. What is the normal balance of accounts?

6. Explain the double entry accounting system.

7. What is the chart of accounts? What is the use of the chart of accounts?

8. How is the transaction analysis chart used in facilitating transaction analysis?

9. What are the steps in using the T account in analyzing transactions?

10. Why are the transaction analysis chart and the T account not considered as formal accounting record?

CHAPTER 03   ACCOUNTING PROCESS: ANALYZING TRANSACTIONS

REVIEW EXAMINATION

TRUE or FALSE: *WRITE TRUE or FALSE IN THE SPACE PROVIDED.*

_____ 1.   A business transaction is any event or happening measured in terms of money that has no affect on the financial condition or results of operations of a business entity.

_____ 2.   Each business transaction results in balanced effect to at least two accounts.

_____ 3.   The increase in liability is recorded as a debit to accounts payable.

_____ 4.   Footing is the process of evaluating the effects of business transactions on the accounting elements.

_____ 5.   It is imperative that the correct transaction analysis be made in order to arrive at accurate financial reports.

_____ 6.   According to the accounting principle of separate business entity, the business entity is the same as its owners.

_____ 7.   Transactions must be analyzed from the point of view of the owners and not from the point of view of the business.

_____ 8.   Transactions happen continuously and repetitiously as the business entity goes through its usual operations.

_____ 9.   In the process of analyzing transactions, the rules of debit and credit dictate the action to take, based on effect on the accounting elements affected by the transaction.

_____ 10.   An asset is anything that the business owes.

_____ 11.   A liability is anything that the business owns.

_____ 12.   Capital represents the claim of the owner in the asset of the business.

_____ 13.   Debit simply means the right side of the account and credit simply means the left side of the account.

_____ 14.   The rules of debit and credit are directly related to the expanded accounting equation.

_____ 15.   The debit and credit rule for the assets, expenses and drawing/dividends is the opposite of the debit and credit rule for liabilities, capital and revenues.

_____ 16.   Debit balance is the normal balance of assets, expenses and revenues.

_____ 17. Credit balance is the normal balance of liabilities, capital, drawing and revenues.

_____ 18. According to the double entry accounting system, a business transaction affects at least two accounts and the debit and credit amounts recorded for the affected accounts must be balanced.

_____ 19. A transaction can affect more than two accounts.

_____ 20. The chart of accounts is a list of account titles with their corresponding account codes that the business will use in recording and posting in the books of accounts and in reporting the financial statements.

FILL IN THE BLANKS: *WRITE THE ANSWER IN THE SPACE PROVIDED.*

1. The balance of an account is computed by deducting the _____ footing from the _____ footing and the resulting balance is placed on the side with the _____ footing.

2. _____ is the process of computing the balance or net amount of an account by getting the difference between the debit footing and the credit footing.

3. _____ is the process of computing the total of each side of the T account by adding all the amounts on each side.

4. The _____ is an accounting device in the form of letter T that facilitates the analysis of transactions.

5. A T account has three parts, namely, the _____, _____ and _____.

6. For very transaction analyzed, at least one _____ account and one _____ account are affected, that is, at least two accounts are affected.

7. In recording transactions, the account titles as shown exactly in the _____ must be used.

8. The chart of accounts is a list of _____ with their corresponding account codes.

9. A transaction can affect more than _____ accounts.

10. According to the _____ system, a business transaction affects at least two accounts and the debit and credit amounts recorded for the affected accounts must be balanced.

11. _____ balance is the normal balance of liabilities, capital and revenues.

Fundamentals of Accounting

12. Debit balance is the normal balance of _____, _____ and _____.

13. _____ are the loans or payables of a business.

14. The debit and credit rule for the assets, expenses and drawing/dividends is the _____ of the debit and credit rule for liabilities, capital and revenues.

15. _____ represent the claim of the owner in the asset of the business.

16. _____ simply means the right side of the account.

17. _____ simply means the left side of the account.

18. In the process of analyzing transactions, the _____ dictate the action to take, based on effect on the accounting elements affected by the transaction.

19. _____ happen continuously and repetitiously as the business entity goes through its usual operations.

20. Transactions must be analyzed from the point of view of the _____ and not from the point of view of the owners.

21. According to the accounting principle of _____, the business entity is separate and distinct from its owners.

22. _____ is the process of evaluating the effects of business transactions on the accounting elements.

23. The increase in liability is recorded as a _____.

24. Each business transaction results in _____ effect to at least two accounts.

25. A _____ is any event or happening measured in terms of money that has an affect on the financial condition or results of operations of a business entity.

PROBLEMS:

A. Prepare the transaction analysis chart for the transactions of the following service businesses identified in Chapter 2. Sample transaction analysis chart form is attached.

	BUSINESS NAME	PERIOD ENDED
1.	Global Delivery Services	June 2006
2.	Garden Landscaping & Pool Services	December 2005
3.	Grade A Plus Tutorial Services	October 2005
4.	Jolie Kids Day Care Services	September 2005
5.	James Deane Tours	June 2005
6.	Have Fun Day Camp	December 2005
7.	Beautiful Hollywood	March 2006
8.	Reliable Security Services	May 2002

B. Post the transactions of the above businesses in T accounts. Samples of the T account form are attached. Since Cash account normally has many entries, the T account for Cash is provided. For all other accounts, use the other T accounts in the T account forms.

REMINDER: Post the trial balance amounts identified as BEG BAL (Beginning Balance) as the first entry in the T accounts for Garden Landscaping & Pool Services and Have Fun Day Camp.

Foot (add) the amounts on each side of the T account. Footing is done only for the side that has more than one posted amount.

Compute the balance of each T account. Balancing is done only for accounts with posted amounts on both sides of the T account. Balance is equal to the difference between the debit side and credit side.

TRANSACTION ANALYSIS CHART FORM

TRANSACTION ANALYSIS CHART
FOR THE _____ ENDED _____

DATE	ACCTG ELEMENT	ACCOUNT TITLE	EFFECT	ACTION	DEBIT AMOUNT	CREDIT AMOUNT

T ACCOUNT FORM

CASH

T ACCOUNT FORM

T ACCOUNT FORM

T ACCOUNT FORM

T ACCOUNT FORM

T ACCOUNT FORM

T ACCOUNT FORM

CHAPTER 04 ACCOUNTING PROCESS: THE BOOKS OF ACCOUNTS

LEARNING OBJECTIVES

L01 Differentiate accounting cycle, accounting period and accounting process.

L02 Describe the steps in the accounting process.

L03 Identify and describe the books of accounts.

L04 Describe the general journal and the information shown in the general journal.

L05 Discuss the rules in recording general journal entries in the general journal.

L06 Identify and describe the types of accounting entries.

L07 Describe the general ledger and the information shown in the general ledger.

L8 Discuss the rules in posting to the general ledger.

L09 Differentiate the three-column general ledger from the four-column general ledger.

CHAPTER 04   ACCOUNTING PROCESS: THE BOOKS OF ACCOUNTS

THE ACCOUNTING CYCLE

The **accounting cycle** involves a series of activities undertaken during the accounting period to process business transactions and produce financial statements. The **accounting period** or **reporting period** is the period (can be one month, one quarter, six months, one year, etc.) covered in the heading of the income statement. An **accounting year** is any twelve-month period. An accounting year can be a calendar year or a fiscal year. A **calendar year** follows the calendar; it starts on January 1 and ends on December 31. A **fiscal year** is any twelve-month period that does not start on January 1.

The steps undertaken during the accounting cycle comprise the **accounting process**. The accounting process has three basic phases, the input, the processing and the output. The inputs in the accounting process are the source documents which support the business transactions. These source documents provide the information needed in the processing of the transactions in the accounting records. The source documents can be sales invoices, official receipts, checks, suppliers' invoices, etc. The processing phase involves analyzing the effects of the transaction in the accounting elements and recording them in the books of accounts. In the output phase (sometimes called the reporting phase), financial statements, namely, the income statement, equity statement, balance and statement of cash flows are produced. The accounting process is illustrated below:

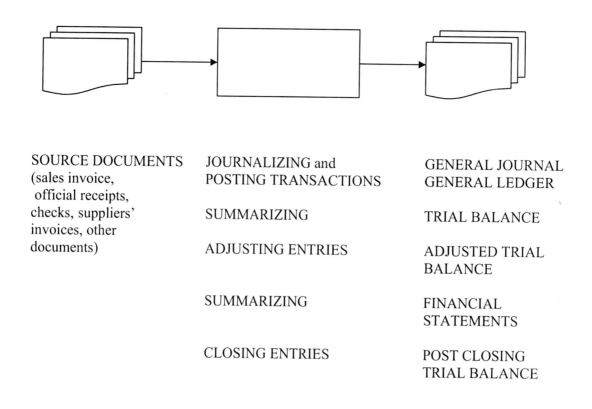

INPUT	PROCESSING	OUTPUT
SOURCE DOCUMENTS (sales invoice, official receipts, checks, suppliers' invoices, other documents)	JOURNALIZING and POSTING TRANSACTIONS	GENERAL JOURNAL GENERAL LEDGER
	SUMMARIZING	TRIAL BALANCE
	ADJUSTING ENTRIES	ADJUSTED TRIAL BALANCE
	SUMMARIZING	FINANCIAL STATEMENTS
	CLOSING ENTRIES	POST CLOSING TRIAL BALANCE

The steps in the accounting process are grouped into three major classifications, those that are done (1) during the current accounting period to record and post transactions as they happen, (2) at the end of the current accounting period to summarize and report financial statements and (3) at the beginning of the next accounting period to simplify the accounting process.

The steps in the accounting process are shown below:

I. During the current accounting period

    1. Analyzing business transactions
    2. Journalizing (recording) accounting entries in the general journal
    3. Posting (classifying) to the general ledger

II. At the end of the current accounting period

    4. Preparing (summarizing) the trial balance
    5. Preparing and recording the adjusting entries in the general journal and posting them to the general ledger
    6. Preparing the worksheet
    7. Preparing the adjusted trial balance
    8. Preparing the financial statements (income statement, equity statement, balance sheet and statement of cash flows)
    9. Preparing and recording the closing entries in the general journal and posting them to the general ledger
    10. Preparing the post-closing trial balance (also called after closing trial balance)

III. At the start of the next accounting period

    11. Preparing and recording reversing entries in the general journal and posting them in the general ledger

BOOKS OF ACCOUNTS

There are two general books of accounts in accounting. These are the **general journal** and the **general ledger**.

THE GENERAL JOURNAL

The **general journal** is called the **book of original entry** because it is the **first formal record** of accounting transactions. **Journalizing,** which is the **recording phase** of accounting is the process of recording business transactions in the general journal in **chronological order** as they happen. Using the information obtained from source documents, transactions are analyzed and their effects in the accounting elements are recorded in the general journal through the general journal entries. **For every transaction, a general journal entry is prepared. Each general journal entry must have at least one debit account and one credit account and the total of the debit amount/s must equal the total of the credit amount/s.** A *simple entry* is a journal entry that has one debit and one credit, only two accounts are affected by the transaction. A *compound entry* is a journal entry that has more than one debit and/or credit, 3 or more accounts are affected by the transaction.

The general journal is actually a thick book with several pages that are sequentially pre-numbered and each page contains the following columns of information:

    Date
    Document Reference
    Account Code
    Description
    Posting Reference
    Debit Amount
    Credit Amount

The information shown in the above columns are:

Date	date when the transaction happened as reflected in the source document, for instance, the date of the check issued to pay an expense or the date of the official receipt issued to customers when cash is received
Document Reference	source document that supports the transaction and provides the details (date, description, amount, etc.) about the transaction; it is very likely that **one transaction has more than one source document,** for instance cash payment is backed up by the check issued by the business **and** the official receipt received from the payee; or cash receipt is supported by the official receipt issued by the business and the bill or statement received from the creditor who is paid

    It is practical to write down all the source documents to support a specific transaction and a two-letter prefix is written before the source document number, such as OR for official receipt for cash receipt and CK for check issued for cash payment. Recommended prefixes for source documents are:

OR	Official receipt for cash received
CK	Check for payments made
CKV	Check voucher
BSR	Billing statement received
CIN	Customer invoice

    Businesses usually assign any meaningful two to four letter prefix related to their nature of operations. In other words there is no fixed or standard prefix that businesses must follow; they can develop their own sets of prefixes that must be known to the persons in the organization who make use of the general journal.

Description	two types of information are shown in this column; (1) the account title to be debited or credited; one line for each account title and (2) after the last credit account title, a brief explanation of the transaction is shown in the last line of the general journal entry
Account Code	account code, usually a 3 or 4 digit code of the account taken from the chart of account
Posting Reference	in the format prefix GLnnn where GL stands for general ledger and nnn is the page number of the general ledger where this journal entry is posted; this field is filled up **after the general journal entry is posted in the general ledger,** not during the journalizing process; therefore this column is left blank during journalizing and is filled up only immediately after the specific journal entry is posted in the general ledger
Debit Amount	amount of the debit account title
Credit Amount	amount of the credit account title

PARTS OF A GENERAL JOURNAL ENTRY

Based on the above, the parts of a general journal entry are the transaction date, source document, account code, debit account/s, debit amount/s, credit account/s, credit amount/s, posting reference and a brief description of the transaction.

RECORDING GENERAL JOURNAL ENTRY IN THE GENERAL JOURNAL

Certain specific rules must be followed in recording general journal entries. These rules are:

1. The date is written on the first line of the general journal entry, on the same line as the first debit entry. The complete date, (month, day and year) is written on the first general journal entry on a page, but only the day is written for subsequent general journal entries. If there are several transactions for one day, the date is indicated only in the first transaction recorded for that specific date and no date is written for subsequent transactions for the same date.

2. The source document is shown in the first line of the general journal entry. To distinguish the source document from each other, use the prefix OR for official receipt; CK for check, PN for promissory note, SI for suppliers' invoice and CI for customer invoice.

3. **All debits must be written before credits**.

4. Debits **can not be intermingled or interspersed with credits and vice versa.**

5. **Debits** are **written in any order ahead of credits** and **credits are written in any order after the debits**. There is no space line or blank line in between the debit and credit entries.

6. **Credits are indented** and not aligned with the debits.

7. The **first letter of account titles must be in capital letter.**

8. **Do not abbreviate the account titles**. Account titles must be written exactly the same way as they are shown in the chart of accounts.

9. In order to maintain the equality of debits and credits in a dual accounting system, the **total debit amount must equal the total credit amount**.

10. The **last line** of each general journal entry is a **brief description of the transaction.**

11. A blank line or a space line separates the general journal entries.

12. The **posting reference is left blank while journalizing** but **the page number of the general ledger is written after the entry is posted in the general ledger.**

In order to understand the rules in recording general journal entries the following transactions are used:

On January 8, 2006, Elmer & Erica Company purchased office equipment amounting to $30,000 and office furniture for $15,000 from ABC, with a cash down payment of $5,000 and the balance payable on January 20, 2006. Check 78 was issued for $5,000 and invoice 96 in the amount of $45,000 was received from ABC.

On January 20, 2006, Elmer & Erica Company settled the balance of the account for the office equipment bought on January 8 by paying $15,000 cash (check 88) and giving the ABC promissory note 08 in the amount of $25,000 to be paid on January 30, 2006.

On January 30, 2006, Elmer & Erica Company issued check 98 for $25,000 to settle the promissory note. On the same date issued check 99 to pay rent $5,000.

Fundamentals of Accounting

GENERAL JOURNAL

Page 095

DATE	DOC REF	ACCT CODE	DESCRIPTION	POST REF	DEBIT AMOUNT	CREDIT AMOUNT
2006						
01-08	BI96	120	Office Equipment		30,000.00	
	CK78	125	Office Furniture		15,000.00	
		101	Cash			5,000.00
		201	Accounts Payable – ABC			40,000.00
			bought equipment & furniture			
20	CK88	201	Accounts Payable - ABC		40,000.00	
	PN08	101	Cash			15,000.00
		203	Notes Payable – ABC			25,000.00
			paid account & issued note			
30	CK98	203	Notes Payable - ABC		25,000.00	
		101	Cash			25,000.00
			paid note due today			
	CK99	505	Rent Expense		5,000.00	
		101	Cash			5,000.00
			paid rent			

NOTE THE FOLLOWING:

Rule #1: The complete date is written for the first debit entry on January 8 and only the day is written for subsequent journal entries. No date is indicated for the payment of rent expense on January 30 because it follows the same date of the first transaction for January 30.

Rule #2: All debits are written before credits.

Rule #3: On January 08, 2006, it is also acceptable to write Office Furniture before Office Equipment and Accounts Payable before Cash. Is it also acceptable to write Notes Payable before Cash on January 20, 2006?

Rule #5: Credits are indented in every general journal entry.

Rule #6: The first letter in the account title is in capital letter.

Rule #7: The account titles are not abbreviated. It is unacceptable to write down Acct Payble, instead of Accounts Payable.

Rule #8: Total debit must equal total credit. For January 8, total debit is $45,000 ($30,000 + $15,000) and $45,000 is also the total credit ($5,000 + $40,000).

Rule #9: At the end of each general journal entry, a brief description of the transaction is indicated.

Rule #10: A blank line separates the general journal entries.

SPECIAL COMBINATION JOURNALS

Businesses maintain **special combination journals** to record transactions that occur **very frequently**. **Sales journal** is a special combination journal where sales transactions are recorded in a chronological order. **Purchases journal** keeps a record of all purchases of merchandise for sale by a merchandising business. **Cash receipts journal** keeps a record of all cash received by the business while **cash disbursements journal** keeps a record of all cash payments made during the accounting period. Companies show information in combination journals according to their requirements. Detailed discussion of combination journals is purposely left out in this book. At the end of the accounting period, the **totals of the monetary columns in a specific special combination journal are used to prepare one general journal entry** to be recorded in the general journal. For example, if the sales journal total for December 2005 of the columns for Cash is $100,000 (meaning cash sales total $100,000); Accounts Receivable is $250,000 (meaning sales on account total $250,000), then there will be a general journal entry in the general journal to reflect these sales (see below).

GENERAL JOURNAL

Page 398

DATE	DOC REF	ACCT CODE	DESCRIPTION	POST REF	DEBIT AMOUNT	CREDIT AMOUNT
2005						
12 30	SJ99	101	Cash		100,000.00	
		103	Accounts Receivable		250,000.00	
		401	Sales			350,000.00
			record December 2005 sales			

TYPES OF ACCOUNTING ENTRIES

Accounting entries are classified into several types based on the transactions that they document, the timing when they are recorded and the objective that they attain. In addition, accounting entries are also classified based on the number of accounts affected by the transaction.

General journal entries are recorded **chronologically in the general journal during the accounting period as the transactions occur**. Source documents, such as sales invoices, official receipts, checks, etc. are used to provide information in the preparation of general journal entries. Before the general journal entries are recorded in the general journal, the effects of the transactions in the accounting elements are analyzed and the rules of debits and credits are used in the transaction analysis and recording of the general journal entries.

Adjusting entries or adjustments are recorded in the general journal at the **end of the accounting period after the trial balance is prepared** in order to reflect the correct balances of accounts that are affected by the adjustments. After all adjustments are posted to the general ledger, an **adjusted trial balance** is prepared which serves as the basis in the preparation of the **financial statements. Financial statements** are formal accounting reports that include the (1) **income statement,** (2) **equity statement (statement of owner's equity for single proprietorship; statement of partner's equity for partnership; statement of retained earnings and stockholders' equity for corporation)** and (3) **balance sheet**. Some businesses include the **statement of cash flows** in their financial statements.

Closing entries are recorded in the general journal at the **end of the accounting period after the financial statements are prepared in order to zero out the balances of temporary** or **nominal** accounts. Temporary or nominal accounts include (1) **revenues** (such as sales, service fees, interest revenues, rental revenues, etc.), (2) **costs and expenses** (such as purchases, salaries expense, rent expense, depreciation expense, telephone expense, etc.) and (3) **drawing** (single proprietorship and partnership) or **dividends** (corporation). Notice that these accounts, **revenues, costs, expenses and drawing or dividends are sometimes called temporary equity accounts because they are closed to the permanent equity account capital (single proprietorship and partnership) or retained earnings (corporation)** The balances of temporary accounts are zeroed out at end of the current accounting period so that they will not be carried over in the next accounting period.

Correcting entries are recorded **any time** in the general journal and posted to the general ledger in order to **correct accounting entries that were previously recorded erroneously.** Correcting entries should be recorded **as soon as the error is identified.**

Memorandum or memo entries are made only as notation in the general journal to describe certain transactions that need to be documented, which do not affect the balances of accounts and therefore no debit or credit account and amount are recorded in the general journal. An example of a memo entry is the declaration of stock dividends or stock splits for corporations.

Reversing entries are recorded in the general journal on the **first day of the next accounting period before any transactions for the next accounting period are recorded** in order to **reverse the adjustments or adjusting entries that increase assets or liabilities**. Note that not all adjusting entries are reversed.

It is important to note that **except for memorandum or memo entries all the above accounting entries are recorded in the general journal and posted in the general ledger.**

Accounting entries can also be classified based on the number of account titles affected by the transaction. A **simple entry** is an accounting entry that affects only one debit account title and one credit account title; only two accounts are affected. A **compound entry** is an accounting entry that affects more than two account titles; three or more accounts are affected.

THE GENERAL LEDGER

The general ledger is called the **book of final entry** because it is the last book of accounts that reflect the effect of business transactions on the accounting elements. **Posting or classifying** is the process of transcribing or transferring information from the general journal to the general ledger. Each account in the general journal entry is posted in the general ledger in the same order that they appear in the general journal, however, accounting information are presented in the general ledger arranged **by account code according to the chart of accounts.**

Just like the general journal, the general ledger is a book of many pages that are sequentially **pre-numbered.** A page in the general ledger contains the following columns:

GENERAL LEDGER

PAGE:_____

ACCOUNT CODE: _____   TITLE: _____

DATE	DESCRIPTION	POST REF	TRANSACTION DEBIT	CREDIT	BALANCE DEBIT	CREDIT

The above columns contain the following information:

DATE: date of the transaction copied from the general journal

DESCRIPTION: explanation of the transaction copied from the last line of the general journal entry in the general journal

POST REF: constant letters GJ nnn; GJ means general journal and nnn is the page number of the general journal where the general journal entry is recorded

TRANSACTION DEBIT AMOUNT: copy the debit amount from the general journal

TRANSACTION CREDIT AMOUNT:	copy the credit amount from the general journal
BALANCE DEBIT AMOUNT:	debit balance is computed by adding the last debit balance to the debit transaction amount OR subtracting the credit transaction amount from the previous debit balance
BALANCE CREDIT AMOUNT:	credit balance is computed by adding the last credit balance to the credit transaction amount OR subtracting the debit transaction amount from the previous credit balance

Note that for **every posting** in the general ledger a **running balance of the account is always computed.**

The above illustrates the **four-column** general ledger which shows four money columns, a pair of debit and credit column for transaction and balance. It is more practical to use the four-column general ledger because the balance easily reflects whether the account has a debit balance or a credit balance. Some businesses use the **three-column** general ledger. As the name suggests, there are only three money columns in the general ledger, namely, the debit transaction amount, the credit transaction amount and the balance column. For a three-column general ledger, the balance column does not specifically identify whether the account has a debit or credit balance and it is up to the user of the general ledger to decide the account side (debit or credit) of the balance. An illustration of the three-column general ledger follows:

GENERAL LEDGER

PAGE:_____

ACCOUNT CODE: _____   TITLE: _____

DATE	DESCRIPTION	POST REF	TRANSACTION DEBIT	CREDIT	BALANCE AMOUNT

POSTING TO THE GENERAL LEDGER

Certain specific rules must be followed when posting general journal entry to the general ledger. These rules are:

1. On the heading line, put a plus "+" sign on the increased side or the normal balance of the account for transaction amount and balance columns. For example, if the account is CASH, put a + on the transaction debit amount and the debit balance columns. If the account is ACCOUNTS PAYABLE, put a + on the transaction credit amount and the credit balance columns. Put a minus "-" sign on the two remaining money

columns. In actual business practice, this step is not done. This step is done as a guide to help the accounting student use the correct arithmetic operation (addition or subtraction) in the computation of the balance of the account every time a posting is made. **The rules of debit and credit are used in identifying the normal balance of an account.** Remember that **assets, costs, expenses, drawing** and **dividends normally have debit balance; liabilities, revenues and capital normally have credit balance.**

2. Copy the date from the general journal of the general journal entry being posted.

3. Indicate in the posting reference of the **general ledger** the letters GJ and the page number of the general journal where the general journal entry is located.

4. If the account is debited in the general journal, put the amount in the transaction debit amount. If the account is credited in the general journal, put the amount in the transaction credit amount.

5. Compute the balance of the account. If the **previous balance and the transaction amount belong to the same side (both are debit or both are credit) add the amounts and the result is the new balance on the same side of the previous balance. If the transaction amount and the previous balance do not belong to the same side (one is debit and the other is credit), the new balance is the difference between the transaction amount and the previous balance and put the result on the side that has a bigger amount** (if previous balance is $1,000.00 debit and transaction amount is $200.00 credit, then new balance is debit $800.00 ($1,000.00 minus $200.00; if previous balance is $200.00 debit and transaction amount is $500 credit, then new balance is $300.00 credit because credit of $500 is greater than debit of $200.00).

6. After indicating the running account balance in the appropriate balance column, **go back to the general journal and in the post reference column of the general journal, write the constant letters GL and the page number of the general ledger where the general journal entry is posted.**

Cross-referencing facilitates the process of matching the general journal entry in the general journal to the posting in the general ledger through the page numbers reflected in the posting reference of both books of accounts. By writing the GL page number in the general journal, the accountant is guided that the particular general journal entry has been posted and therefore, it will not be posted more than once. In addition, it is easier to trace errors (for instance, trial balance is out of balance) in accounting records if both books of accounts are cross-referenced.

To better understand the above rules, let us use the transactions of Elmer & Erica Company and post the general journal entries in the general ledger. Based on the transactions for January 8, 20 and 30, there 6 accounts affected and the beginning balances on January 7, 2006 are shown below:

ACCOUNT TITLE	CODE	GL PAGE	DEBIT	CREDIT
Cash	101	011	85,000.00	
Office Equipment	120	051	25,000.00	
Office Furniture	125	061	10,000.00	
Accounts Payable	201	101		75,000.00
Notes Payable	203	151		12,000.00
Rent Expense	505	601	0.00	

The general ledgers for these accounts are shown in the following illustration after the general journal entries are posted.

The first line is the balance as of January 7, 2006.

GENERAL LEDGER

PAGE: 011

ACCOUNT CODE: 101   TITLE: CASH

DATE	DESCRIPTION	POST REF	TRANSACTION DEBIT (+)	CREDIT (-)	BALANCE DEBIT (+)	CREDIT (-)
01-07-06					85,000.00	
08	bought equipment	GJ095		5,000.00	80,000.00	
20	paid acct/issued note	GJ095		15,000.00	65,000.00	
30	paid note due	GJ095		25,000.00	40,000.00	
	paid rent	GJ095		5,000.00	35,000.00	

GENERAL LEDGER

PAGE: 051

ACCOUNT CODE: 120   TITLE: OFFICE EQUIPMENT

DATE	DESCRIPTION	POST REF	TRANSACTION DEBIT (+)	CREDIT (-)	BALANCE DEBIT (+)	CREDIT (-)
01-07-06					25,000.00	
08	bought equipment	GJ095	30,000.00		55,000.00	

GENERAL LEDGER

PAGE: 061

ACCOUNT CODE: 125   TITLE: OFFICE FURNITURE

DATE	DESCRIPTION	POST REF	TRANSACTION DEBIT (+)	CREDIT (-)	BALANCE DEBIT (+)	CREDIT (-)
01-07-06					10,000.00	
08	bought furniture	GJ095	15,000.00		25,000.00	

GENERAL LEDGER

PAGE: 101

ACCOUNT CODE: 201   TITLE: ACCOUNTS PAYABLE

DATE	DESCRIPTION	POST REF	TRANSACTION DEBIT (-)	CREDIT (+)	BALANCE DEBIT (-)	CREDIT (+)
01-07-06						75,000.00
08	bought equipment	GJ095		40,000.00		115,000.00
20	paid acct/issued note	GJ095	40,000.00			75,000.00

GENERAL LEDGER

PAGE: 151

ACCOUNT CODE: 203   TITLE: NOTES PAYABLE

DATE	DESCRIPTION	POST REF	TRANSACTION DEBIT (-)	CREDIT (+)	BALANCE DEBIT (-)	CREDIT (+)
01-07-06						12,000.00
20	issued note	GJ095		25,000.00		37,000.00
30	paid note due	GJ095	25,000.00			12,000.00

GENERAL LEDGER

PAGE: 601

ACCOUNT CODE: 505 TITLE: RENT EXPENSE

DATE	DESCRIPTION	POST REF	TRANSACTION DEBIT (+)	CREDIT (-)	BALANCE DEBIT (+)	CREDIT (-)
01-30	paid rent	GJ095	5,000.00		5,000.00	

ILLUSTRATION PROBLEM: EFFICIENT SERVICES

REQUIRED: Record the general journal entries in the general journal. Post the general journal entries in the general ledger. Use the chart of accounts below.

CHART OF ACCOUNTS

Code	Account Title
ASSETS	
101	Cash
103	Accounts Receivable
103.1	Allowance for Bad Debts
105	Office Supplies
107	Prepaid Insurance
109	Prepaid Rent
110	Notes Receivable
112	Interest Receivable
120	Land
122	Building
122.1	Accumulated Depreciation – Building
124	Car
124.1	Accumulated Depreciation – Car
126	Delivery Van
126.1	Accumulated Depreciation – Delivery Van
127	Computer
127.1	Accumulated Depreciation – Computer
128	Furniture
128.1	Accumulated Depreciation – Furniture

Code	Account Title
LIABILITIES	
201	Accounts Payable
203	Notes Payable
205	Interest Payable
207	Wages Payable
208	Unearned Rental Revenues
221	Loans Payable

Code	Account Title
CAPITAL	
301	Clark Kent, Capital

Code	Account Title
REVENUES	
501	Revenues
EXPENSES	
600	Bad Debts Expense
601	Rent Expense
602	Wages Expense
603	Telephone Expense
604	Electricity Expense
605	Transportation Expense
606	Gasoline Expense
607	Office Supplies Expense
608	Entertainment Expense
609	Depreciation Expense - Building
610	Depreciation Expense - Car
611	Depreciation Expense – Delivery Van
612	Depreciation Expense – Computer
613	Depreciation Expense – Furniture
615	Van Maintenance Expense
617	Insurance Expense
618	Taxes and Licenses Expense
699	Miscellaneous Expenses

Code	Account Title
OTHER REVENUES	
701	Earned Rental Revenues
703	Interest Revenues

Code	Account Title
OTHER EXPENSES	
801	Interest Expense

Code	Account Title
DRAWING	
401	Clark Kent, Drawing

Transactions for the month of December, 2005.

Dec	01 2005	Received $150,000 investment from Clark Kent to start Efficient Services. Issued official receipt (OR) 001.
	02	Issued check (CK) 001 for office supplies, $3,000
	03	Bought computer equipment from Best Buy, $15,000. Issued CK 002 for $3,000 down payment. Balance is on account.
	06	Bought delivery van from A-J Car Dealership, $25,000. Issued CK 003 for $2,000 down payment. Balance is on account.
	07	Paid one year rent, $3,000. Issued CK 004.
	08	Performed services for cash, $5,000. Issued OR 002 and sales invoice (SI) 001.
	09	Performed services, $10,000. Issued OR 003 for the $4,000 down payment and SI 002 for the full amount. Balance is on account.
	13	Obtained bank loan, $50,000. Issued promissory note (PN) 001.
	14	Paid $300 for van maintenance. Issued CK 005.
	15	Paid wages, $3,000. Issued CK 007. CK 006 was voided.
	16	Performed services, $20,000. Issued OR 004 for the $4,000 down payment and SI 003 for the full amount. Balance is on account.
	17	Issued OR 005 for $6,000 collected from customers (see on Dec 10).
	18	Issued CK 008 as payment for telephone expense, $400.
	19	Issued CK 009 as payment for electricity expense, $600.
	20	Issued CK 010 partial payment to Best Buy, $6,000 (see Dec 03).
	21	Issued CK 011 payment to A-J Dealership, $5,000 (see Dec 06).
	22	Issued CK 012 to Clark Kent for cash withdrawal, $4,000.
	23	Collected $2,000 from customers on account. Issued OR 007.
	28	Paid entertainment expense, $400. Issued CK 013.
	30	Paid wages, $5,000. Issued CK 014.

GENERAL JOURNAL

Page 001

DATE	DOC REF	ACCT CODE	DESCRIPTION	POST REF	DEBIT AMOUNT	CREDIT AMOUNT
2005						
12/01	OR001	101	Cash		150,000	
		301	Clark Kent, Capital			150,000
			initial investment			
02	CK001	105	Office Supplies		3,000	
		101	Cash			3,000
			bought supplies			
03	CK002	127	Computer		15,000	
		101	Cash			3,000
		103	Accounts Payable			12,000
			bought computer			
06	CK003	126	Delivery Van		25,000	
		101	Cash			2,000
		103	Accounts Payable			23,000
			bought delivery van			
07	CK004	107	Prepaid Rent		3,000	
		101	Cash			3,000
			paid one year rent			
08	SI001	101	Cash		5,000	
	OR002	501	Revenues			5,000
			performed services			
09	SI002	101	Cash		4,000	
	OR003	103	Accounts Receivable		6,000	
		501	Revenues			10,000
			performed services			
13	PN001	101	Cash		50,000	
		221	Loans Payable			50,000
			obtained bank loan			
14	CK005	615	Van Maintenance Expense		300	
		101	Cash			300
			paid van maintenance			

GENERAL JOURNAL

Page 002

DATE	DOC REF	ACCT CODE	DESCRIPTION	POST REF	DEBIT AMOUNT	CREDIT AMOUNT
12/15	CK007	602	Wages Expense		3,000	
		101	Cash			3,000
			paid wages			
16	OR004	101	Cash		4,000	
	SI003	103	Accounts Receivable		16,000	
		501	Revenues			20,000
			performed services			
17	OR005	101	Cash		6,000	
		103	Accounts Receivable			6,000
			collected from customers			
18	CK008	603	Telephone Expense		400	
		101	Cash			400
			paid telephone bill			
19	CK009	604	Electricity Expense		600	
		101	Cash			600
			paid electricity			
20	CK010	201	Accounts Payable		6,000	
		101	Cash			6,000
			paid account			
21	CK011	201	Accounts Payable		5,000	
		101	Cash			5,000
			paid account			
22	CK012	401	Clark Kent, Drawing		4,000	
		101	Cash			4,000
			owner withdrawal			
23	OR007	101	Cash		2,000	
		103	Accounts Receivable			2,000
			collected from customer			
28	CK013	608	Entertainment Expense		400	
		101	Cash			400
			paid entertainment expense			

GENERAL JOURNAL

Page 003

DATE	DOC REF	ACCT CODE	DESCRIPTION	POST REF	DEBIT AMOUNT	CREDIT AMOUNT
12/30	CK014	602	Wages Expense		5,000	
		101	Cash			5,000
			paid wages			

GENERAL LEDGER

PAGE: 001

ACCOUNT CODE: 101   TITLE: CASH

DATE	DESCRIPTION	POST REF	TRANSACTION DEBIT (+)	TRANSACTION CREDIT (-)	BALANCE DEBIT (+)	BALANCE CREDIT (-)
2005						
12/01	Investment	GJ001	150,000		150,000	
12/02	bought supplies	GJ001		3,000	147,000	
12/03	bought computer	GJ001		3,000	144,000	
12/06	bought van	GJ001		2,000	142,000	
12/07	paid one year rent	GJ001		3,000	139,000	
12/08	performed services	GJ001	5,000		144,000	
12/09	performed services	GJ001	4,000		148,000	
12/13	bank loan	GJ001	50,000		198,000	
12/14	paid van maintenance	GJ001		300	197,700	
12/15	paid wages	GJ002		3,000	194,700	
12/16	collected customer account	GJ002	4,000		198,700	
12/17	collected customer account	GJ002	6,000		204,700	
12/18	paid telephone bill	GJ002		400	204,300	
12/19	paid electricity	GJ002		600	203,700	
12/20	paid account – Best Buy	GJ002		6,000	197,700	
12/21	paid account – A-J Dealer	GJ002		5,000	192,700	
12/22	owner withdrawal	GJ002		4,000	188,700	
12/23	collected customer account	GJ002	2,000		190,700	
12/28	paid entertainment expense	GJ002		400	190,300	
12/30	paid wages	GJ003		5,000	185,300	

IMPORTANT: After posting an entry in the general ledger, the *post reference column in the general journal must be filled in with the page number of the general ledger where the entry is posted.* For example, the general journal entry on Dec 01 for the initial investment of $150,000 will have GL001 in the posting reference for the debit to Cash and GL008 in the posting reference for the credit to Clark Kent, Capital.

Filling in the post reference column of the general journal indicates that the entry has been posted to the general ledger.

GENERAL LEDGER

PAGE: 002

ACCOUNT CODE: 103   TITLE: ACCOUNTS RECEIVABLE

DATE	DESCRIPTION	POST REF	TRANSACTION DEBIT (+)	TRANSACTION CREDIT (-)	BALANCE DEBIT (+)	BALANCE CREDIT (-)
2005						
12/09	performed services	GJ001	6,000		6,000	
12/16	performed services	GJ002	16,000		22,000	
12/17	collected customer account	GJ002		6,000	16,000	
12/23	collected customer account	GJ002		2,000	14,000	

GENERAL LEDGER

PAGE: 003

ACCOUNT CODE: 105   TITLE: OFFICE SUPPLIES

DATE	DESCRIPTION	POST REF	TRANSACTION DEBIT (+)	TRANSACTION CREDIT (-)	BALANCE DEBIT (+)	BALANCE CREDIT (-)
2005						
12/02	bought supplies	GJ001	3,000		3,000	

GENERAL LEDGER

PAGE: 004

ACCOUNT CODE: 107   TITLE: PREPAID RENT

DATE	DESCRIPTION	POST REF	TRANSACTION DEBIT (+)	TRANSACTION CREDIT (-)	BALANCE DEBIT (+)	BALANCE CREDIT (-)
2005						
12/07	paid one year rent	GJ001	3,000		3,000	

GENERAL LEDGER

PAGE: 005

ACCOUNT CODE: 126 TITLE: DELIVERY VAN

DATE	DESCRIPTION	POST REF	TRANSACTION DEBIT (+)	TRANSACTION CREDIT (−)	BALANCE DEBIT (+)	BALANCE CREDIT (−)
2005						
12/06	bought van	GJ001	25,000		25,000	

GENERAL LEDGER

PAGE: 006

ACCOUNT CODE: 127 TITLE: COMPUTER

DATE	DESCRIPTION	POST REF	TRANSACTION DEBIT (+)	TRANSACTION CREDIT (−)	BALANCE DEBIT (+)	BALANCE CREDIT (−)
2005						
12/03	bought computer	GJ001	15,000		15,000	

GENERAL LEDGER

PAGE: 007

ACCOUNT CODE: 201 TITLE: ACCOUNTS PAYABLE

DATE	DESCRIPTION	POST REF	TRANSACTION DEBIT (−)	TRANSACTION CREDIT (+)	BALANCE DEBIT (−)	BALANCE CREDIT (+)
2005						
12/03	bought computer	GJ001		12,000		12,000
12/06	bought delivery van	GJ001		23,000		35,000
12/20	paid account – Best Buy	GJ002	6,000			29,000
12/21	paid account – A-J Dealers	GJ002	5,000			24,000

GENERAL LEDGER

PAGE: 008

ACCOUNT CODE: 221　　TITLE:　LOANS PAYABLE

DATE	DESCRIPTION	POST REF	TRANSACTION DEBIT (-)	TRANSACTION CREDIT (+)	BALANCE DEBIT (-)	BALANCE CREDIT (+)
2005						
12/13	bank loan	GJ001		50,000		50,000

GENERAL LEDGER

PAGE: 009

ACCOUNT CODE: 301　　TITLE:　CLARK KENT, CAPITAL

DATE	DESCRIPTION	POST REF	TRANSACTION DEBIT (-)	TRANSACTION CREDIT (+)	BALANCE DEBIT (-)	BALANCE CREDIT (+)
2005						
12/01	initial investment	GJ001		150,000		150,000

GENERAL LEDGER

PAGE: 010

ACCOUNT CODE: 401　　TITLE:　CLARK KENT, DRAWING

DATE	DESCRIPTION	POST REF	TRANSACTION DEBIT (+)	TRANSACTION CREDIT (-)	BALANCE DEBIT (+)	BALANCE CREDIT (-)
2005						
12/22	owner withdrawal	GJ002	4,000		4,000	

GENERAL LEDGER
PAGE: 011

ACCOUNT CODE: 501   TITLE: REVENUES

DATE	DESCRIPTION	POST REF	TRANSACTION DEBIT (-)	TRANSACTION CREDIT (+)	BALANCE DEBIT (-)	BALANCE CREDIT (+)
2005						
12/08	performed services	GJ001		5,000		5,000
12/09	performed services	GJ001		10,000		15,000
12/16	performed services	GJ002		20,000		35,000

GENERAL LEDGER
PAGE: 012

ACCOUNT CODE: 602   TITLE: WAGES EXPENSE

DATE	DESCRIPTION	POST REF	TRANSACTION DEBIT (+)	TRANSACTION CREDIT (-)	BALANCE DEBIT (+)	BALANCE CREDIT (-)
2005						
12/15	paid wages	GJ002	3,000		3,000	
12/30	paid wages	GJ003	5,000		8,000	

GENERAL LEDGER
PAGE: 013

ACCOUNT CODE: 603   TITLE: TELEPHONE EXPENSE

DATE	DESCRIPTION	POST REF	TRANSACTION DEBIT (+)	TRANSACTION CREDIT (-)	BALANCE DEBIT (+)	BALANCE CREDIT (-)
2005						
12/18	paid telephone bill	GJ002	400		400	

GENERAL LEDGER

PAGE: 014

ACCOUNT CODE: 604　　　　TITLE:　　ELECTRICITY EXPENSE

DATE	DESCRIPTION	POST REF	TRANSACTION DEBIT (+)	CREDIT (-)	BALANCE DEBIT (+)	CREDIT (-)
2005						
12/19	paid electric bill	GJ002	600		600	

GENERAL LEDGER

PAGE: 015

ACCOUNT CODE: 608　　　　TITLE:　　ENTERTAINMENT EXPENSE

DATE	DESCRIPTION	POST REF	TRANSACTION DEBIT (+)	CREDIT (-)	BALANCE DEBIT (+)	CREDIT (-)
2005						
12/28	paid entertainment expense	GJ002	400		400	

GENERAL LEDGER

PAGE: 016

ACCOUNT CODE: 615　　　　TITLE:　　VAN MAINTENANCE EXPENSE

DATE	DESCRIPTION	POST REF	TRANSACTION DEBIT (+)	CREDIT (-)	BALANCE DEBIT (+)	CREDIT (-)
2005						
12/14	paid maintenance expense	GJ001	300		300	

Fundamentals of Accounting

Note that the running balance is computed every time an entry is posted in the general ledger. The ***T account* is referred to as a simplified version of the general ledger.** If you refer back to the chapter on analyzing transactions with the use of the T account, the balance in the T accounts for Efficient Services for the above transactions reflect the same balance in the general ledger accounts after all the general journal entries are posted to the general ledger.

The balances of the general ledger accounts are shown below:

Account Code	Account Title	Debit	Credit
101	Cash	185,300	
103	Accounts Receivable	14,000	
105	Office Supplies	3,000	
107	Prepaid Rent	3,000	
126	Delivery Van	25,000	
127	Computer	15,000	
201	Accounts Payable		24,000
221	Loans Payable		50,000
301	Clark Kent, Capital		150,000
401	Clark Kent, Drawing	4,000	
501	Revenues		35,000
602	Wages Expense	8,000	
603	Telephone Expense	400	
604	Electricity Expense	600	
608	Entertainment Expense	400	
615	Van Maintenance Expense	300	
		259,000	259,000

These balances will be used in the summarizing process, the preparation of the Trial Balance as of December 31, 2005.

SUMMARY OF BASIC BUSINESS TRANSACTIONS FOR A SERVICE BUSINESS IN A SOLE PROPRIETORSHIP

TRANSACTION	ANALYSIS	SAMPLE TRANSACTION	GENERAL JOURNAL ENTRY DESCRIPTION	DEBIT	CREDIT

Owner investment	Debit Cash
	Credit Capital
		John Jones invested $50,000 to start Jones Co.	Cash
			  John Jones, Capital
			  initial investment
				50,000	50,000

Purchase asset for cash	Debit Asset bought
	Credit Cash
		Bought car, $15,000	Car
			  Cash
			  bought car
				15,000	15,000

Purchase asset on account	Debit Asset bought
	Credit Accounts Payable
		Bought computer on account, $5,000	Computer
			  Accounts Payable
			  bought computer
				5,000	5,000

Purchase asset with cash down payment, balance on account	Debit Asset bought
	Credit Cash (down payment)
	Credit Accounts Payable
		Bought car, $25,000 paid $5,000, balance on account	Car
			  Cash
			  Accounts Payable
			  bought car
				25,000	5,000
					20,000

Payment of expense	Debit _____ Expense
	Credit Cash
		Paid wages, $17,000	Wages Expense
			  Cash
			  paid wages
				17,000	17,000

Performance of services for cash	Debit Cash
	Credit Revenues
		Performed services, $10,000 and received cash	Cash
			  Revenues
			  performed services
				10,000	10,000

Performance of services on account	Debit Accounts Receivable
	Credit Revenues
		Performed services, $12,000 on account	Accounts Receivable
			  Revenues
			  performed services
				12,000	12,000

TRANSACTION	ANALYSIS	SAMPLE TRANSACTION	GENERAL JOURNAL ENTRY DESCRIPTION	DEBIT	CREDIT
Performance of services with cash down payment, balance on account	Debit Cash (down payment) Debit Accounts Receivable Credit Revenues	Performed services, $15,000 received $1,000 cash and balance on account	Cash Accounts Receivable Revenues performed services	1,000 14,000	 15,000
Collection of customer account	Debit Cash Credit Accounts Receivable	Collected $14,000 for services previously rendered	Cash Accounts Receivable collected customer account	14,000	14,000
Receipt of promissory note as payment for account due	Debit Notes Receivable Credit Accounts Receivable	Customer issued note for account due, $14,000	Notes Receivable Accounts Receivable received note for account	14,000	14,000
Payment of supplier account	Debit Accounts Payable Credit Cash	Paid supplier account for computer bought, $5,000	Accounts Payable Cash paid computer account	5,000	5,000
Issuance of promissory for supplier account due	Debit Accounts Payable Credit Notes Payable	Issued promissory note for account due, $5,000	Accounts Payable Notes Payable issued note to settle account	5,000	5,000
Owner cash withdrawal for personal use	Debit Drawing Credit Cash	Mr. John Jones withdrew $3,000 for personal use	John Jones, Drawing Cash owner withdrawal	3,000	3,000

NOTE: This chart illustrates the basic transactions for a service business in a sole proprietorship. The general journal entry on the rightmost column will always be the same every time the specific transaction on the leftmost column occurs. The accounting student must study this chart as these are representative transactions that happen repeatedly throughout the accounting cycle.

CHAPTER 04 ACCOUNTING PROCESS: THE BOOKS OF ACCOUNTS

REVIEW QUESTIONS

1. What are the two books of accounts? Briefly describe each one.

2. Why is the general journal called the book of original entry?

3. What is journalizing? Name some rules followed in journalizing.

4. What are the parts of a general journal entry?

5. What are the types of accounting entries based on the number of accounts affected by the transaction.

6. What are the types of accounting entries based on the timing of recording the accounting entry in the general journal?

7. Why is the general ledger called the book of final entry?

8. Distinguish between the three-column and the four-column general ledger.

9. What is posting? Name some rules followed in posting to the general ledger.

10. How is the balance computed in the general ledger?

CHAPTER 04 ACCOUNTING PROCESS: THE BOOKS OF ACCOUNTS

REVIEW EXAMINATION

TRUE or FALSE: *WRITE TRUE or FALSE IN THE SPACE PROVIDED.*

1. _____ The four-column general ledger shows four money columns, a pair of debit and credit column for transaction and balance.

2. _____ It is more practical to use the two-column general ledger because the balance easily reflects whether the account has a debit balance or a credit balance.

3. _____ The general ledger is called the book of original entry because it is the last book of accounts that reflect the effect of business transactions on the accounting elements.

4. _____ Journalizing is the process of transcribing or transferring information from the general journal to the general ledger.

5. _____ A simple entry is general journal entry that affects only one debit account title and one credit account title.

6. _____ A compound entry is a general journal entry that affects more than two accounts.

7. _____ Except for memorandum entries all the accounting entries are not recorded in the general journal and posted in the general ledger.

8. _____ All adjusting entries are reversed.

9. _____ Adjusting entries are recorded in the general journal on the first day of the next accounting period before any transactions for the next accounting period are recorded in order to reverse the adjustments or adjusting entries that increase assets or liabilities.

10. _____ Correcting entries are recorded any time in the general journal in order to correct accounting entries that were previously recorded erroneously.

11. _____ Correcting entries should be recorded as soon as the error is identified.

12. _____ Memorandum entries are made only as notation in the general journal to describe certain transactions that need to be documented, which do not affect the balances of accounts.

13. _____ Reversing entries are recorded in the general journal at the end of the accounting period after the financial statements are prepared in order zero out the balances of or nominal accounts.

14. _____ Adjusting entries are recorded in the general journal at the end of the accounting period after the trial balance is prepared in order to reflect the correct balances of accounts that are affected by the adjustments.

15. _____ After all adjustments are posted to the general ledger, an adjusted trial balance is prepared which serves as the basis in the preparation of the financial statements.

16. _____ General journal entries are recorded chronologically in the general journal during the accounting period as the transactions occur.

17. _____ Source documents, such as sales invoices, official receipts, checks, etc. are used to provide information in the preparation of financial statements.

18. _____ Businesses maintain special combination journals to record transactions that occur very frequently.

19. _____ At the end of the accounting period, the totals of the monetary columns in a specific special combination journal are used to prepare one general journal entry to be recorded in the general journal.

20. _____ The T account is referred to as a simplified version of the general journal.

21. _____ The running balance of an account is computed every time an entry is posted in the general journal.

22. By writing the GL page number in the general journal, the accountant is guided that the particular general journal entry has been posted.

23. Journalizing facilitates the process of matching the general journal entry in the general journal to the posting in the general ledger.

24. It is easier to trace errors in accounting records if both books of accounts are cross-referenced.

25. The two books of accounts are the general journal and the trial balance.

COMPLETION: *WRITE THE ANSWER IN THE SPACE PROVIDED.*

1. _____ entries are made only as notation in the general journal to describe certain transactions that need to be documented, which do not affect the balances of accounts.

2. Closing entries are recorded in the general journal at the end of the accounting period after the financial statements are prepared in order zero out the balances of _____ accounts.

3. The _____ is referred to as a simplified version of the general ledger.

4. The _____ is computed every time an entry is posted in the general ledger.

5. By writing the GL _____ in the general journal, the accountant is guided that the particular general journal entry has been posted

6. _____ facilitates the process of matching the general journal entry in the general journal to the posting in the general ledger.

7. It is easier to _____ in accounting records if both books of accounts are cross-referenced.

8. _____ are recorded in the general journal at the end of the accounting period after the trial balance is prepared in order to reflect the correct balances of affected accounts.

9. After all adjustments are posted to the general ledger, an _____ is prepared which serves as the basis in the preparation of the financial statements.

10. The _____ general ledger which shows four money columns, a pair of debit and credit column for transaction and balance.

11. It is more practical to use the four-column general ledger because the balance easily reflects whether the account has a _____ balance or a _____ balance.

12. The general ledger is called the _____ because it is the last book of accounts that reflect the effect of business transactions on the accounting elements

13. General journal entries are recorded _____ in the general journal during the accounting period as the transactions occur.

14. _____ entries should be recorded as soon as the error is identified.

15. _____ are used to record transactions that occur very frequently.

16. Posting is the process of transcribing or transferring information from the _____ to the _____.

17. Each account in the general journal entry is posted in the general ledger in the _____ that they appear in the general journal

18. A _____ is general journal entry that affects only one debit account title and one credit account title

19. A _____ is a general journal entry that affects more than two account titles; three or more accounts are affected.

20. Except for _____ entries all the accounting entries are recorded in the general journal and posted in the general ledger.

21. At the end of the accounting period, the _____ of the monetary columns in a special combination journal are used to prepare one general journal entry.

21. Some _____ entries are reversed at the start of the next accounting period.

22. Reversing entries are recorded in the general journal on the _____ of the next accounting period before any transactions for the next accounting period are recorded in order to reverse the some adjusting entries.

23. Correcting entries are recorded any time in the general journal in order to correct accounting entries that were previously recorded _____.

24. Source documents, such as sales invoices, official receipts, checks, etc. are used to provide information in the preparation of _____.

25. Filling in the _____ column of the general journal indicates that the entry has been posted to the general ledger.

26. _____ balance is the normal balance for assets, costs, expenses, drawing and dividends.

27. Credit balance is the normal balance for _____, _____ and _____.

28. Accounting information is presented in the general ledger arranged according to _____ as indicated in the chart of accounts.

29. _____ is the recording phase of accounting.

30. The balances of nominal accounts are zeroed out at end of the current accounting period so that they will not be _____ in the next accounting period.

EXERCISE:

Indicate DEBIT or CREDIT in the ACTION column.

	TRANSACTION	ACTION	ACCOUNT TITLE
1.	Owner invested cash	_____	Cash
2.	Performed services on account	_____	Revenues
3.	Bought office supplies	_____	Office Supplies
4.	Bought computer	_____	Computer
5.	Paid electricity bill	_____	Electricity Expense
6.	Paid telephone bill	_____	Cash
7.	Owner withdrew cash for personal use	_____	Drawing
8.	Owner invested land in the business	_____	Capital
9.	Performed services for cash	_____	Cash
10.	Paid accounts payable	_____	Accounts Payable
11.	Paid wages	_____	Wages Expense
12.	Bought car on account	_____	Accounts Payable
13.	Bought office furniture on account	_____	Office Furniture
14.	Owner invested a delivery truck	_____	Delivery Truck
15.	Collected customer accounts	_____	Accounts Receivable
16.	Paid suppliers accounts	_____	Accounts Payable
17.	Performed services on account	_____	Accounts Receivable
18.	Paid magazine ads	_____	Advertising Expense
19.	Paid car maintenance bill	_____	Cash
20.	Collected accounts receivable	_____	Cash

PROBLEMS:

A. **JOURNALIZING:** Prepare the general journal entries to record the transactions of the following service businesses identified in Chapter 2. Sample general journal form is provided. Use the starting page number shown below as the page number of the first general journal page.

	BUSINESS NAME	PERIOD ENDED	GENERAL JOURNAL STARTING PAGE
1.	Global Delivery Services	June 2006	001
2.	Garden Landscaping & Pool Services	December 2005	025
3.	Grade A Plus Tutorial Services	October 2005	001
4.	Jolie Kids Day Care Services	September 2005	001
5.	James Deane Tours	June 2005	001
6.	Have Fun Day Camp	December 2005	037
7.	Beautiful Hollywood	March 2006	001
8.	Reliable Security Services	May 2002	001

B. **POSTING:** Post general journal entries recorded in the general journal in the general ledger. Be sure to copy the trial balance amounts for Garden Landscaping & Pool Services and Have Fun Day Camp as the first entry in the general ledger for affected accounts. Samples of general ledger forms are provided. Since the Cash account normally has many entries, the general ledger form for Cash is on a whole page sheet. For all other accounts, use the other general ledger form.

REMINDER: The balances of each account in the general ledger should equal the balances of the corresponding accounts in the T accounts prepared in Chapter 03.

GENERAL JOURNAL

PAGE _____

DATE	DOC REF	ACCT CODE	DESCRIPTION	POST REF	DEBIT	CREDIT

GENERAL LEDGER

ACCOUNT CODE: __101__ TITLE: __CASH__ PAGE

DATE	DESCRIPTION	POST REF	TRANSACTION		BALANCE	
			DEBIT	CREDIT	DEBIT	CREDIT

GENERAL LEDGER

ACCOUNT CODE: _____ TITLE: _____ PAGE _____

DATE	DESCRIPTION	POST REF	TRANSACTION DEBIT	TRANSACTION CREDIT	BALANCE DEBIT	BALANCE CREDIT

GENERAL LEDGER

ACCOUNT CODE: _____ TITLE: _____ PAGE _____

DATE	DESCRIPTION	POST REF	TRANSACTION DEBIT	TRANSACTION CREDIT	BALANCE DEBIT	BALANCE CREDIT

CHAPTER 05 ACCOUNTING PROCESS: THE TRIAL BALANCE

LEARNING OBJECTIVES

L01 Describe the trial balance.

L02 Identify the purpose of the trial balance.

L03 Describe the types of trial balance.

CHAPTER 05   ACCOUNTING PROCESS: THE TRIAL BALANCE

THE SUMMARIZING PROCESS

The summarizing process is the first in a series of steps done at the end of the accounting period. During the summarizing process, the **trial balance is prepared using the ending account balances in the general ledger.** The trial balance is an accounting report prepared at the end of the accounting period that shows the account titles and their corresponding balances with the total debit column amount equal to the total credit column amount. The trial balance shows the equality of debit total and credit total.

The heading of the trial balance shows the name of the business on the first line, the title of the report (trial balance) on the second line and the date of the trial balance on the third line. To prepare the trial balance, simply copy the account titles and the corresponding balances from the general ledger. Add the amounts in the debit and credit columns. The total for both columns must equal. Follow the format in the illustration below.

Using the balances of the general ledger accounts in Chapter 4, the trial balance for Efficient Services as of December 31, 2005 is shown below:

EFFICIENT SERVICES
Trial Balance
December 31, 2005

ACCOUNT TITLE	DEBIT	CREDIT
Cash	185,300	
Accounts Receivable	14,000	
Office Supplies	3,000	
Prepaid Rent	3,000	
Computer	15,000	
Delivery Van	25,000	
Accounts Payable		24,000
Loans Payable		50,000
Clark Kent, Capital		150,000
Clark Kent, Drawing	4,000	
Revenues		35,000
Wages Expense	8,000	
Telephone Expense	400	
Electricity Expense	600	
Entertainment Expense	400	
Van Maintenance Expense	300	
	259,000	259,000

Note that accounts with zero balances are not shown in the trial balance. So even if there are so many accounts in the chart of accounts, only the ones with balances are reflected in the trial balance.

TYPES OF TRIAL BALANCE

At the end of the accounting period, three types of trial balance are prepared, based on the timing when they are done. The three types of trial balance are:

1. The **trial balance** is prepared after all general journal entries are posted to the general ledger. The preparation of the trial balance is the first step done at the end of accounting period. The trial balance provides the initial balance in the worksheet.

2. The **adjusted trial balance** is prepared after all adjusting entries/adjustments are recorded in the general journal and posted in the general ledger, incorporating the effect of the adjustments in the affected accounts. The adjusted trial balance provides the information used in the preparation of the financial statements (the income statement, equity statement, balance sheet and statement of cash flows).

3. The **post closing trial balance also called the after closing trial balance** is prepared after all closing entries are recorded in the general journal and posted in the general ledger. It contains only balance sheet or permanent accounts (assets, liabilities and capital). The post closing trial balance provides the beginning balance of the accounts for the next accounting period.

CHAPTER 05   ACCOUNTING PROCESS: THE TRIAL BALANCE

REVIEW QUESTIONS

1. What is the summarizing process?

2. What is the trial balance? Why is it prepared?

3. How is the general ledger connected to the trial balance?

4. What is the adjusted trial balance? Why is it prepared?

5. What is the post closing trial balance? How is it used?

CHAPTER 05 ACCOUNTING PROCESS: THE TRIAL BALANCE

REVIEW EXAMINATION

TRUE or FALSE: *WRITE* TRUE or FALSE *IN THE SPACE PROVIDED.*

1. _____ The summarizing process is the first in a series of steps done at the end of the accounting period.

2. _____ The trial balance is prepared using the ending account balances in the general journal.

3. _____ The general journal is an accounting report prepared at the end of the accounting period that shows the account titles and their corresponding balances with the total debit column amount equal to the total credit column amount.

4. _____ The trial balance shows the equality of debit total and credit total.

5. _____ The adjusted trial balance provides the beginning balance of the accounts for the next accounting period.

6. _____ Only the accounts with balances are reflected in the trial balance even if there are so many accounts in the chart of accounts.

7. _____ The amounts in the trial balance are copied from the general ledger.

8. _____ The post closing balance is prepared after all adjusting entries are recorded in the general journal and posted in the general ledger.

9. _____ The adjusted trial balance provides the information used in the preparation of the financial statements.

10. _____ Accounts with zero balances are shown in the trial balance.

11. _____ At the end of the accounting period, three types of trial balance are prepared, based on the timing when they are done.

12. _____ The trial balance is prepared after all general journal entries are posted to the general ledger.

13. _____ The trial balance provides the initial balance in the worksheet.

14. _____ The post closing trial balance is prepared after all adjusting entries are recorded in the general journal and posted in the general ledger.

15. _____ The post closing trial balance shows only permanent accounts such as assets, liabilities and capital.

COMPLETION: *WRITE THE ANSWER IN THE SPACE PROVIDED.*

1. Even if there are so many accounts in the chart of accounts, only the ones with _____ are reflected in the trial balance.

2. The summarizing process is the first in a series of steps done at the _____ of the accounting period.

3. The trial balance is prepared using the ending account balances in the _____.

4. The trial balance is an accounting report prepared at the end of the accounting period that shows the account titles and their corresponding balances with the total debit column amount _____ to the total credit column amount.

5. The trial balance shows the _____ of debit total and credit total.

6. To prepare the trial balance, the account titles and the corresponding balances are copied from the _____.

7. Accounts with _____ balances are not shown in the trial balance.

8. At the end of the accounting period, _____ types of trial balance are prepared, based on the timing when they are done.

9. The _____ is prepared after all general journal entries are posted to the general ledger.

10. The trial balance provides the initial balance in the _____.

11. The _____ is prepared after all adjusting entries are recorded in the general journal and posted in the general ledger, incorporating the effect of the adjustments in the affected accounts.

12. The _____ provides the information used in the preparation of the financial statements.

13. The _____ is prepared after all closing entries are recorded in the general journal and posted in the general ledger.

14. The post closing trial balance contains only _____ accounts.

15. The post closing trial balance provides the beginning balance of the accounts for the _____ accounting period.

PROBLEMS:

A. SUMMARIZING: Prepare the trial balance using the ending balances in the general ledger from Chapter 4 for the following service businesses identified in Chapter 2. Sample trial balance form is provided.

	BUSINESS NAME	TRIAL BALANCE DATE
1.	Global Delivery Services	June 30, 2006
2.	Garden Landscaping & Pool Services	December 31, 2005
3.	Grade A Plus Tutorial Services	October 31, 2005
4.	Jolie Kids Day Care Services	September 30, 2005
5.	James Deane Tours	June 30, 2005
6.	Have Fun Day Camp	December 31, 2005
7.	Beautiful Hollywood	March 31, 2006
8.	Reliable Security Management Services	May 31, 2002

GLOBAL DELIVERY SERVICES
TRIAL BALANCE
AS OF _____

ACCOUNT TITLE	DEBIT	CREDIT

GARDEN LANDSCAPING & POOL SERVICES
TRIAL BALANCE
AS OF _____

ACCOUNT TITLE	DEBIT	CREDIT

GRADE A PLUS TUTORIAL SERVICES
TRIAL BALANCE
AS OF _____

ACCOUNT TITLE	DEBIT	CREDIT

JOLIE KIDS DAY CARE SERVICES
TRIAL BALANCE
AS OF _____

ACCOUNT TITLE	DEBIT	CREDIT

JAMES DEANE TOURS
TRIAL BALANCE
AS OF _____

ACCOUNT TITLE	DEBIT	CREDIT

HAVE FUN DAY CAMP
TRIAL BALANCE
AS OF _____

ACCOUNT TITLE	DEBIT	CREDIT

BEAUTIFUL HOLLYWOOD
TRIAL BALANCE
AS OF _____

ACCOUNT TITLE	DEBIT	CREDIT

RELIABLE SECURITY MANAGEMENT SERVICES
TRIAL BALANCE
AS OF _____

ACCOUNT TITLE	DEBIT	CREDIT

CHAPTER 06　ACCOUNTING PROCESS: THE ADJUSTING ENTRIES

LEARNING OBJECTIVES

L01　Nature and importance of adjusting entries in the accounting process

L02　Types of business transactions

L03　Matching of costs and revenues principle

L04　Cost recovery principle

L05　Cash method vs. accrual method of accounting

L06　Types of adjusting entries

L07　Accounting for prepaid expenses – asset method vs. expense method

L08　Accounting for unearned revenues – liability method vs. revenue method

L09　Accounting for depreciation of long-term asset

L10　Accounting for bad debts expense

L11　Accounting for accrual of unpaid expenses

L12　Accounting for accrual of uncollected revenues

CHAPTER 06   ACCOUNTING PROCESS: THE ADJUSTING ENTRIES

ADJUSTING ENTRIES

Adjusting entries or adjustments are recorded at the end of the accounting period after the trial balance, but before the financial statements are prepared in order to reflect the correct balance of accounts. If adjusting entries are not made, the balance of some accounts will be overstated while the balance of some accounts will be understated. In order to understand the concept of adjusting entries it is important to discuss the (1) **matching of costs and revenues and the cost recovery principles**, (2) **two types of business transactions,** *the expressed or explicit transactions and the implied or implicit transactions* and the (3) **two accounting methods of income measurement,** *the cash basis and accrual basis of accounting.*

MATCHING OF COSTS and REVENUES and COST RECOVERY PRINCIPLES

The matching of costs and revenues principle states that costs and expenses must be recorded in the same accounting period that the related revenues are recorded. For example, bad debts expense for uncollectible accounts receivable are recorded in the same accounting period when the credit was extended to the customer for products sold or services rendered. Under the **cost recovery principle**, certain purchases of goods or services or prepayments of expenses in the current period, the benefits of which are applicable to future periods (like the payment of one-year insurance premium) are initially recorded as assets. When these goods, services or prepaid expenses are used, consumed or expired as time passes by, then these assets are reduced and correspondingly transferred to the appropriate expense accounts. For example, businesses usually buy office supplies in bulk, to be consumed for several months. At the time of purchase, an asset account, Office Supplies is debited. As the office supplies are consumed, no accounting entries are recorded; it will be impractical and time consuming to make an accounting entry every time ball pens, copy papers, paper clips, staples, etc. are consumed. The accounting practice is to count the office supplies at the end of the accounting period and allocate the cost corresponding to the office supplies on hand. The difference between the available office supplies (beginning balance of office supplies plus purchases of office supplies during the period) and the ending balance of office supplies resulting from the inventory count is considered as the office supplies consumed. The office supplies consumed is then transferred from the asset Office Supplies to an expense account Office Supplies Expense.

EXPRESSED (EXPLICIT) TRANSACTIONS and IMPLIED (IMPLICIT) TRANSACTIONS

Expressed or explicit transactions are the routinary, ordinary and repetitive transactions that occur during the ordinary course of business. These transactions are supported by source documents. Examples of expressed transactions are the purchase of assets, payment of expenses, sale of products or performance of services to earn revenues, collection of receivables, payment of liabilities, etc. All these transactions are evidenced by source documents such as official receipts, delivery receipts, checks, suppliers' invoices, etc. **In recording expressed transactions, the information used is definite and specific, and**

the actual amounts, not estimates are used because they come from the source documents that serve as the evidence of the business transaction.

On the other hand, **implied or implicit transactions** are incidents or events, such as the passage of time, that are not recorded during the course of ordinary business, but are accounted only at the end of the accounting period as adjusting entries or adjustments. Examples of implied transactions are the recording of depreciation expense for long-term assets, bad debts expense for uncollectible accounts, the transfer from asset to expense of expired insurance, office supplies used, used rent, used interest, etc. Unlike the actual amount used in the recording of expressed transactions, **the amount recorded for implied transactions are derived from calculations, not directly as indicated in the source documents.** Sometimes, the amounts are based on estimates using the historical experience of the business, such as the recording of depreciation expense and bad debts expense. **It must be remembered however that before an implied transaction can happen, it is preceded by a related expressed transaction.** Before the implied transaction of recording depreciation expense can be made, an expressed transaction, the purchase of asset must happen beforehand. The recording of bad debts expense is preceded by the recording of accounts receivable for the performance of services on account or sale of products on account. The recording of office supplies expense is preceded by the purchase of office supplies.

ACCOUNTING METHODS OF INCOME MEASUREMENT

Under the **cash basis of accounting, transactions are recorded only when cash is received or when cash is paid**. In other words, when services are rendered on account or when a product is sold on account, or when an asset is bought on account, these transactions are not reflected in the accounting records, because no cash is received or paid. Effectively, under the cash basis of accounting, there are no liability accounts and no receivable accounts. The **cash basis violates the matching of costs and revenues principle of accounting. The cost recovery principle of recording expenses is also violated by the cash basis.** The cash basis results in incomplete records of business transactions and it is therefore very difficult to reconcile non-cash transactions as they are not even recorded. **Under the cash basis of accounting, no adjusting entries are recorded at the end of the accounting period.** The cash basis results in incomplete accounting records and consequently if users of financial statements will use financial statements produced under the cash basis, it is very likely that they will make erroneous decisions.

The deficiencies of the cash basis of accounting are corrected by the accrual basis. Under the **accrual basis, the effects of all transactions on the financial statements are recognized, even though no cash is received or no cash is paid.** Revenues are recorded when they are earned or rendered whether or not cash is received. Expenses are recorded when they are incurred, whether or not cash is paid. For example, if the business renders services on account, Accounts Receivable is debited and Revenues is credited. Under the cash basis of accounting, this transaction will not be recorded because no cash was received. If the business has an outstanding loans payable, and the monthly interest payments are paid every 15th of the month, the month-end financial statements must reflect the effect of an adjusting entry debiting Interest Expense and crediting Interest Payable for the accrual of the half-month interest from the 16th to month-end, even though it has not yet paid said interest at month-end. **Under the accrual basis, adjusting entries are recorded at the end of the accounting period to reflect the correct balance of accounts.**

TYPES OF ADJUSTING ENTRIES

The different types of adjusting entries are:

1. Expiration or consumption of prepaid expenses
   a. Asset method of recording prepaid expenses
   b. Expense method of recording prepaid expenses
2. Accrual of unrecorded expenses and payables
3. Accrual of unrecorded revenues and receivables
4. Realization or earning of unearned revenues (deferred credit)
   a. Liability method of recording unearned revenues
   b. Revenue method of recording unearned revenues
5. Depreciation of long-term tangible assets
6. Bad debts expense for accounts receivable

EXPIRATION OR CONSUMPTION OF PREPAID EXPENSES

Prepaid expenses are expenses paid in advance, the benefit, use or consumption of which is chargeable to the current period and to future accounting period/s after the payment was made. Prepaid expenses are classified as current assets if they will benefit the business for a period of one year or less; if the benefit is for more than one year, then they are shown in the balance sheet as current assets for the portion good for one year and long term assets for the portion beyond one year. For example, on December 31, 2004 the business paid $3,600 for a three-year insurance policy covering the period January 1, 2005 to December 31, 2007. The December 31, 2004 balance sheet will show in the Current Assets section Prepaid Insurance for $1,200 and in the Long-Term Assets section, Prepaid Insurance for $2,400.

There are two ways to account for prepaid expenses, namely:

A. **Asset method: Upon payment, an asset account, such as Prepaid Expense** (ex. Prepaid Insurance or Office Supplies) **is debited and Cash is credited. When adjusting entries are made at the end of the accounting period, the portion of the asset Prepaid Expense that expired/used/consumed from the date of payment up to the end of the accounting period is expensed and must be recorded as debit to an expense account** (ex. Supplies Expense or Insurance Expense). The **reduction in the asset Prepaid Expense is recorded as credit to Prepaid Expense,** such as Prepaid Insurance or Office Supplies.

B. **Expense Method: Upon payment, an expense account** (ex. Insurance Expense or Supplies Expense) **is debited and Cash is credited. When adjusting entries are made at the end of the accounting period, the** portion **NOT YET expired/used/consumed is an asset and must be recorded as debit to Prepaid Expense** (ex. Office Supplies or Prepaid Insurance). The **unexpired or unused portion is a reduction from the expense account and is recorded as a credit to the appropriate expense account**, such as Office Supplies Expense or Insurance Expense.

RECORDING PREPAID EXPENSES USING THE ASSET METHOD: An asset account is debited when the prepaid expense is paid.

Sep 01 2005   Issued check 1001 as payment for office supplies, $2,800.

Issued check 1002 as payment for one year car insurance premium, $2,400.

Issued check 1003 as payment for one-year advanced rent, $9,600.

REQUIRED: Record the above transactions on Sep 01, 2005. Record the adjusting entries on December 31, 2005. The Office Supplies on hand on Dec 31 amount to $300.

GENERAL JOURNAL ENTRIES USING THE ASSET METHOD (an asset account is debited and cash is credited at the time of payment)

GENERAL JOURNAL

DATE	DOC REF	DESCRIPTION	POST REF	DEBIT	CREDIT
Sep 01 05	CK1001	Office Supplies		2,800	
		Cash			2,800
		bought office supplies			
	CK1002	Prepaid Insurance		2,400	
		Cash			2,400
		paid one year car insurance (Sep 01 05 to Aug 31 06)			
	CK1003	Prepaid Rent		9,600	
		Cash			9,600
		paid one year rent (Sep 01 05 to Aug 31 06)			

ANALYSIS and COMPUTATION

1. Used Office Supplies
   Cost of Office Supplies bought on Sep 01 $ 2,800
   Office Supplies on Hand (unused) as of Dec 31   300
   Used Office Supplies - Sep 01 to Dec 31 (charged to expense)   2,500

2. Expired Insurance from Sep 01 to Dec 31, 2005
   Prepaid one year insurance (Sep 01, 2005 to Aug 31, 2006) $ 2.400
   Monthly insurance (2,400/12)   200
   Months expired (Sep 01 to Dec 31, 2005)   4
   Expired Insurance (charged to expense) ($200 x 4)   800
   As of Dec 31, Prepaid Insurance for Jan 1-Aug 31, 2006 is $1,600 ($2,400 - $800).

3. Used Rent from Sep 01 to Dec 31, 2005
   Prepaid one year advanced rent (Sep 01, 2005 to Aug 31, 2006) $ 9,600
   Monthly rent (9,600/12)   800
   Months expired (Sep 01 to Dec 31, 2005)   4
   Used Rent (charged to expense) ($800 x 4)   3,200
   As of Dec 31, Prepaid Rent for Jan 1-Aug 31, 2006 is $6,400 ($9,600 - $3,200).

ADJUSTING ENTRIES TO RECORD THE USED/EXPIRED/CONSUMED PORTION
(debit expense account for the used or expired portion and credit an asset account)

GENERAL JOURNAL

DATE	DOC REF	DESCRIPTION	POST REF	DEBIT	CREDIT

123105	ADJ001	Office Supplies Expense
		    Office Supplies
		    used office supplies
				2,500	2,500

	ADJ002	Insurance Expense
		    Prepaid Insurance
		    expired insurance Sep1-Dec31
				800	800

	ADJ003	Rent Expense
		    Prepaid Rent
		    used rent Sep 1-Dec 31
				3,200	3,200

To better understand the general journal entries and the adjusting entries, let us post them to the affected T accounts.

```
     OFFICE SUPPLIES              PREPAID INSURANCE              PREPAID RENT
  09/01  2,800 | 12/31  2,500   09/01  2,400 | 12/31  800     09/01  9,600 | 12/31  3,200
  BAL     300  |                 BAL    1,600|                 BAL    6,400|


  OFFICE SUPPLIES EXPENSE          INSURANCE EXPENSE              RENT EXPENSE
  12/31  2,500 |                   12/31   800  |                 12/31  3,200 |
```

RECORDING PREPAID EXPENSES USING THE EXPENSE METHOD (debit an expense account and credit cash at the time of payment). Let us process the same transactions illustrated earlier under the ASSET method of accounting for prepaid expenses.

Sep 01 2005   Issued check 1001 as payment for office supplies, $2,800.

Issued check 1002 as payment for one year car insurance premium, $2,400.

Issued check 1003 as payment for one-year advanced rent, $9,600.

REQUIRED: Record the above transactions on Sep 01, 2005. Record the adjusting entries on December 31, 2005. The Office Supplies on hand on Dec 31 amount to $300.

GENERAL JOURNAL ENTRIES USING THE EXPENSE METHOD (an expense account is debited and cash is credited at the time of payment)

GENERAL JOURNAL

DATE	DOC REF	DESCRIPTION	POST REF	DEBIT	CREDIT
Sep 01 05	CK1001	Office Supplies Expense 　　Cash bought office supplies		2,800	2,800
	CK1002	Insurance Expense 　　Cash paid one year car insurance (Sep 01 05 to Aug 31 06)		2,400	2,400
	CK1003	Rent Expense 　　Cash paid one year rent (Sep 01 05 to Aug 31 06)		9,600	9,600

ANALYSIS and COMPUTATION

1. The cost of unused office supplies is $300. This amount must be recorded as debit to asset Office Supplies and the Office Supplies Expense must be credited for the same amount. The adjusting entry will reduce Office Supplies Expense by $300, from $2,800 to $2,500.

2. Prepaid Insurance from Jan 1, 2006 to Aug 31, 2006

Insurance Expense recorded on Sep 01 (for Sep 01 05 to Aug 31 06)	$ 2,400
Monthly insurance ($2,400/12)	200
Months unexpired (prepaid) Jan 01 to Aug 31 06	8
Prepaid Insurance ($200 x 8)	1,600

3. Prepaid Rent from Jan 1, 2006 to Aug 31, 2006

Rent Expense recorded on Sep 01 (for Sep 01 05 to Aug 31 06)	$ 9,600
Monthly rent ($9,600/12)	800
Months unexpired (prepaid) Jan 01 to Aug 31 06	8
Prepaid Rent ($800 x 8)	6,400

ADJUSTING ENTRIES TO RECORD THE UNUSED/UNEXPIRED ASSET PORTION
(debit asset account for the unexpired or unused portion and credit an expense account)

GENERAL JOURNAL

DATE	DOC REF	DESCRIPTION	POST REF	DEBIT	CREDIT
123105	ADJ001	Office Supplies		300	
		Office Supplies Expense			300
		office supplies on hand			
	ADJ002	Prepaid Insurance		1,600	
		Insurance Expense			1,600
		prepaid insurance Jan 1-Aug 31, 2006			
	ADJ003	Prepaid Rent		6,400	
		Rent Expense			6,400
		prepaid rent Jan 1-Aug 31, 2006			

To better understand the general journal entries and the adjusting entries, let us post them to the affected T accounts.

OFFICE SUPPLIES EXPENSE		INSURANCE EXPENSE		RENT EXPENSE	
09/01 2,800	12/31 300	09/01 2,400	12/31 1,600	09/01 9,600	12/31 6,400
BAL 2,500		BAL 800		BAL 3,200	

OFFICE SUPPLIES		PREPAID INSURANCE		PREPAID RENT	
12/31 300		12/31 1,600		12/31 6,400	

Compare the balances of the T accounts under the asset method and expense method. What do you notice?

NOTE: The balances of the affected accounts are the same regardless of the method used (asset method or expense method) after the adjusting entries are posted to the general ledger. For the above transactions, the balance of the affected accounts, using either method is shown below.

ACCOUNT TITLE	DEBIT	CREDIT
Office Supplies	300	
Prepaid Insurance	1,600	
Prepaid Rent	6,400	
Office Supplies Expense	2,500	
Insurance Expense	800	
Rent Expense	3,200	

ACCRUAL OF EXPENSES AND PAYABLES

At the end of the accounting period, it is very likely that there are some expenses that the business already incurred, although, they are not yet paid in cash. These expenses are called **accrued expenses (also called unpaid expenses)**. At the end of the accounting period, accrued expenses must be recorded because if they are left unrecorded, the corresponding expense item will be understated, resulting in overstatement of net income. Since accrued expenses are not yet due for payment, a liability account must be recorded to recognize that the business has an obligation to pay the accrued expenses on due date. If accrued liabilities are not recorded at the end of the accounting period, the total liabilities of the business will be understated. Many businesses use the word **accrued** before the liability account title to distinguish accrued liability (used only in adjusting entries) from ordinary liability. However, it is also acceptable simply to use directly the liability account, without using the word accrued. What is important is to record the accrued expenses and the corresponding liability at the end of the accounting period.

Suppose the business uses a calendar year accounting period. It obtained a $300,000 ten-year long-term loan on December 15, 2000 at 6%, interest payment to be made every 15th of the month, with a balloon payment of principal at maturity date. Every year-end until the loan is fully paid on December 15, 2010, it must record accrued interest expense and accrued interest payable in the amount of $800, the interest for 16 days from Dec 16-31.

Remember that **accrued expenses always go with accrued liabilities.**

Computation of Interest (I)

$I = PRT$ P is Principal; R is interest rate and T is time (days/360)
$I = 300,000 \times .06 \times 16/360$ (in business computation, the denominator for time is always 360 days, not 365)
$I = \$800$

The adjusting entry to record accrued expense is to **debit the expense account and credit the accrued liability account.** In the above example, the following adjusting entry must be recorded in the general journal:

GENERAL JOURNAL

DATE	DESCRIPTION	DEBIT	CREDIT
12-31-nn	Interest Expense	800	
	Accrued Interest Payable		800
	Interest on loan Dec 16-31		

ACCOUNTING FOR ACCRUED EXPENSES and ACCRUED LIABILITIES

Some of the more commonly known accrued expenses are:

1. Accrued interest on notes payable, loans payable or mortgage payable
2. Accrued salaries or wages for work already rendered by employees
3. Accrued rent
4. Accrued income tax

ACCRUED INTEREST ON NOTES PAYABLE

In accounting for accrued interest, the first step is to determine the number of days that will be used in the computation of accrued interest. Remember to exclude the date of issuance of the note, for example if the note was issued on December 5, start counting from December 6 up to the end of the accounting period. Mathematically, the number of days for the month of issue is equal to the number of days for that month minus the date of issue. If the note was issued on December 5, the number of days used in the computation of interest is 26 days, computed as 31 (there are 31 days in December) minus 5 (date of issue), which corresponds to December 6 to December 31. It is important to know the number of days of each month of the year, as notes may be issued for longer term that cover many months, say 180 days (see computation below). The second step is to compute the interest due for the number of days computed in step one. Interest is computed using the formula $I = PRT$. I stands for interest, P stands for principal or the face amount of the note, R stands for the interest rate of the note and T stands for time or term of the note. Rate is the annual interest rate, expressed as a percentage, say 6%. Time is expressed as a fraction, where the numerator is the number of days computed in step 1 and the denominator is always 360. Note that in business computations, one year is equal to 360 days, not 365 days. When the accrued interest is already computed the adjusting entry to record accrued interest expense is to **debit Interest Expense for the amount computed in step 2 and to credit Interest Payable for the same amount.**

Fundamentals of Accounting

ILLUSTRATION PROBLEM

REQUIRED: Record the following transactions of ABC Company.

Oct 05, 2005 Bought computer, $15,000. Issued promissory note PN001, a 6% 90 day note to Best Staples.

Dec 31, 2005 Record accrued interest on notes payable.

ANALYSIS and COMPUTATION

Step 1 Compute the number of days from Oct 6 to Dec 31

Number of days in October	31
Less: Issue date of the promissory note Oct 5	-5
Number of days from Oct 6 to Oct 31	26 days
Number of days in Nov	30
Number of days in Dec	31
Total number of days from Oct 6 to Dec 31	87 days

Step 2 Compute the accrued interest for 87 days

$I = PRT = \$15,000 \times 6/100 \times 87/360 = \$217.50$

GENERAL JOURNAL

DATE	DOC REF	DESCRIPTION	POST REF	DEBIT	CREDIT
2005					
Oct 06	PN001	Computer		15,000	
		Notes Payable			15,000
		bought computer with 6%-90 day note			
Dec 31	ADJ001	Interest Expense		217.50	
		Interest Payable			217.50
		accrued interest Oct 6-Dec31			

Note that if the above adjusting entry is not recorded on December 31, Interest Expense is understated by $217.50, therefore net income is overstated and owner's capital is also overstated. Interest payable will be understated. Therefore the income statement, equity statement and balance sheet will reflect incorrect balances.

ACCRUED SALARIES or ACCRUED WAGES

Employees' salaries or wages are usually paid either on a weekly, bi-weekly, semi-monthly or monthly basis. In the past, salaries refer to the compensation computed on a periodic basis, such as weekly, semi-annually, monthly or annually and not expressed based on an hourly rate while wages are compensation computed based on an hourly rate basis. Nowadays, salaries and wages are used interchangeably; there is no longer any distinction between these two terms. Businesses usually establish a fixed payroll period and it is very likely that sometimes, the end of the accounting period will not coincide with the payroll date. **When the payroll date does not fall on the same date as the end of the accounting period, it gives rise to accrued payroll (accrued wages or accrued salaries).** The employees have already rendered work up to the end of the accounting period and the business must recognize and record the wages expense or salaries expense while at the same time, it must also record the liability, accrued salaries payable or accrued wages payable. For example, ABC Company pays its workers every Friday for work done from Monday to Friday. ABC Company uses the calendar year accounting period. The weekly payroll is $100,000. If December 31 falls on a Wednesday, the accrued payroll for three days (Monday, Tuesday, Wednesday) must be recorded on December 31, even though, the weekly payroll will be paid on Friday, January 2, the following year. The **adjusting entry to record accrued wages is to debit Wages Expense and credit Wages Payable**. Therefore, ABC Company must record the following adjusting entry on December 31:

GENERAL JOURNAL

DATE	DOC REF	DESCRIPTION	POST REF	DEBIT	CREDIT
Dec 31	ADJ001	Wages Expense		60,000	
		Wages Payable			60,000
		payroll Mon-Wed			

ANALYSIS and COMPUTATION

Weekly payroll for 5 days (Monday-Friday)	$100,000
Daily payroll ($100,000/5)	20,000
Unpaid days already worked (Monday-Wednesday)	3
Accrued Wages ($20,000 x 3)	$ 60,000

ACCRUED RENT

The standard business practice is to pay rent on a specific date every month, as specified in the lease agreement. **If the rental payment date does not coincide with the end of the accounting period, accrued rent must be computed and recorded corresponding to the number of days from the last payment date to the end of the accounting period.** In business computations, one month is equal to 30 days. For example, ABC Company pays its monthly rent every 10th day of the month. Accrued rent must be recorded for the remaining days of December. If monthly rent is $3,000, then accrued rent in the amount of $2,000 must be recorded on December 31. The **adjusting entry to record accrued rent is to debit Rent Expense and credit Rent Payable.** Therefore, ABC Company must record the following adjusting entry on December 31:

GENERAL JOURNAL

DATE	DOC REF	DESCRIPTION	POST REF	DEBIT	CREDIT
Dec 31	ADJ002	Rent Expense		2,000	
		Rent Payable			2,000
		rent Dec 11-31			

ANALYSIS and COMPUTATION

Monthly rent (30 days)	$3,000
Daily rent ($3,000/30 days)	100
Accrued number of days (30-10)	10
Accrued Rent	$2,000

ACCRUED INCOME TAX

Accrued income tax refers to the income tax due to the government based on current year's taxable income, which remains unremitted to the government as of the end of the accounting period. The income tax expense for the year must be recorded and the corresponding income tax liability for the year must be recognized in the books even though the payment of the income tax will happen a few months after the close of the accounting year. The deadline for the filing of the annual tax returns and the payment of income tax is on the 15th day on the third month following the close of the corporation's tax year.

Accrued income tax is recognized only in the books of corporations. Sole proprietorships and partnerships do not pay income taxes, because the profits of the business are reflected as income by the owners or partners in their individual tax returns. In the corporate business structure, double taxation exists. The corporate business pays income tax on its profits or income and the stockholders also pay income tax on the dividend income that they receive from the corporation. In the United States, in addition to the federal income tax, some corporations also pay state and city income tax if they are based in states and cities that impose income tax. The tax rates vary depending on the amount of taxable income before income tax. The federal income tax rates range from 15% for the first $50,000 taxable income to 38% for taxable income between $15,000,000 and $18,333,333 and 35% for taxable income in excess of $18,333,333. The tax rates are graduated based on the taxable income. The United States Congress, in the case of federal tax rates and the state and city legislatures, in the case of state and city income tax rates are empowered to revise the income tax rates. Corporations usually report in their income statement the income before income tax and show as a separate line the provision for income tax as a deduction to arrive at the net income after income tax. Sometimes corporations use the account titles **Provision for Federal Income Tax or Provision for State Income Tax or simply Provision for Income Tax instead of Federal Income Tax Expense or State Income Tax Expense. In the income statement, the federal, state and city income taxes are combined and shown simply as one line item.**

The accrual of income tax is recorded monthly as pretax income (income before tax) is earned by the business. Businesses usually establish their own combined tax rates based on past experience and use this tax rate in estimating their monthly provision for income tax. To compute the estimated monthly accrual amount, simply multiply the average tax rate by the pretax income earned for the period. At the end of the accounting year, the actual amount of accrued income tax is computed using the federal, state and city graduated tax tables.

The adjusting entry to record accrued income tax is shown below:

	Debit	Credit
Federal Income Tax Expense	xxx	
State Income Tax Expense	xxx	
City Income Tax Expense	xxx	
Federal Income Tax Payable		xxx
State Income Tax Payable		xxx
City Income Tax Payable		xxx
record accrued federal and state income tax		

ILLUSTRATION PROBLEM

ABC Company earned a pretax income of $50,000 in December 2005, the first month of its operation. The applicable federal tax rate is 15% while the applicable state income tax rate is 5%. Record the accrued federal and state income taxes on December 31, 2005.

ANALYSIS and COMPUTATION

Accrued federal income tax (15% x $50,000)	$7,500
Accrued state income tax (5% x 50,000)	2,500

The adjusting entry to record the accrued federal income tax and the accrued state income tax for ABC Company will be:

GENERAL JOURNAL

DATE	DOC REF	DESCRIPTION	POST REF	DEBIT	CREDIT
Dec 31	ADJ003	Federal Income Tax Expense		7,500	
		State Income Tax Expense		2,500	
		Federal Income Tax Payable			7,500
		State Income Tax Payable			2,500
		accrued income taxes			

ACCRUAL OF UNRECORDED REVENUES and RECEIVABLES

Accrued revenues are revenues already earned but have not yet been collected at the end of the accounting period. Accrued revenues give rise to accrued receivables. Accrued revenues are recorded at the end of the accounting period in order to reflect the correct balance of the revenues of the business. If accrued revenues are not recorded then the revenues of the business will be understated resulting in understatement of net income in the income statement and understatement of the owner's equity account in the balance sheet. Since accrued revenues are not yet due for collection, an asset account, accrued receivable is recorded in order to recognize that the business has a right to collect from a customer for services already rendered or an implicit transaction already happened, such as the passage of time in the case of notes receivable. For instance, XYZ Consulting Services sends a monthly billing every 15th of the month for a fixed monthly retainer fee of $25,000. XYZ follows the calendar year as its accounting year. On December 31, XYZ Consulting must record accrued service fees amounting to $12,500 since it will only charge for services rendered from the 16th-31st of December in next year's January billing statement to be sent on January 15. Another example of accrued revenues is accrued interest revenues on notes receivable. Suppose that XYZ Consulting received a 12% 90 day note from one of its clients on December 01, 2005 in the amount of $150,000. On December 31, 2005, it must record accrued interest revenues and accrued interest receivable amounting to $1,500 (I=PRT = $150,000 x .12 x 30/360).

The adjusting entry to record the accrual of unrecorded revenues is to debit the asset account accrued receivable and credit revenues.

In the above examples, XYZ Consulting Services must prepare the following adjusting entries on December 31, 2005:

GENERAL JOURNAL

DATE	DOC REF	DESCRIPTION	POST REF	DEBIT	CREDIT
2005					
Dec 31	ADJ007	Retainer Fees Receivable		12,500	
		Retainer Fees			12,500
		retainer fees Dec16-31			
	ADJ008	Interest Receivable		1,500	
		Interest Revenues			1,500
		interest earned Dec 01-31			

ILLUSTRATION PROBLEM

Johney Kochran is a famous lawyer. He sends his monthly billing for his legal services to his retainer clients every 20th day of each month. He charges each of his 50 retainer clients $7,500 every month. Mr. Kochran uses the fiscal year ending November 30 as his accounting year. On October 25, 2005, Mr. Kochran received a $50,000 120 day 12% promissory note from Orenthal Samson.

REQUIRED: Prepare the adjusting entries on November 30, 2005 to record the accrued retainer fees and the accrued interest on the promissory note.

ANALYSIS and COMPUTATION

Accrued Retainer Fees

Monthly retainer fees	$7,500
Daily retainer fees ($7,500/30)	250
Accrued number of days (30-20)	10
Accrued retainer fees per client	$2,500
Number of retainer clients	50
Total accrued retainer fees (2,500 x 50)	$125,000

Accrued Interest Revenues

Step 1 Compute the number of days from October 26 to November 30.

Days in October (31 – 25)	6 days
Days in November	30
Total number of days	36 days

Step 2 Compute accrued interest revenues

$I = PRT$ $I = \$50,000 \times .12 \times 36/360 = \$600$

GENERAL JOURNAL

DATE	DOC REF	DESCRIPTION	POST REF	DEBIT	CREDIT
2005					
Nov 30	ADJ009	Retainer Fees Receivable		125,000	
		Retainer Fees			125,000
		accrued retainer fees			
	ADJ010	Interest Receivable		600	
		Interest Revenues			600
		accrued interest revenues			

REALIZATION or EARNING OF UNEARNED REVENUES

Unearned revenues (also called deferred credit or deferred revenues) are revenues collected in advance even though they are not yet earned. In other words, the business already collected cash before it performed the services or sold the product to its customers. **Unearned revenues are classified as current liabilities** because the business is obligated to perform a service or sell a product in the future in exchange for the cash that it collected in advance. Typical examples of unearned revenues are collecting advanced subscription payment for magazines or newspapers, selling season tickets to sports events, collecting advanced rent from tenants, restaurants collecting deposits for reservations, lottery ticket receipts good for several drawings collected in advance, etc. It is important to record properly what portion of customer advances have been earned, which should be appropriately recorded as revenues and what portion is unearned which should be appropriately recorded as liability.

The two methods of accounting for unearned revenues are the liability method and the revenue method.

(1) Under **the liability method**, at the time of the collection of the advanced payment, a liability account, unearned revenues is credited and asset cash is debited for the same amount. At the end of the year, an adjusting entry is recorded whereby the earned portion is credited to earned revenues and the liability account unearned revenues is debited for the same amount.

(2) Under the **revenue method**, a revenue account is credited at the time of the collection of the advanced payment and asset cash is debited for the same amount. At the end of the year, an adjusting entry is recorded whereby the unearned portion is credited to a liability account, unearned revenues and the revenue account is debited for the same amount.

ILLUSTRATION PROBLEMS

UNEARNED SEASON TICKETS

On November 1, 2005 Madison Square Garden (MSG) sold 5,000 season tickets to the 2005-2006 NBA season for the 35 Knicks games to be played at MSG. The cost of each season ticket is $3,500. As of December 31, 2005, 5 games have been played at MSG.

REQUIRED: Record the sale of the season tickets on November 1, 2005.
Record the adjusting entry on December 31, 2005 for the 5 games already played
Record the above entries using the revenue method and the liability method.

UNEARNED REVENUES USING THE LIABILITY METHOD

ANALYSIS and COMPUTATION

Cost per season ticket	$3,500
Number of season tickets sold	5,000
Total Advanced Collection ($3,500 x 5,000)	$17,500,000

GENERAL JOURNAL ENTRY TO RECORD THE SALE OF SEASON TICKET
(liability, unearned revenues is credited at the time of collection of advanced payment)

GENERAL JOURNAL

DATE	DOC REF	DESCRIPTION	POST REF	DEBIT	CREDIT
2005					
Nov 01		Cash		17,500,000	
		Unearned Knicks Season Tickets			17,500,000
		5,000 tickets @ $3,500			

ADJUSTING ENTRY TO RECORD THE EARNED PORTION (liability, unearned revenues is debited for the earned portion and revenue is credited for the same amount)

ANALYSIS and COMPUTATION

Cost per season ticket	$3,500
Total number of games at MSG	35
Average cost per game ($3,500/35)	$ 100
Total games played up to Dec 31	5
Earned portion per season ticket ($100 x 5)	$ 500
Total earned portion ($500 x 5,000 tickets)	$2,500,000

GENERAL JOURNAL

DATE	DOC REF	DESCRIPTION	POST REF	DEBIT	CREDIT
2005					
Dec 31	ADJ011	Unearned Knicks Season Tickets		2,500,000	
		Earned Knicks Season Tickets			2,500,000
		5 games played @ $100 for 5,000 tickets			

Let us post these two entries to T accounts.

UNEARNED KNICKS SEASON TICKETS		EARNED KNICKS SEASON TICKETS
12/31/05 2,500,000	11/01/05 17,500,000	12/31/05 2,500,000
	- 2,500,000	
	BAL 15,000,000	

Fundamentals of Accounting

UNEARNED REVENUES USING THE REVENUE METHOD

ANALYSIS and COMPUTATION

Cost per season ticket	$3,500
Number of season tickets sold	5,000
Total Advanced Collection ($3,500 x 5,000)	$17,500,000

GENERAL JOURNAL ENTRY TO RECORD THE SALE OF SEASON TICKET
(earned revenues is credited at the time of collection of advanced payment)

GENERAL JOURNAL

DATE	DOC REF	DESCRIPTION	POST REF	DEBIT	CREDIT
2005					
Nov 01		Cash		17,500,000	
		Earned Knicks Season Tickets			17,500,000
		5,000 tickets @ $3,500			

ADJUSTING ENTRY TO RECORD THE UNEARNED PORTION (earned revenues is debited for the unearned portion and unearned revenues is credited for the same amount)

ANALYSIS and COMPUTATION

Cost per season ticket	$3,500
Total number of games at MSG	35
Average cost per game ($3,500/35)	$ 100
Total games not yet played as of Dec 31 (35-5)	30
Unearned portion per ticket ($100 x 30)	$3,000
Total unearned portion ($3,000 x 5,000 tickets)	$15,000,000

GENERAL JOURNAL

DATE	DOC REF	DESCRIPTION	POST REF	DEBIT	CREDIT
2005					
Dec 31	ADJ001	Earned Knicks Season Tickets		15,000,000	
		Unearned Knicks Season Tickets			15,000,000
		unearned portion ($3,000 x 5,000 tickets)			

Let us post the above entries to T accounts

UNEARNED KNICKS SEASON TICKETS		EARNED KNICKS SEASON TICKETS	
	12/31/05 15,000,000	12/31/05 15,000,000	11/01/05 17,500,000
			-15,000,000
		BAL	2,500,000

Compare the balance of the T accounts for Unearned Knicks Season Tickets and Earned Knicks Season Tickets under the liability method and the revenue method. What do you notice?

The balances in the T accounts show that in both methods, the resulting balances for earned revenues and unearned revenues are the same. The Earned Knicks Season Tickets balance under the liability method is $$2,500,000. This is the same balance of Earned Knicks Season Tickets under the revenue method. The liability account, Unearned Knicks Season Tickets has a balance of $15,000,000 under both the liability method and revenue method.

UNEARNED SUBSCRIPTIONS REVENUE

Magazine Publishers gets annual subscriptions to Business Weekly. The annual subscription is $104 for 52 issues of Business Weekly. On September 1, 2005, Magazine Publishers received 9,000 subscriptions. There were 18 issues of Business Weekly from September 1 to December 31, 2005.

REQUIRED: Record the sale of the 9,000 subscriptions on September 01, 2005.
Record the adjusting entry on December 31, 2005 for the 18 issues already delivered.
Record the above entries using the revenue method and the liability method.

UNEARNED REVENUES USING THE LIABILITY METHOD

ANALYSIS and COMPUTATION

Cost of an annual subscription	$ 104
Number of subscriptions sold	9,000
Total Advanced Collection ($104 x 9,000)	$936,000

GENERAL JOURNAL ENTRY TO RECORD THE SALE OF SUBSCRIPTIONS
(unearned revenues is credited at the time of collection of advanced payment)

GENERAL JOURNAL

DATE	DOC REF	DESCRIPTION	POST REF	DEBIT	CREDIT
2005					
Sep 01		Cash		936,000	
		Unearned Magazine Subscriptions			936,000
		9,000 @ $104			

ADJUSTING ENTRY TO RECORD THE EARNED PORTION (unearned revenues is debited for the earned portion and revenues is credited for the same amount)

ANALYSIS and COMPUTATION

Cost of annual subscription	$ 104
Total number of issues of Business Weekly	52
Average cost per issue ($104/52)	$ 2
Total issues delivered (Sep 01 – Dec 31)	18
Earned portion per subscription ($2 x 18)	$ 36
Total earned portion ($36 x 9,000 subscriptions)	$324,000

GENERAL JOURNAL

DATE	DOC REF	DESCRIPTION	POST REF	DEBIT	CREDIT
2005					
Dec 31	ADJ011	Unearned Magazine Subscriptions		324,000	
		Earned Magazine Subscriptions			324,000
		18 issues ($36 x 9,000)			

Let us post the above entries to T accounts.

UNEARNED MAGAZINE SUBSCRIPTIONS

12/31/05	324,000	09/01/05	936,000
			-324,000
		BAL	612,000

EARNED MAGAZINE SUBSCRIPTIONS

		12/31/05	324,000

UNEARNED REVENUES USING THE REVENUE METHOD

ANALYSIS and COMPUTATION

Cost per subscription	$ 104
Number of subscriptions sold	9,000
Total Advanced Collection ($104 x 9,000)	$936,000

GENERAL JOURNAL ENTRY TO RECORD THE SALE OF SUBSCRIPTIONS
(earned revenues is credited at the time of collection of advanced payment)

GENERAL JOURNAL

DATE	DOC REF	DESCRIPTION	POST REF	DEBIT	CREDIT
2005					
Sep 01		Cash		936,000	
		Earned Magazine Subscriptions			936,000
		9,000 subscriptions @ $104			

ADJUSTING ENTRY TO RECORD THE UNEARNED PORTION (earned revenues is debited for the unearned portion and unearned revenues is credited for the same amount)

ANALYSIS and COMPUTATION

Cost per subscription	$ 104
Total number of issues	52
Average cost per issue ($104/52)	$ 2
Total not yet delivered as of Dec 31 (52 – 18)	34
Unearned portion per subscription ($2 x 34)	$ 68
Total unearned portion ($68 x 9,000 subscriptions)	$612,000

GENERAL JOURNAL

DATE	DOC REF	DESCRIPTION	POST REF	DEBIT	CREDIT
2005					
Dec 31	ADJ011	Earned Magazine Subscriptions		612,000	
		Unearned Magazine Subscriptions			612,000
		unearned portion ($68 x 9,000 subscriptions)			

Let us post the above entries to T accounts

UNEARNED MAGAZINE SUBSCRIPTIONS

	12/31/05 612,000

EARNED MAGAZINE SUBSCRIPTIONS

12/31/05 612,000	09/01/05 936,000
	-612,000
	BAL 324,000

The balances in the T accounts show that under both methods, the resulting balances for earned revenues and unearned revenues are the same. The Earned Magazine Subscriptions balance under the liability method is $324,000. This is the same balance of Earned Magazine Subscriptions under the revenue method. The liability account, Unearned Magazine Subscriptions has a balance of $612,000 under both the liability method and revenue method.

UNEARNED RENTAL REVENUES

Mall Stores For Rent (MSFR) is a realty company that rents out store space in various malls. On August 1, 2005, MSFR collected $36,000,000 advanced rent for one year covering the period from August 1, 2005 to July 31, 2006.

REQUIRED: Record the collection of $36,000,000 advanced rent on August 01, 2005

Record the adjusting entry on December 31, 2005 for the unearned rental revenues and earned rental revenues

Record the above entries using the revenue method and the liability method.

UNEARNED REVENUES USING THE LIABILITY METHOD

GENERAL JOURNAL ENTRY TO RECORD THE COLLECTION OF ONE YEAR ADVANCED RENT (unearned revenues is credited at the time of collection of advanced payment)

GENERAL JOURNAL

DATE	DOC REF	DESCRIPTION	POST REF	DEBIT	CREDIT
2005 Aug 01		Cash		36,000,000	
		Unearned Rental Revenues			36,000,000
		collection of one year advanced rent			

ADJUSTING ENTRY TO RECORD THE EARNED PORTION (unearned revenues is debited for the earned portion and revenues is credited for the same amount)

ANALYSIS and COMPUTATION

One year advanced annual rent	$36,000,000
Total number of months in a year	12
Monthly rent ($36,000,000/12)	$ 3,000,000
Total expired months (Aug1 – Dec 31)	5
Earned Rental Revenues ($3,000,000 x 5)	$15,000,000

GENERAL JOURNAL

DATE	DOC REF	DESCRIPTION	POST REF	DEBIT	CREDIT
2005 Dec 31	ADJ011	Unearned Rental Revenues		15,000,000	
		Earned Rental Revenues			15,000,000
		Aug 01 – Dec 31 earned rent			

Let us post the above entries to T accounts.

UNEARNED RENTAL REVENUES

12/31/05	15,000,000	09/01/05	36,000,000
			-15,000,000
		BAL	21,000,000

EARNED RENTAL REVENUES

	12/31/05	15,000,000

UNEARNED REVENUES USING THE REVENUE METHOD

GENERAL JOURNAL ENTRY TO RECORD THE COLLECTION OF ONE YEAR ADVANCED RENT (earned revenues is credited at the time of collection of advanced payment)

GENERAL JOURNAL

DATE	DOC REF	DESCRIPTION	POST REF	DEBIT	CREDIT
2005 Aug 01		Cash		36,000,000	
		Earned Rental Revenues			36,000,000
		collection of one year advanced rent			

ADJUSTING ENTRY TO RECORD THE UNEARNED PORTION (earned revenues is debited for the unearned portion and unearned revenues is credited for the same amount)

ANALYSIS and COMPUTATION

One year advanced rent	$36,000,000
Total number of months	12
Average monthly rent ($36,000,000/12)	$ 3,000,000
Number of unexpired months (Jan1 05 – Jul 31 06)	7
Unearned rent ($3,000,000 x 7)	$21,000,000

GENERAL JOURNAL

DATE	DOC REF	DESCRIPTION	POST REF	DEBIT	CREDIT
2005					
Dec 31	ADJ011	Earned Rental Revenues		21,000,000	
		Unearned Rental Revenues			21,000,000
		unearned rent (Jan 01, 2005 to Jul 31, 2006)			

Let us post the above entries in T accounts

UNEARNED RENTAL REVENUES

		12/31/05	21,000,000

EARNED RENTAL REVENUES

12/31/05	21,000,000	08/01/05	36,000,000
			-21,000,000
		BAL	15,000,000

The balances in the T accounts show that in both methods, the resulting balances for earned revenues and unearned revenues are the same. The Earned Rental Revenues balance under the liability method is $15,000,000. This is the same balance of Earned Rental Revenues under the revenue method. The liability account, Unearned Rental Revenues has a balance of $21,000,000 under both the liability method and revenue method.

DEPRECIATION OF LONG-TERM TANGIBLE ASSETS

Depreciation is the cost allocation of long-term tangible assets over its useful life. Long-term assets are also called (1) plant assets, (2) fixed assets, (3) property plant and equipment and (4) long-lived assets. These are assets that serve the business for many years. Long term assets are classified into tangible assets (such as land, building, office equipment, delivery equipment, trucks, van, etc.), intangible assets (such as copyrights, patents, goodwill, trademarks, etc.) and wasting assets or natural resources (such as gold mine, oil deposits, marble deposits, diamond mines, etc.). For purposes of this chapter, only the straight line method of depreciation of long-term tangible assets will be discussed. The other depreciation methods (units of production and the accelerated methods such declining balance methods and sum of the years digits) will be discussed in accounting for fixed assets.

Tangible long term assets are assets that have physical substance. These are assets that are sensible to the senses (can be seen, heard, touched, etc.). When a long term asset is acquired, its cost (also called acquisition cost) is recorded as debit to the corresponding asset account and reflected in the balance sheet. As the long term asset is used in the business, the cost applicable to the period that the asset was used is charged to expense, by transferring the allocated cost portion from asset to expense. This is in compliance with the principle of matching of cost and revenues. As long as the asset is used to produce revenues, the portion of the asset used to earn the revenues is allocated to expense. If depreciation expense is not recorded, the book value of the asset will remain the same, hence will be overstated. As the asset is depreciated, its book value diminishes over time. Sometimes, obsolescence or the state at which the asset loses its usefulness also demands that the asset be depreciated. In addition, mere passage of time also reduces the book value of the asset. The **book value** is the undepreciated cost of the asset and it is equal to cost minus accumulated depreciation. **Accumulated depreciation (also called allowance for depreciation)** is the depreciated cost of the asset, which is the cumulative total of the depreciation expenses over the years from the first year that the asset was placed in production. Accumulated depreciation is a contra asset account and it is presented in the balance sheet as a deduction from the related asset account.

When a long-term asset is acquired, the business *estimates* the useful life of the asset. **Useful life** is the number of years that the business will use the asset; it is the number of years that the asset will be productive. Sometimes, useful life is expressed as the number of units of product that the asset will produce. For a fabric making machine, useful life is expressed in the number of yards of cloth that the machine will produce. For transportation equipment, useful life is sometimes expressed as the number of miles that the vehicle will cover over its life. At the time of asset acquisition, the business also *estimates* the **salvage value (also called residual value or scrap value or disposal value)** of the asset. **Salvage value** is the amount that the business will receive when the asset is disposed or sold at the end of its useful life, when it is fully depreciated.

The **straight line depreciation method** assumes that assets are depreciated based on a uniform depreciation rate every year; the annual depreciation expense is fixed, constant and the same throughout the useful life of the asset. Depreciation rate is equal to 1 divided by the useful life of the asset. If the useful life is 10 years, then the depreciation rate is 10% (1/10). The **depreciable cost of an asset is equal to cost minus salvage value.**

Two ways to compute the annual depreciation expense using the straight line method are shown below:

> (1) Annual depreciation expense = (Cost minus salvage value) x 1/useful life
> Note that cost minus salvage value is the depreciable cost of the asset and 1/useful life is the depreciation rate

> (2) Annual depreciation expense = (Cost minus salvage value) / useful life
> Again, in the above formula, the numerator is the depreciable cost of the asset.

The same amount of annual depreciation expense will result using either one of the above formula.

The adjusting entry to record depreciation expense is to debit the depreciation expense (asset) and credit accumulated depreciation (asset) or allowance for depreciation (asset). The asset being depreciated must be identified in both the depreciation expense and accumulated depreciation expense accounts.

ILLUSTRATION PROBLEM

On July 1, 2005, ABC Company issued check 1105 to pay for 5 delivery trucks bought for $100,000. It is estimated that the trucks will be useful for 5 years and each truck will have a salvage value of $2,000 at the end of its useful life. Straight line depreciation method is used.

REQUIRED: (1) Prepare the general journal entry to record the purchase of the trucks on July 1, 2005

(2) Prepare the adjusting entry to record the depreciation expense on December 31, 2005

(3) Compute the book value of the trucks on December 31, 2005

ANALYSIS and COMPUTATION

Note that each truck has a salvage value of $2,000, therefore the total salvage value of the 5 trucks amount to $10,000 ($2,000 x 5).

The trucks were bought on July 1, 2005. Therefore depreciation expense in 2005 shall be calculated only for half year from July 1 to December 31. Depreciation expense for 2006, 2007, 2008 and 2009 will be for one full year. During the last year of its useful life on 2010 the depreciation expense will be for half year.

Depreciation Expense By Year

2005	Half year (Jul 01 – Dec 31)	½
2006	Full Year (Jan 01 – Dec 31)	1
2007	Full Year (Jan 01 – Dec 31)	1
2008	Full Year (Jan 01 – Dec 31)	1
2009	Full Year (Jan 01 – Dec 31)	1
2010	Half Year (Jan 01 – Jun 30)	½
	Total Years (useful life)	5

Step 1 Compute Annual depreciation

FORMULA 1

(Cost minus salvage value) x 1/useful life
($100,000 – 10,000) x 1/5
$90,000 x .20 = $18,000

FORMULA 2

(Cost minus salvage value) / useful life
($100,000 – 10,000) / 5
$90,000 / 5 = $18,000

Step 2 Compute depreciation expense for 2005 (6 months - July 1 to December 31)

Depreciation Expense for 2005 = Annual depreciation x (6/12)
= $18,000 x (6/12) = $9,000

GENERAL JOURNAL

DATE	DOC REF	DESCRIPTION	POST REF	DEBIT	CREDIT
2005					
July 01	CK1105	Trucks		100,000	
		Cash			100,000
		bought trucks			
Dec 31	ADJ005	Depreciation Expense (Trucks)		9,000	
		Accumulated Depreciation (Trucks)			9,000
		depreciation July 01-Dec 31			

Book Value as of December 31, 2005 = Cost Minus Accumulated Depreciation
= $100,000 - 9,000 = $91,000

Remember that salvage value is not used in the computation of the book value of the asset. Salvage value is only used in the computation of the annual depreciation expense.

BAD DEBTS EXPENSE FOR ACCOUNTS RECEIVABLE

Accounts receivable arises when the business earns revenues and it does not receive full payment when services are rendered or when products are sold. Accounts receivable is a current asset because it gives right to the business to collect money from its customers in the future. As a common practice, businesses perform services or sells products on account to increase revenues. Customers do not always have cash at the time they require services or need to buy the products provided by businesses. Credit sales or selling on account therefore enhances the sales of many businesses. In the United States many stores have their own store-issued credit cards and the stores even offer special discounts to holders of store-issued credit cards to entice them to patronize the store. Stores earn additional revenues by way of the interests that they charge to cardholders who maintain outstanding balances on their credit card accounts. Maintaining a database of credit card customers enables the store to keep track of their purchases which benefits the store in using the available information when it designs marketing and customer services related programs.

Despite the advantages of selling on account, businesses assume a certain amount of risk when customers are unable to pay their accounts on time. During economic downturn, when people lose their jobs, their ability to pay their debts suffers. Businesses experience difficulty in collecting customers' accounts and their outstanding accounts receivable build up. Sometimes, businesses have to write off customers accounts that have no chance of being collected. The costs associated with selling on account are called **bad debts expense. Bad debts expense (also called uncollectible accounts)** is considered an ordinary operating business expense.

The **two methods of accounting for bad debts are the direct write off method and the allowance method.** Under the **direct write off method**, bad debts expense is recorded only when it is certain and definite that the accounts receivable is not collectible; therefore the amount recorded as bad debts expense is an actual amount and not an estimate. It is very likely that the revenues arising from the uncollectible accounts were recorded during the accounting period before recording the bad debts expense. Therefore the **direct write off method may result in mismatching of costs and revenues**; when the revenues and actual write off of bad accounts are recorded in different accounting periods. The **principle of matching costs and revenues** requires that bad debts expense be charged against the revenues in the same accounting period that the revenues were recognized and recorded. The direct write off method does not provide for adjusting entry to record an estimated bad debts expense at the end of the accounting period. The **direct write off method violates both the principle of matching of costs and revenues and the principle of conservatism.** According to the **principle of conservatism**, when there is a choice between selecting a method of income measurement, it is prudent for businesses to **choose the method that will result in lower net income, lower assets and lower owner's equity during the earlier years of business operation.** In other words, businesses must select the method that will produce a less favorable immediate result and this less favorable result should be recognized and recorded right away, not later. It is a known fact that businesses are unable to collect 100% of their outstanding accounts receivable. In accordance with the principle of conservatism, businesses must record a certain percentage of the accounts receivable as bad debts expense, during the same accounting period when the credit sales were made, not later, when the accounts receivable are certain to be uncollectible. Recording the uncollectible accounts later will result in higher net income, higher assets and higher owner's equity in the immediate year. The only advantage of the direct write off method is that it is simple to use; since only actual uncollectible accounts are written off, there is no need to make adjusting entry and make calculations at year end.

The deficiencies of the direct write off method are resolved by the allowance method of accounting for bad debts. **Under the allowance method, bad debts expense is recognized and recorded in the same accounting period that the credit sales are earned and recorded**. The allowance method results in proper matching of costs and revenues. At the same time, since bad debts expense is immediately recorded, it adheres to the principle of conservatism, because in the immediate year when the bad debts is recognized, it results in higher operating expenses thereby resulting in lower net income, lower assets and lower owner's equity, even though it is uncertain that the accounts are not uncollectible. Based on experience and the state of the economy, businesses usually establish a reasonable rate of uncollectible accounts which they use as basis in estimating the bad debts expense. **At the end of the accounting period, an adjusting entry, debit to Bad Debts Expense and credit to Allowance for Bad Debts is made to record bad debts expense using a calculated estimate**.

The two methods of calculating bad debts expense under the allowance method are the percentage of sales and percentage of receivables. **Under the percentage of sales method, bad debts expense is equal to an established percentage of uncollectible accounts multiplied by the net credit sales during the accounting period**. Note that cash sales are not considered since the business is not exposed to any credit risk from cash sales. Under the percentage of receivable method, the "should be" allowance for bad debts (effectively, the uncollectible accounts receivable) is equal to an established percentage of uncollectible accounts multiplied by the outstanding accounts receivable at the end of the accounting period. Bad debts expense is then calculated depending on the beginning balance of the allowance for bad debts before the adjusting entry is made. If the allowance for bad debts has a beginning credit balance, bad debts expense is equal to the difference between the "should be" allowance for bad debts and the beginning credit balance of the allowance for bad debts. If the allowance for bad debts has a beginning debit balance before the adjusting entry, bad debts expense is equal to the sum of the "should be" allowance for bad debts and the beginning debit balance of the allowance for bad debts.

For purposes of this chapter, only the allowance method of accounting for bad debts using the percentage of sales method of calculating the bad debts expense will be discussed. The direct write off method and the allowance method using the percentage of receivables in calculating bad debts expense are appropriately covered in accounting for accounts receivable and bad debts expense.

ILLUSTRATION PROBLEM

You Are Great records Bad Debts Expense on December 31, the end of the accounting calendar year. 2% of net credit sales are uncollectible. In 2005, net credit sales amount to $1,595,000.

ANALYSIS and COMPUTATION

Bad Debts Expense = 2% of net credit sales = .02 x $1,595,000 = $31,900

ADJUSTING ENTRY TO RECORD BAD DEBTS EXPENSE

GENERAL JOURNAL

DATE	DOC REF	DESCRIPTION	POST REF	DEBIT	CREDIT
2005 Dec 31	ADJ012	Bad Debts Expense Allowance for Bad Debts bad debts (2% x $1,595,000)		31,900	31,900

CHAPTER 06   ACCOUNTING PROCESS: THE ADJUSTING ENTRIES

REVIEW QUESTIONS

1. Why are adjusting entries prepared at the end of the accounting period?

2. What are the types of business transactions? Differentiate one from the other.

3. Explain the principle of matching of costs and revenues.

4. Explain the cost recovery principle.

5. Differentiate cash basis from accrual basis of accounting.

6. Identify and describe the types of adjusting entries,

7. Identify and describe the two methods of accounting for prepaid expense.

8. Identify and describe the two methods of accounting for unearned revenues.

9. Describe accounting for unearned season tickets.

10. What are long-term assets?

11. Identify and describe the types of long-term assets.

12. Why are long-term tangible assets subjected to depreciation?

13. Explain the need to recognize bad debts expense.

14. What are accrued expenses? Give examples.

15. What are accrued revenues? Give examples.

CHAPTER 06   ACCOUNTING PROCESS: THE ADJUSTING ENTRIES

REVIEW EXAMINATION

TRUE or FALSE: *WRITE TRUE or FALSE IN THE SPACE PROVIDED.*

1. _____ Adjusting entries are recorded at the beginning of the accounting period before the trial balance are prepared in order to reflect the correct balance of accounts.

2. _____ If adjusting entries are not made, the balance of some accounts will be overstated while the balance of some accounts will be understated.

3. _____ The principle of materiality states that costs and expenses must be recorded in the same accounting period that the related revenues are recorded.

4. _____ Under the cost recovery principle, certain purchases of goods or services or prepayments of expenses in the current period which will benefit future periods are initially recorded as assets.

5. _____ implied or implicit transactions are incidents or events, such as the passage of time, that are not recorded during the course of ordinary business, but are accounted only at the end of the accounting period as adjusting entries.

6. _____ The amount recorded for explicit transactions are derived from calculations and not from source documents.

7. _____ The accrual basis of accounting violates the matching of costs and revenues principle.

8. _____ Under the accrual basis, the effects of all transactions on the financial statements are recognized, even though no cash is received or no cash is paid.

9. _____ Expressed or explicit transactions are the routinary, ordinary and repetitious transactions that occur during the ordinary course of business.

10. _____ When the payroll date falls on the same date as the end of the accounting period, it gives rise to accrued payroll.

11. _____ The adjusting entry to record accrued wages is to debit Wages Expense and credit Accrued Wages Payable.

12. _____ The adjusting entry to record accrued rent is to debit Rent Expense and credit Accrued Rent Payable.

13. _____ In recording expressed transactions, the information used is definite and specific, and the actual amounts, not estimates are used because they come from the source documents that serve as the evidence of the business transaction.

14. _____ Prepaid expenses are expenses paid in advance, the benefit, use or consumption of which is chargeable to the current period and to future accounting period/s after the payment was made.

15. _____ Under the asset method of accounting for prepaid expenses, upon payment an asset account, Prepaid Expense is credited and Cash is debited.

16. _____ Before an implied transaction can happen, it is preceded by a related expressed transaction.

17. _____ Under the accrual basis of accounting, transactions are recorded only when cash is received or when cash is paid.

18. _____ Under the liability method of accounting for unearned revenues, the adjusting entry at the end of the accounting period is a debit to the unearned revenues and a credit to earned revenues.

19. _____ Expenses that are already incurred but remain unpaid at the end of the accounting period are called prepaid expenses.

20. _____ The adjusting entry to record accrued expense is to debit the expense account and credit the accrued liability account.

21. _____ In the computation of interest, the first step is to determine the number of days that will be used in the computation of accrued interest.

22. _____ The adjusting entry to record accrued interest expense is to debit Accrued Interest Payable and to credit Interest Expense.

23. _____ The balances of the accounts are the same regardless of whether the asset method or expense method is used in accounting for prepaid expenses.

24. _____ At the end of the accounting period, it is very likely that there are some expenses that the business already incurred, although, they are not yet paid in cash.

25. _____ The adjusting entry to record accrued rent is to debit Rent Expense and credit Accrued Rent Payable.

COMPLETION: *WRITE THE ANSWER IN THE SPACE PROVIDED.*

1. The _____ principle states that costs and expenses must be recorded in the same accounting period that the related revenues are recorded.

2. Under the _____ certain purchases of goods or services or prepayments of expenses in the current period are initially recorded as assets in the current period even though the benefits will extend to future accounting periods.

3. _____ are the routinary, ordinary and repetitious transactions that occur during the ordinary course of business.

4. In recording expressed transactions, the information used is definite and specific, and the actual amounts, not estimates are used because they come from the _____ that serve as the evidence of the business transaction.

5. _____ transactions are incidents or events, such as the passage of time, that are not recorded during the course of ordinary business, but are accounted only at the end of the accounting period as adjusting entries.

6. The amount recorded for implied transactions are derived from _____, not directly as indicated in the source documents.

7. Before an implied transaction can happen, it is preceded by a related _____ transaction.

8. Under the _____ basis of accounting, transactions are recorded only when cash is received or when cash is paid.

9. Under the _____ basis, the effects of all transactions on the financial statements are recognized, even though no cash is received or no cash is paid.

10. _____ expenses are expenses paid in advance, the benefit, use or consumption of which is chargeable to the current period and to future accounting period/s.

11. Under the _____ method of accounting for prepaid expenses, at the end of the accounting period, an adjusting entry is made to debit the expense account and credit the prepaid asset account.

12. Under the _____ method of accounting for prepaid expense, at the time of pre-payment, an expense account is debited and cash is credited.

13. The adjusting entry to record earned revenues under the _____ method of accounting for unearned revenues is to debit unearned revenues and credit earned revenues.

14. At the time of collecting revenues in advance, cash is debited and earned revenues is credited under the _____ method.

15. After posting the adjusting entries to the general ledger, the balances of the affected accounts are the _____ regardless of the method used in accounting for prepaid expenses.

16. At the end of the accounting period, it is very likely that there are some expenses that the business already _____ although they are not yet paid.

17. Accrued expenses always go with _____.

18. Before an _____ transaction can happen, it is preceded by a related expressed transaction.

19. The adjusting entry to record accrued expense is to debit the _____ account and credit the _____ account.

20. In accounting for accrued interest, the first step is to determine the _____ that will be used in the computation of accrued interest.

21. The adjusting entry to record accrued interest expense is to debit _____ to credit _____.

22. When the payroll date does not fall on the same date as the end of the accounting period, it gives rise to _____.

23. The adjusting entry to record accrued wages is to debit _____ and to credit _____.

24. The adjusting entry to record accrued interest on notes receivable is to debit _____ and credit _____.

25. The adjusting entry to record accrued rent is to debit _____ and credit _____.

26. _____ are recorded at the end of the accounting period after the trial balance, but before the financial statements are prepared in order to reflect the correct balance of accounts.

27. If adjusting entries are not made, the balance of some accounts will be _____ while the balance of some accounts will be _____.

28. The adjusting entry to record used office supplies under the asset method is to debit _____ and credit _____.

29. To record uncollectible accounts under the allowance method, an adjusting entry is made debiting _____ and crediting _____.

30. Depreciation is recorded debiting _____ and crediting _____.

EXERCISES: Use the general journal form provided.

1. ABC Janitorial Services received a $20,000 60 day-12% promissory note on December 1, 2005 from XYZ Corporation. Compute the accrued interest revenues and prepare the adjusting entry to record the accrued interest revenues on December 31, 2005.

2. On March 1, 2005, Able Moving Services bought a moving truck for $35,000. It is estimated that the truck will be useful for 5 years with a salvage value of $5,000. Compute the depreciation expense and record the depreciation expense on December 31, 2005.

3. On November 1, 2005, Shea Stadium sold 20,000 season tickets at $800 per season ticket for the forty (40) games that the METS will play at Shea for the 2005-2006 baseball season. As of December 31, 2005, there were 8 games already played. Prepare the journal entry to record the sale of the season tickets on November 1 under the liability method and under the revenue method. Prepare the adjusting entries on December 31 under each method. Post the journal entries in T accounts under each method.

4. On July 1, 2005, Publishers House sold 25,000 annual subscriptions to Monthly Children's Magazine at $12 per subscription. Prepare the journal entry to record the sale of the annual subscriptions using the revenue method and the liability method. Prepare adjusting entry on December 31 under each method. Post the journal entries to T accounts under each method.

5. Dr. Excel Care earned $200,000 in professional fees. It is estimated that 2% of professional fees is uncollectible. Compute the bad debts expense and prepare the adjusting entry to record bad debts expense on December 31, 2005.

6. On October 1, 2005, Beautiful You paid $36,000 for one year advanced rent. Compute the expired rent as of December 31, 2005. Prepare the journal entry to record the prepayment of rent under the asset method and under the expense method. Record the adjusting entry on December 31, 2005 under the asset method and under the expense method. Post the accounting entries to T accounts under each method.

7. ABC bought office supplies worth $5,000 on January 1, 2005. ABC uses the asset method in accounting for prepaid expense. On December 31, 2005, a physical count of office supplies showed that $750 worth of supplies were on hand. Prepare the (1) journal entry on January 1 to record the purchase of office supplies and (2) adjusting entry on December 31 to record the office supplies used.

8. Wella Day Care paid the $1,200 annual insurance premium on its delivery van on March 1, 2005. Wella Day Care uses the expense method in accounting for prepaid expense. Prepare the (1) journal entry on March 1 to record the payment of the annual insurance premium and (2) adjusting entry to record prepaid insurance on December 31.

9. The workers of Metro Construction are paid every Saturday for six days work done from Monday to Saturday. The weekly payroll is $12,000. December 31 falls on a Thursday. Compute the accrued wages on December 31. Prepare the adjusting entry on December 31 to record accrued wages.

10. MGM Stunts Services issued a $250,000 promissory note to Stunts Tools for stuntmen tools on June 1, 2005. The note is for 360 days at 12% interest. Compute the accrued interest expense as of December 31. Prepare the journal entry on June 1 to record the issuance of the promissory note and the adjusting entry on December 31 to record the accrued interest.

GENERAL JOURNAL

PAGE _____

DATE	DOC REF	ACCT CODE	DESCRIPTION	POST REF	DEBIT	CREDIT

GENERAL JOURNAL

PAGE

DATE	DOC REF	ACCT CODE	DESCRIPTION	POST REF	DEBIT	CREDIT

GENERAL JOURNAL

PAGE _____

DATE	DOC REF	ACCT CODE	DESCRIPTION	POST REF	DEBIT	CREDIT

PROBLEMS: Use the general journal form provided.

A. GLOBAL DELIVERY SERVICES

REQUIRED: Prepare the adjusting entries for the month of June 2006. Depreciation is recorded at full month rate if the asset is bought before the 16th of the month and at half month rate if the asset is bought after the 15th of the month. The same half-month convention is used in accounting for prepaid expenses. The asset method of accounting for prepaid expense is used. Straight line depreciation method is used. The allowance method is used in recording bad debts expense.

1. Bad debts expense is equal to 1% of Delivery Fees amounting to $20,000.

2. An inventory count of office supplies on June 30 showed $1,200 worth of office supplies remain on hand. Office supplies on June 1 amount to $1,500.

3. One month expired insurance. Prepaid insurance for one year, $2,400 was paid on June 2, 2006.

4. One month expired rent. Prepaid annual rent, $12,000 was paid on June 3.

5. Depreciation on the truck. Estimated useful life is ten years with no salvage value. Juan del Mundo invested the truck on June 1. Cost of truck is $20,000.

6. Depreciation on the computer equipment. Computer was bought on June 9 for $5,000. Salvage value at the end of three-year useful life is $500.

7. Depreciation on furniture. Furniture was bought on June 4 for $2,400. Useful life is ten years with salvage value of $400.

8. Accrued interest on notes payable, Principal is $1,000; interest rate is 6%; term is 90 days and the note was issued on June 2.

9. One employee was unable to submit his time sheet on time, so he was not paid as of June 30. Unpaid wages amount to $800.

B. GARDEN LANDSCAPING & POOL SERVICES

REQUIRED: Prepare the adjusting entries for the year ended December 31, 2005. Depreciation is recorded at full month rate if the asset is bought before the 16th of the month and at half month rate if the asset is bought after the 15th of the month. The same half-month convention is used in accounting for prepaid expenses. The asset method of accounting for prepaid expense is used. All adjusting entries are recorded on December 31. Straight line depreciation method is used.

1. Used pool and garden supplies amount to $8,300.

2. Used office supplies, $1,000.

3. Expired insurance. One year prepaid insurance, $3,600 was paid on May 1, 2005.

4. Expired rent. One year advanced rent, $12,000 was paid on September 1, 2005.

5. Depreciation on the truck. Truck was bought on January 1, 2004 for $25,000. It is estimated that the truck will be in service for five years and salvage value is estimated at $5,000.

6. Depreciation on the computer equipment. The computer cost $5,000 when it was bought on January 1, 2004. It is estimated that it will have no salvage value at the end of its five-year useful life.

7. Depreciation on the pool & yard equipment bought on January 10, 2004 for $22,000. It is estimated that it will be productive for ten years and it will be discarded at the end of its useful life.

8. Unearned service fees amount to $15,850. These were collected in advance but lawn moving services will be done in the summer of 2006. The revenue method was used when the service fees were collected.

9. One employee had been absent for three days and was unable to submit his time sheet for the last payroll. Accrued wages for this employee is $800.

C. GRADE A PLUS TUTORIAL SERVICES

REQUIRED: Prepare the adjusting entries for the month of October 2005. Depreciation is recorded at full month rate if the asset is bought before the 16th of the month and at half month rate if the asset is bought after the 15th of the month. The same half-month convention is used in accounting for prepaid expenses. The asset method of accounting for prepaid expense is used. Straight line depreciation method is used. The allowance method is used in recording bad debts.

1. Bad debts expense, $500. One student gave notice that he lost his job and would not be able to pay tutorial fees billed to him.

2. Expired insurance. Prepaid insurance for one year, $1,800 was paid on October 1.

3. Used office supplies. Office supplies on hand as of October 31 amount to $100. Balance of office supplies on October 1 is $500.

4. Depreciation on the car invested by Mr. Teach on October 1. Car is worth $20,000 with salvage value of $2,000 and useful life of 9 years.

5. Depreciation on the computer equipment bought on October 3 for $12,000. It is estimated that the computer equipment will have no salvage value at the end of its five-year useful life.

6. Depreciation on furniture bought on October 4 for $10,000. Salvage value is $500 and useful life is 10 years.

D. JOLIE KIDS DAY CARE SERVICES

REQUIRED: Prepare the adjusting entries for the month ended September 2005. Depreciation is recorded at full month rate if the asset is bought before the 16th of the month and at half month rate if the asset is bought after the 15th of the month. The same half-month convention is used in accounting for prepaid expenses. The asset method of accounting for prepaid expense is used. Straight line depreciation method is used.

1. Expired rent. Prepaid rent for one year was paid on September 1, $12,000.

2. Used day care supplies, $300.

3. Day care fees for two days already rendered but not yet billed and still uncollected, $2,000.

4. Accrued interest on promissory note issued on September 12. Principal is $3,000; term is 90 days and interest rate is 6%.

5. Depreciation on van bought on September 1. Cost was $10,000. No salvage value is expected at the end of the service life of five years.

6. Depreciation on the computer equipment bought on September 12 for $3,000. No salvage value is expected at the end of five-year useful life.

7. Depreciation on furniture bought on September 1 for $1,500. No salvage value is expected at the end of five-year useful life.

8. Unpaid wages of one assistant, $500.

E. JAMES DEANE TOURS

REQUIRED: Prepare the adjusting entries for the month of June 2005. Depreciation is recorded at full month rate if the asset is bought before the 16th of the month and at half month rate if the asset is bought after the 15th of the month. The same half-month convention is used in accounting for prepaid expenses. The asset method of accounting for prepaid expense is used. James Deane Tours uses the straight line depreciation method. The allowance method is used in accounting for bad debts.

1. Bad debts expense amount to 2% of tour service fees. Tour service fees amount to $36,000.

2. Video and DVD supplies used, $350.

3. Expired Insurance. One year insurance premium, $24,000 was paid on June 3.

4. Expired rent. One year rent, $2,400 was paid on June 8.

5. Depreciation on tour busses bought on June 2 for $100,000. Estimated useful life is ten years and salvage value is $10,000.

6. Depreciation on computer equipment bought on June 4 for $3,000. It is estimated that the computer equipment will have no salvage value at the end of its useful life of five years.

7. Depreciation on video and DVD equipment bought on June 1 for $1,800. Salvage value is zero at the end of its five-year useful life.

8. Accrued interest on notes payable issued on June 2. Principal is $80,000, interest rate is 6% and term is 120 days.

9. Accrued wages, $6,000.

F   HAVE FUN DAY CAMP

REQUIRED: Prepare the adjusting entries for the year ended December 2005. Operations started on October 1, 2005 but the business follows the calendar year as its accounting year. So for 2005, the business operated only for three months. Long-term assets are depreciated using the straight line method. Depreciation is recorded at full month rate if the asset is bought before the 16th of the month and at half month rate if the asset is bought after the 15th of the month. Depreciation is recorded only in December of each year. The same half-month convention is used in accounting for prepaid expenses. The asset method of accounting for prepaid expense is used. Revenue method is used to account for unearned revenues.

1. Depreciate computer equipment. On October 10 $12,000 worth of playground equipment were purchased. Additional computer equipment worth $8,000 were bought on December 2. The computers are expected to be useful for five years and no salvage value estimated.

2. Depreciate furniture bought on October 17 for $2,200. Useful life is five years and salvage value is $200.

3. Depreciate van. The van was purchased on October 10 for $25,000. It is estimated that the van will be in service for seven years with a salvage value of $4,000.

4. Depreciate playground equipment. The playground equipment was installed in service on November 7 at a cost of $1,800. The estimated useful life is ten years with no salvage value.

5. Day camp fees amount to $118,700. It is estimated that 2% of day camp fees is uncollectible.

6. Used school supplies amount to $400.

7. It is determined by an inventory that $700 of toys and crafts supplies are still on hand. Toys and crafts supplies costing $1,000 were bought on October 1

8. Expired insurance for December. One year insurance premium was paid on October 1, $1,200. Insurance expense was already recorded in October and November.

9. Expired rent for December. One year advanced rent was paid on October 5, $24,000. Rent expense was already recorded in October and November.

10. Unearned day camp fees. Day camp fees of $118,700 include $4,500 collected in advance applicable to January 2006 services.

G   BEAUTIFUL HOLLYWOOD

REQUIRED: Prepare the adjusting entries for the month ended March 2006. Long-term assets are depreciated using the straight line method. Depreciation is recorded at full month rate if the asset is bought before the 16th of the month and at half month rate if the asset is bought after the 15th of the month. The same half-month convention is used in accounting for prepaid expenses. The asset method of accounting for prepaid expense is used. Revenue method is used to account for unearned revenues.

1. Office supplies used, $350.

2. An inventory count determined that beauty supplies on hand amount to $1,700. Beauty supplies on March 1 amount to $2,200.

3. Expired insurance. Prepaid one year insurance premium was paid on March 15, $1,800.

4. Depreciation on van. Van was bought on March 15 for $15,000. At the end of its ten-year useful life, it is estimated that the van will have no salvage value.

5. Depreciation on beauty parlor equipment. Beauty parlor equipment was bought on March 5 for $1,800. Useful life is ten years and salvage value is zero.

6. Accrued interest on notes payable. Promissory note was issued on March 5; Principal is $2,500; Interest rate is 6% and term is 90 days.

7. One beautician failed to submit her time sheet on time so she was not paid her weekly wages on March 31. Accrued wages amount to $500.

H   RELIABLE SECURITY MANAGEMENT SERVICES

REQUIRED: Prepare the adjusting entries for the month ended May 2002. Long-term assets are depreciated using the straight line method. Depreciation is recorded at full month rate if the asset is bought before the 16th of the month and at half month rate if the asset is bought after the 15th of the month. The same half-month convention is used in accounting for prepaid expenses. The expense method of accounting for prepaid expense is used. Revenue (income) method is used to account for unearned revenues.

1   Expired insurance. Prepaid insurance premium for twelve months was paid on May 3, $2,400.

2.   Expired rent. Six months advanced rent was paid on May 9, $2,400.

3.   Depreciation on van. Van was bought on May 3 for $22,000. It is estimated that the useful life is ten years and salvage value is $2,000.

4.   Depreciation on computer equipment. Computer was bought on May 4 for $3,000. No salvage value is assigned at the end of the five-year useful life.

5.   Depreciation on security services equipment. Amount paid on May 2 was $20,000. Estimated useful life is eight years and salvage value is $4,000.

6.   Depreciation on surveillance equipment bought on May 5 for $1,800. Useful life is estimated at five years and salvage value is zero.

7.   Accrued interest on notes payable issued on May 2 for principal amount of $15,000. Interest rate is 3% and term is 60 days.

8.   Security services already completed for Downstate Bank but bill was not yet prepared, $ 3,000.

GENERAL JOURNAL

PAGE

DATE	DOC REF	ACCT CODE	DESCRIPTION	POST REF	DEBIT	CREDIT

GENERAL JOURNAL

PAGE

DATE	DOC REF	ACCT CODE	DESCRIPTION	POST REF	DEBIT	CREDIT

GENERAL JOURNAL

PAGE

DATE	DOC REF	ACCT CODE	DESCRIPTION	POST REF	DEBIT	CREDIT

GENERAL JOURNAL

PAGE

DATE	DOC REF	ACCT CODE	DESCRIPTION	POST REF	DEBIT	CREDIT

GENERAL JOURNAL

PAGE

DATE	DOC REF	ACCT CODE	DESCRIPTION	POST REF	DEBIT	CREDIT

GENERAL JOURNAL

PAGE _____

DATE	DOC REF	ACCT CODE	DESCRIPTION	POST REF	DEBIT	CREDIT

GENERAL JOURNAL

PAGE

DATE	DOC REF	ACCT CODE	DESCRIPTION	POST REF	DEBIT	CREDIT

GENERAL JOURNAL

PAGE _____

DATE	DOC REF	ACCT CODE	DESCRIPTION	POST REF	DEBIT	CREDIT

GENERAL JOURNAL

PAGE

DATE	DOC REF	ACCT CODE	DESCRIPTION	POST REF	DEBIT	CREDIT

GENERAL JOURNAL

PAGE _____

DATE	DOC REF	ACCT CODE	DESCRIPTION	POST REF	DEBIT	CREDIT

GENERAL JOURNAL

PAGE

DATE	DOC REF	ACCT CODE	DESCRIPTION	POST REF	DEBIT	CREDIT

CHAPTER 07　　ACCOUNTING PROCESS:　　THE WORKSHEET

LEARNING OBJECTIVES

L01　Discuss how the worksheet facilitates the preparation of the financial statements.

L02　Describe the worksheet and the money columns shown in the worksheet.

L03　Describe the steps in the preparation of the worksheet.

CHAPTER 07 ACCOUNTING PROCESS: THE WORKSHEET

THE WORKSHEET

At the end of the accounting period, the worksheet is prepared to facilitate the preparation of the financial statements. The worksheet is an accounting device or tool, not an accounting report. It contains the account titles and 5 pairs of debit and credit money columns for trial balance, adjustments, adjusted trial balance, income statement and balance sheet. The account titles are shown in the order that they appear in the chart of accounts, i.e. assets, liabilities, owner's equity, revenues, costs and expenses.

The **first pair of money column** shows the trial balance and serves as the beginning balance used in the worksheet. The **second pair of money column** shows the adjustments or adjusting entries that affect accounts that need to be adjusted at the end of the accounting period. Adjustments must be made for some accounts because the balances of these accounts will be overstated or understated if the adjustments are not made. The **third pair of money column** shows the adjusted trial balance, which reflects the accurate balances of the accounts, with the effect of adjustments already effected in the balances. In the adjusted trial balance money columns, the accounts affected by the adjustments will show a different balance from the trial balance amount, whereas accounts not affected by the adjustments will show the same balance as the trial balance amount because the trial balance amounts are simply extended or copied to the appropriate column in the adjusted trial balance. The total debit and total credit must equal for the trial balance, adjustments and the adjusted trial balance, the first three pairs of money columns. The **fourth pair of money column** shows the balance of income statement accounts. The balances of revenues, costs and expenses in the adjusted trial balance are simply extended or copied to the income statement column. The total debit and total credit in the income statement column are not equal. The difference between the debit total and credit total is the result of operations for the period. If the total debit is larger than the total credit, the difference is the net loss of the business and if the total credit is larger than the total debit, the difference is the net income for the period. The **last pair of money column** shows the balance of balance sheet accounts. The balances of assets, liabilities and equity accounts are copied to the balance sheet column. Just like in the income statement column, the total debit and total credit in the balance sheet column are not equal. The difference between the total debit and total credit in the balance sheet column must equal the difference between the total debit and total credit in the income statement column. This difference must be added to the column with the smaller amount for both the income statement and balance sheet columns, and when this difference (net income or net loss) is added to the column with the smaller amount then the debit total and credit total for the income statement and balance sheet columns will equal. It is only after adding the net income or net loss to the money columns with smaller amount that the total debit and total credit of the income statement and balance sheet will equal.

PREPARING THE WORKSHEET

Many students get confused and find it difficult to prepare the worksheet. As a matter of fact, worksheet preparation is mostly a process of transferring or copying information from one column to another. The most common mistake that students commit is to copy an amount to the wrong column; copy from debit column to credit column and vice-versa. For instance if the cash amount in the adjusted trial balance is on the debit side, it should be transferred to the debit side of the balance sheet. A student can not be careless in preparing the worksheet, because he can not balance the columns, if the amounts are extended or copied to the wrong columns. If the amount is on the debit side of the source column, the amount must be copied to the debit side of the destination column. If the amount is on the credit side of the source column, the amount must be copied to the credit side of the destination column.

1. HEADING

Write the heading of the worksheet in three lines with the name of the business as the first line, the word "worksheet" as the second line and the reporting period ended as the third line. The heading of the worksheet for Best Deal Tutorial Services is shown below:

Best Deal Tutorial Services
Worksheet
For the year ended December 31, 2005

2. TRIAL BALANCE COLUMN

Copy the trial balance in the first three columns of the worksheet. The first column contains the account titles and the next two columns are the debit and credit balance of the accounts. Separately add debit and credit balances. The total debit must equal the total credit.

3. ADJUSTMENTS COLUMN

Post the adjusting entries in the appropriate money column in the adjustments. Separately add the debit column amounts and credit column amounts. Again, the total debit must equal the total credit.

4. ADJUSTED TRIAL BALANCE COLUMN

For accounts that are not affected by the adjusting entries, extend (copy or transfer) the trial balance amount to the appropriate column in the adjusted trial balance. If the trial balance amount is a debit balance, copy this amount to the debit column in the adjusted trial balance. If the trial balance amount is a credit balance, copy this amount to the credit column of the adjusted trial balance. **For accounts that are affected by the adjusting entries, compute the new balance of the account and write this new balance in the appropriate column in the adjusted trial balance. To compute the new balance, use the following rule:**

a. If the trial balance amount and the adjustment amount belong to the *same* column (both are debit OR both are credit), *add the trial balance amount and the adjustment amount and put the sum in the same column in the adjusted trial balance column.*

b. If the trial balance amount and the adjustment amount belong to *different* columns (trial balance amount is debit and adjustment is credit OR trial balance amount is credit and adjustment is debit), *subtract the smaller amount from the larger amount and put the difference on the column with the larger amount in the adjusted trial balance column.*

Add the debit column amount and credit column amounts. The total debit must equal the total credit.

5. THE INCOME STATEMENT COLUMN

The income statement column contains the adjusted trial balance of revenues, costs and expenses. Make sure that the amounts are copied to the appropriate debit column or credit column in the income statement. Separately add the debit column amounts and credit column amounts. **This time the total debit will not equal the total credit. The difference is either the net income or net loss for the period.** If the total debit is larger than the total credit, the difference is the net loss for the period. If the total credit is larger than the total debit, the difference is the net income for the period. **Add the difference of the total debit and total credit to the smaller total to make the final debit total equal to the final credit total.**

6. THE BALANCE SHEET COLUMN

The balance sheet column contains the adjusted trial balance of assets, liabilities and equity accounts (capital and drawing/dividends). It is important that the amounts are extended to the appropriate column in the balance sheet, i.e. debit amounts in the adjusted trial balance must be extended to the debit column and credit amounts must be extended to the credit column. Separately add the debit column amounts and the credit column amounts. **Just like the income statement column, the total debit will not equal the total credit. Add the difference of the total debit and total credit to the smaller total to make the final debit total equal to the final credit total.**

ILLUSTRATION PROBLEM

In Chapters 2, 3 and 4 the transactions of Efficient Services for the month of December 2005 were processed. In Chapter 2 the expanded accounting equation chart was prepared. The transactions were processed in the transaction analysis chart and posted to T accounts in Chapter 3. The general journal entries were recorded in the general journal and posted to the general ledger in Chapter 4.

REQUIRED: Prepare the worksheet for Efficient Services for the month ended December 31, 2005. Use the trial balance amounts as the starting balances. Post the adjustments in the adjustments column of the worksheet. The total debit and total credit of the adjustments column must equal. Compute the adjusted trial balance amounts for each account using the amount from the trial balance and adjustments columns. The total debit and total credit of the adjusted trial balance column must equal. Copy the adjusted trial balance amounts of revenues and expenses to the income statement column. The total debit and total credit of the income statement column will not be equal. Find the difference between the total debit and credit columns of the income statement and add this difference to the column with the smaller amount. Total the debit and credit columns of the income statement. This time the debit and credit totals of the income statement columns must equal. Copy the adjusted trial balance amounts of assets, liabilities, capital and drawing to the balance sheet column. The total debit and total credit of the balance sheet column will not be equal. Find the difference between the total debit and credit columns of the balance sheet and add this difference to the column with the smaller amount. Total the debit and credit columns of the balance sheet. This time the debit and credit totals of the balance sheet columns must equal.

The trial balance of Efficient Services as of December 31, 2005 is shown below:

EFFICIENT SERVICES
TRIAL BALANCE
AS OF DECEMBER 31, 2005

ACCOUNT TITLE	DEBIT	CREDIT
Cash	185,300	
Accounts Receivable	14,000	
Office Supplies	3,000	
Prepaid Rent	3,000	
Computer	15,000	
Delivery Van	25,000	
Accounts Payable		24,000
Loans Payable		50,000
Clark Kent, Capital		150,000
Clark Kent, Drawing	4,000	
Revenues		35,000
Van Maintenance Expense	300	
Wages Expense	8,000	
Telephone Expense	400	
Entertainment Expense	400	
Electricity Expense	600	
Van Maintenance Expense	300	
	259,000	259,000

ADJUSTING ENTRIES

Long-term assets are depreciated using the straight line method. Depreciation is recorded at full month rate if the asset is bought before the 16th of the month and at half month rate if the asset is bought after the 15th of the month. The same half-month convention is used in accounting for prepaid expenses. The asset method of accounting for prepaid expense is used.

01. Bad debts expense is 1% of revenues.

02. Expired rent. One year rent was paid on December 7.

03. Depreciate delivery van bought on December 6. Useful life = 7 years; salvage value is $4,000.

04. Depreciate computer bought on December 3. Useful life = 5years; salvage value is zero.

05. Accrued interest on loans payable. Interest rate is 12%; term is ten years. Loan was obtained on December 13.

06. Office supplies used, $500.

ADJUSTING ENTRIES

GENERAL JOURNAL

DATE	DOC REF	DESCRIPTION	POST REF	DEBIT	CREDIT
2005					
12/31	ADJ01	Bad Debts Expense		350	
		Allowance for Bad Debts			350
		bad debts = 1% of revenues (1% x 35,000)			
	ADJ02	Rent Expense		250	
		Prepaid Rent			250
		expired rent = 3,000/12 = 250			
	ADJ03	Depreciation Expense – Delivery Van		250	
		Accumulated Depreciation - Delivery Van			250
		depreciation expense = [(25,000-4,000)/7] / 12			
	ADJ04	Depreciation Expense – Computer Equipment		250	
		Accumulated Depreciation – Computer Equipment			250
		depreciation expense = (15,000/5) / 12			

ADJ05	Interest Expense	300	
	Interest Payable		300
	interest expense = (50,000 x 12%) x 18/360		
ADJ06	Office Supplies Expense	500	
	Office Supplies		500
	used supplies = 3,000 – 2,500		

Efficient Services
Worksheet
For the month ended December 31, 2005

	TRIAL BALANCE DEBIT	TRIAL BALANCE CREDIT	ADJUSTMENTS	ADJUSTMENTS DEBIT	ADJUSTMENTS CREDIT	ADJ TRIAL BALANCE DEBIT	ADJ TRIAL BALANCE CREDIT	INCOME STATEMENT DEBIT	INCOME STATEMENT CREDIT	BALANCE SHEET DEBIT	BALANCE SHEET CREDIT
Cash	185,300					185,300				185,300	
Accounts Receivable	14,000					14,000				14,000	
Allowance for Bad Debts			01)		350		350				350
Office Supplies	3,000		06)		500	2,500				2,500	
Prepaid Rent	3,000		02)		250	2,750				2,750	
Delivery Van	25,000					25,000				25,000	
Accum Depr - Del. Van			03)		250		250				250
Computer Equipment	15,000					15,000				15,000	
Accum Depr - Computer			04)		250		250				250
Accounts Payable		24,000					24,000				24,000
Interest Payable			05)		300		300				300
Loans Payable		50,000					50,000				50,000
Clark Kent Capital		150,000					150,000				150,000
Clark Kent Drawing	4,000					4,000				4,000	
Revenues		35,000					35,000		35,000		
Wages Expense	8,000					8,000		8,000			
Telephone Expense	400					400		400			
Electricity Expense	600					600		600			
Entertainment Expense	400					400		400			
Van Maintenance Expense	300					300		300			
Bad Debts Expense			01)	350		350		350			
Rent Expense			02)	250		250		250			
Depr. Expense - Del. Van			03)	250		250		250			
Depr. Expense - Computer			04)	250		250		250			
Office Supplies Expense			06)	500		500		500			
Interest Expense			05)	300		300		300			
	259,000	259,000		1,900	1,900	260,150	260,150	11,600	35,000	248,550	225,150
NET INCOME								23,400			23,400
								35,000	35,000	248,550	248,550

CHAPTER 07   ACCOUNTING PROCESS: THE WORKSHEET

REVIEW QUESTIONS

1. Whys is the worksheet considered as a tool that facilitates the preparation of the financial statements?

2. What financial report provides the starting input information in the preparation of the worksheet?

3. Describe the five money columns of the worksheet.

4. What accounting elements are extended to the income statement column?

5. What accounting elements are extended to the balance sheet column?

6. Which column totals must have equal amounts for the debit column and the credit column?

7. Which column totals do not have equal amounts for the debit column and the credit column?

8. What does the difference between the debit and credit column totals of the income statement and balance sheet represent?

CHAPTER 07   ACCOUNTING PROCESS: THE WORKSHEET

REVIEW EXAMINATION

TRUE or FALSE: *WRITE TRUE or FALSE IN THE SPACE PROVIDED.*

_____ 1. It is only after adding the net income or net loss to the money columns with smaller amount that the total debit and total credit of the income statement and balance sheet will equal.

_____ 2. The balances of assets, liabilities and equity accounts of the adjusted trial balance are copied to the income statement column.

_____ 3. The difference between the total debit and total credit of both the income statement and balance sheet columns must be added to the column with the larger amount.

_____ 4. The difference between the total debit and total credit in the income statement column represents the net income or net loss for the period.

_____ 5. When the difference between the debit total and credit total in the income statement and balance sheet columns is added to the column with the smaller amount then the debit total and credit total for the income statement and balance sheet columns not be equal.

_____ 6. The last pair of money column shows the balance of income statement accounts.

_____ 7. The difference between the total debit and total credit in the balance sheet column must equal the difference between the total debit and total credit in the income statement column.

_____ 8. The balances of assets, liabilities and equity accounts are copied to the balance sheet column.

_____ 9. The difference between the debit total and credit total in the income statement column is the result of operation for the period.

_____ 10. The total debit and total credit in the balance sheet column are not equal.

_____ 11. In the adjusted trial balance money columns, the accounts affected by the adjustments will show the same amount as the trial balance amount.

_____ 12. The adjusted trial balance will show the same balance as the trial balance for accounts not affected by the adjustments because the trial balance amounts are simply extended or copied to the appropriate column in the adjusted trial balance.

_____ 13. The balances of revenues, costs and expenses in the adjusted trial balance are simply extended or copied to the balance sheet column.

_____ 14. The total debit and total credit must equal for the first three pairs of money column, the trial balance, adjustments and the adjusted trial balance.

_____ 15. Adjustments must be made for some accounts because the balances of these accounts will be overstated or understated if the adjustments are not made.

_____ 16. The fourth pair of money column shows the adjusted trial balance, which reflects the accurate balances of the accounts, with the effect of adjustments already effected in the balances.

_____ 17. The second pair of money column shows the balance of income statement accounts

_____ 18. The first pair of money column shows the adjustments or adjusting entries that affect accounts that need to be adjusted at the end of the accounting period.

_____ 19. The worksheet contains the account titles and 5 pairs of debit and credit money columns for trial balance, adjustments, adjusted trial balance, income statement and balance sheet.

_____ 20. The first pair of money column shows the adjusted trial balance and serves as the beginning balance used in the worksheet.

_____ 21. The worksheet is an accounting device or tool, not an accounting report.

_____ 22. The account titles are shown in the order that they appear in the chart of accounts, i.e. assets, liabilities, owner's equity, revenues, costs and expenses.

_____ 23. At the beginning of the accounting period, the worksheet is prepared to facilitate the preparation of the financial statements.

_____ 24. If the business did not earn any profit and did not suffer any loss, the total debit and credit of the income statement column will be equal.

_____ 25. The adjusted trial balance column is shown before the adjustments column in the worksheet.

COMPLETION: *WRITE THE ANSWER IN THE SPACE PROVIDED.*

1. At the end of the accounting period, the _____ is prepared to facilitate the preparation of the financial statements.

2. The _____ in the worksheet are shown in the order that they appear in the chart of accounts, i.e. assets, liabilities, owner's equity, revenues, costs and expenses.

3. The first pair of money column shows the _____ and serves as the beginning balance used in the worksheet.

4. The worksheet is an accounting _____ or _____, not an accounting report.

5. The worksheet contains the account titles and 5 pairs of debit and credit money columns for _____, _____, _____, _____ and _____.

6. The second pair of money column shows the _____ that affect accounts that need to be adjusted at the end of the accounting period.

7. The fourth pair of money column shows the balance of _____ accounts

8. Adjustments must be made for some accounts because the balances of these accounts will be _____ or _____ if the adjustments are not made.

9. The third pair of money column shows the _____, which reflects the accurate balances of the accounts, with the effect of adjustments already effected in the balances.

10. In the adjusted trial balance money columns, the accounts affected by the adjustments will show a _____ balance from the trial balance amount, whereas accounts not affected by the adjustments will show _____ balance as the trial balance amount because the trial balance amounts are simply extended or copied to the appropriate column in the adjusted trial balance.

11. In the worksheet, the total debit and total credit must equal for the _____, _____ and the _____.

12. The balances of revenues, costs and expenses in the adjusted trial balance are simply extended or copied to the _____ column.

13. The total debit and total credit in the income statement column are _____.

14. The difference between the debit total and credit total in the income statement column is the _____ of operation for the period.

15. In the income statement column, if the total debit is larger than the total credit, the difference is the _____ of the business and if the total credit is larger than the total debit, the difference is the _____ for the period.

16. The last pair of money column shows the balance of _____ accounts.

17. The balances of _____, _____ and _____ accounts are copied to the balance sheet column.

18. The difference between the total debit and total credit in the _____ column must equal the difference between the total debit and total credit in the income statement column.

19. This difference must be added to the column with the _____ amount for both the income statement and balance sheet columns, and when this difference is added to the column with the _____ amount then the debit total and credit total for the income statement and balance sheet columns will equal.

20. It is only after adding the _____ to the money columns with smaller amount that the total debit and total credit of the income statement and balance sheet will equal.

PROBLEMS

01   GLOBAL DELIVERY SERVICES

The trial balance of Global Delivery Services is shown below:

GLOBAL DELIVERY SERVICES
TRIAL BALANCE
June 30, 2005

	DEBIT	CREDIT
Cash	134,815	
Accounts Receivable	5,000	
Office Supplies	1,500	
Prepaid Insurance	2,400	
Prepaid Rent	12,000	
Truck	20,000	
Computer Equipment	5,000	
Furniture	2,400	
Notes Payable		1,000
Juan del Mundo, Capital		170,000
Juan del Mundo, Drawing	1,000	
Delivery Fees		20,000
Wages Expense	6,000	
Telephone Expense	185	
Electricity Expense	200	
Gasoline Expenses	500	
	191,000	191,000

REQUIRED: (1) Prepare the worksheet for Global Delivery Services for one month ended June 30, 2005. Use the adjusting entries in chapter 6 and post these to the adjustments column. Worksheet form is provided at the end of the chapter.
(2) Prepare the adjusted trial balance as of June 30, 2005.

02 GARDEN LANDSCAPING AND POOL SERVICES

The trial balance of Garden Landscaping and Pool Services as of December 31, 2005 is shown below:

GARDEN LANDSCAPING AND POOL SERVICES
TRIAL BALANCE
DECEMBER 31, 2005

	DEBIT	CREDIT
Cash	336,675	
Accounts Receivable	8,200	
Allowance for Bad Debts		2,000
Pool and Garden Supplies	10,300	
Office Supplies	3,000	
Prepaid Insurance	3,600	
Prepaid Rent	12,000	
Truck	25,000	
Accumulated Depreciation – Truck		4,000
Computer Equipment	5,000	
Accumulated Depreciation – Computer Equipment		1,000
Pool & Yard Equipment	22,000	
Accumulated Depreciation – Pool & Yard Equipment		2,000
Accounts Payable		6,800
John Flowers, Capital		136,350
John Flowers, Drawing	17,000	
Service Fees		388,500
Wages Expense	66,000	
Telephone Expense	1,750	
Electricity Expense	2,325	
Gasoline Expense	12,000	
Advertising Expense	300	
Miscellaneous Expenses	15,500	
	540,650	540,650

REQUIRED: (1) Prepare the worksheet for Garden Landscaping & Pool Services for the year ended December 31, 2005. Use the adjusting entries in chapter 6 and post these to the adjustments column. Worksheet form is provided at the end of the chapter.

(2) Prepare the adjusted trial balance as of December 31, 2005.

03 GRADE A PLUS TUTORIAL SERVICES

The trial balance of Grade A Plus Tutorial Services is shown below:

GRADE A PLUS TUTORIAL SERVICES
TRIAL BALANCE
OCTOBER 31, 2005

	DEBIT	CREDIT
Cash	55,990	
Accounts Receivable	7,000	
Office Supplies	500	
Prepaid Insurance	1,800	
Car	20,000	
Computer Equipment	12,000	
Furniture	10,000	
Accounts Payable		10,500
Charles Teach, Capital		80,000
Charles Teach, Drawing	3,000	
Tutorial Fees		33,000
Wages Expense	12,000	
Telephone Expense	180	
Electricity Expense	200	
Gasoline Expense	450	
Advertising Expense	380	
	123,500	123,500

REQUIRED: (1) Prepare the worksheet for Grade A Plus Tutorial Services for the month ended October 31, 2005. Use the adjusting entries in chapter 6 and post these to the adjustments column. Worksheet form is provided at the end of the chapter.
(2) Prepare the adjusted trial balance as of October 31, 2005.

04   JOLIE KIDS DAY CARE SERVICES

The trial balance for Jolie Kids Day Care Services is shown below:

JOLIE KIDS DAY CARE SERVICES
TRIAL BALANCE
SEPTEMBER 30, 2005

	DEBIT	CREDIT
Cash	72,050	
Day Care Supplies	1,000	
Prepaid Rent	12,000	
Van	10,000	
Computer Equipment	3,000	
Furniture	1,500	
Accounts Payable		1,000
Notes Payable		3,000
Carey Jolie, Capital		90,000
Carey Jolie, Drawing	3,000	
Day Care Fees		14,000
Wages Expense	4,600	
Telephone Expense	150	
Electricity Expense	200	
Advertising Expense	500	
	108,000	108,000

REQUIRED: (1)   Prepare the worksheet for Jolie Kids Day Care Services for the month ended September 30, 2005. Use the adjusting entries in chapter 6 and post these to the adjustments column. Worksheet form is provided at the end of the chapter.
(2)   Prepare the adjusted trial balance as of September 30, 2005.

05   JAMES DEANE TOURS

REQUIRED: (1) Prepare the worksheet for James Deane Tours for the month ended June 30, 2005. Use the adjusting entries in chapter 6 and post these to the adjustments column. Worksheet form is provided at the end of the chapter.
(2) Prepare the adjusted trial balance as of June 30, 2005.

The trial balance for James Deane Tours is shown below:

JAMES DEANE TOURS
TRIAL BALANCE
JUNE 30, 2005

	DEBIT	CREDIT
Cash	260,825	
Accounts Receivable	14,000	
Video & DVD Supplies	500	
Prepaid Insurance	24,000	
Prepaid Rent	2,400	
Tour Bus	100,000	
Computer Equipment	3,000	
Video & DVD Equipment	1,800	
Accounts Payable		1,000
Notes Payable		80,000
James Deane, Capital		300,000
James Deane, Drawing	2,000	
Tour Service, Fees		36,000
Wages Expense	6,000	
Telephone Expense	175	
Electricity Expense	250	
Gasoline Expense	1,300	
Bus Maintenance Expense	500	
Taxes and Licenses Expense	250	
	417,000	417,000

06 HAVE FUN DAY CAMP

REQUIRED:
(1) Use the trial balance shown and prepare the worksheet for Have Fun Day Camp for the three months ended December 31, 2005. Use the adjusting entries in chapter 6 and post these to the adjustments column. Worksheet form is provided at the end of the chapter.
(2) Prepare the adjusted trial balance as of December 31, 2005.

HAVE FUN DAY CAMP
TRIAL BALANCE
DECEMBER 31, 2005

	DEBIT	CREDIT
Cash	108,620	
Accounts Receivable	14,000	
School Supplies	1,800	
Toys and Crafts Supplies	1,000	
Prepaid Insurance	1,000	
Prepaid Rent	20,000	
Van	25,000	
Playground Equipment	1,800	
Furniture	2,200	
Computer Equipment	20,000	
Accounts Payable		9,300
Notes Payable		10,000
Wella Care, Capital		100,000
Wella Care, Drawing	3,000	
Day Camp Fees		118,700
Rent Expense	4,000	
Insurance Expense	200	
Wages Expense	32,000	
Telephone Expense	400	
Electricity Expense	680	
Gasoline Expense	1,000	
Advertising Expense	500	
Miscellaneous Expenses	800	
	238,000	238,000

07   BEAUTIFUL HOLLYWOOD

REQUIRED:
(1) Use the trial balance shown and prepare the worksheet for Beautiful Hollywood for the month ended March 31, 2006. Use the adjusting entries in chapter 6 and post these to the adjustments column. Worksheet form is provided at the end of the chapter.
(2) Prepare the adjusted trial balance as of March 31, 2006.
(3) Prepare another worksheet if the Service Fees amount to $7,000 and Cash amount to $89,180 and the balance of all other accounts are the same as shown in the trial balance as of March 31, 2006..

BEAUTIFUL HOLLYWOOD
TRIAL BALANCE
MARCH 31, 2006

	DEBIT	CREDIT
Cash	101,680	
Office Supplies	800	
Beauty Supplies	2,200	
Prepaid Insurance	1,800	
Van	15,000	
Beauty Parlor Equipment	3,000	
Accounts Payable		13,200
Notes Payable		2,500
Daia Narra, Capital		100,000
Daia Narra, Drawing	3,000	
Service Fees		19,500
Wages Expense	6,000	
Telephone Expense	150	
Gasoline Expense	570	
Advertising Expense	500	
Taxes and Licenses Expense	500	
	135,200	135,200

08 RELIABLE SECURITY MANAGEMENT SERVICES

REQUIRED: (1) Use the trial balance shown and prepare the worksheet for Reliable Security Management Services for the month ended May 31, 2002. Use the adjusting entries in chapter 6 and post these to the adjustments colum Worksheet form is provided at the end of the chapter.
(2) Prepare the adjusted trial balance as of December 31, 2005.

RELIABLE SECURITY MANAGEMENT SERVICES
TRIAL BALANCE
MAY 31, 2002

	DEBIT	CREDIT
Cash	216,595	
Accounts Receivable	10,000	
Prepaid Insurance	2,400	
Prepaid Rent	2,400	
Van	22,000	
Computer Equipment	3,000	
Security Services Equipment	20,000	
Surveillance Equipment	1,800	
Accounts Payable		14,000
Notes Payable		15,000
Reli Able, Capital		200,000
Reli Able, Drawing	8,000	
Security Services Fees		99,000
Wages Expense	39,000	
Telephone Expense	255	
Electricity Expense	450	
Gasoline Expense	800	
Van Maintenance Expense	800	
Taxes and Licenses Expense	500	
	328,000	328,000

PROBLEM 01 GLOBAL DELIVERY SERVICES

	TRIAL BALANCE		ADJUSTMENTS		ADJ TRIAL BALANCE		INCOME STATEMENT		BALANCE SHEET	
	DEBIT	CREDIT	DEBIT	CREDIT	DEBIT	CREDIT	DEBIT	CREDIT	DEBIT	CREDIT
Cash										
Accounts Receivable										
Allowance for Bad Debts										
Office Supplies										
Prepaid Insurance										
Prepaid Rent										
Truck										
Accumulated Depr - Truck										
Computer Equipment										
Accum Depr - Computer Equipment										
Furniture										
Accum Depr - Furniture										
Notes Payable										
Wages Payable										
Interest Payable										
Juan del Mundo, Capital										
Juan del Mundo, Drawing										
Delivery Fees										
Bad Debts Expense										
Rent Expense										
Wages Expense										
Telephone Expense										
Electricity Expense										
Gasoline Expense										
Office Supplies Expense										
Depreciation Expense - Truck										
Depreciation Expense - Computer Eqpt										
Depreciation Expense - Furniture										
Insurance Expense										
Interest Expense										

PROBLEM 02 GARDEN LANDSCAPING AND POOL SERVICES

	TRIAL BALANCE		ADJUSTMENTS		ADJ TRIAL BALANCE		INCOME STATEMENT		BALANCE SHEET	
	DEBIT	CREDIT	DEBIT	CREDIT	DEBIT	CREDIT	DEBIT	CREDIT	DEBIT	CREDIT
Cash										
Accounts Receivable										
Allowance for Bad Debts										
Pool & Garden Supplies										
Office Supplies										
Prepaid Insurance										
Prepaid Rent										
Truck										
Accumulated Depr - Truck										
Computer Equipment										
Accum Depr - Computer Equipment										
Pool & Yard Equipment										
Accum Depr - Pool & Yard Eqpt										
Accounts Payable										
Wages Payable										
Unearned Service Fees										
John Flowers, Capital										
John Flowers, Drawing										
Service Fees										
Rent Expense										
Pool & Garden Supplies Expense										
Wages Expense										
Telephone Expense										
Electricity Expense										
Gasoline Expense										
Office Supplies Expense										
Depreciation Expense - Truck										
Depreciation Expense - Computer Eqpt										
Depreciation Expense - Pool & Yard Eqpt										
Advertising Expense										
Insurance Expense										
Miscellaneous Expense										

PROBLEM 03 GRADE A PLUS TUTORIAL SERVICES

	TRIAL BALANCE		ADJUSTMENTS		ADJ TRIAL BALANCE		INCOME STATEMENT		BALANCE SHEET	
	DEBIT	CREDIT	DEBIT	CREDIT	DEBIT	CREDIT	DEBIT	CREDIT	DEBIT	CREDIT
Cash										
Accounts Receivable										
Allowance for Bad Debts										
Office Supplies										
Prepaid Insurance										
Car										
Accumulated Depr - Car										
Computer Equipment										
Accum Depr - Computer Equipment										
Furniture										
Accum Depr - Furniture										
Accounts Payable										
Charles Teach, Capital										
Charles Teach, Drawing										
Tutorial Fees										
Bad Debts Expense										
Wages Expense										
Telephone Expense										
Electricity Expense										
Gasoline Expense										
Office Supplies Expense										
Advertising Expense										
Depreciation Expense - Car										
Depreciation Expense - Computer Eqpt										
Depreciation Expense - Furniture										
Insurance Expense										

PROBLEM 04 JOLIE KIDS DAY CARE SERVICES

	TRIAL BALANCE		ADJUSTMENTS		ADJ TRIAL BALANCE		INCOME STATEMENT		BALANCE SHEET	
	DEBIT	CREDIT	DEBIT	CREDIT	DEBIT	CREDIT	DEBIT	CREDIT	DEBIT	CREDIT
Cash										
Accounts Receivable										
Day Care Supplies										
Prepaid Rent										
Van										
Accumulated Depr - Van										
Computer Equipment										
Accum Depr - Computer Equipment										
Furniture										
Accum Depr - Furniture										
Accounts Payable										
Notes Payable										
Wages Payable										
Interest Payable										
Carey Jolie, Capital										
Carey Jolie, Drawing										
Day Care Fees										
Rent Expense										
Wages Expense										
Telephone Expense										
Electricity Expense										
Day Care Supplies Expense										
Advertising Expense										
Depreciation Expense - Van										
Depreciation Expense - Computer Eqpt										
Depreciation Expense - Furniture										
Interest Expense										

PROBLEM 05 JAMES DEANE TOURS

	TRIAL BALANCE		ADJUSTMENTS		ADJ TRIAL BALANCE		INCOME STATEMENT		BALANCE SHEET	
	DEBIT	CREDIT	DEBIT	CREDIT	DEBIT	CREDIT	DEBIT	CREDIT	DEBIT	CREDIT
Cash										
Accounts Receivable										
Allowance for Bad Debts										
Video & DVD Supplies										
Prepaid Insurance										
Prepaid Rent										
Tour Bus										
Accumulated Depr - Tour Bus										
Computer Equipment										
Accum Depr - Computer Equipment										
Video & DVD Equipment										
Accum Depr - Video & DVD Equipment										
Accounts Payable										
Notes Payable										
Wages Payable										
Interest Payable										
James Deane, Capital										
James Deane, Drawing										
Tour Service Fees										
Bad Debts Expense										
Rent Expense										
Wages Expense										
Telephone Expense										
Electricity Expense										
Gasoline Expense										
Bus Maintenance Expense										
Depreciation Expense - Tour Bus										
Depreciation Expense - Computer Eqpt										
Depreciation Expense - Video & DVD Eqpt										
Video & DVD Supplies Expense										
Insurance Expense										
Taxes and Licenses Expense										
Interest Expense										

PROBLEM 06 HAVE FUN DAY CAMP

	TRIAL BALANCE		ADJUSTMENTS		ADJ TRIAL BALANCE		INCOME STATEMENT		BALANCE SHEET	
	DEBIT	CREDIT	DEBIT	CREDIT	DEBIT	CREDIT	DEBIT	CREDIT	DEBIT	CREDIT
Cash										
Accounts Receivable										
Allowance for Bad Debts										
School Supplies										
Toys and Crafts Supplies										
Prepaid Insurance										
Prepaid Rent										
Van										
Accum Depr - Van										
Playground Equipment										
Accum Depr - Playground Eqpt										
Furniture										
Accum Depr - Furniture										
Computer Equipment										
Accum Depr - Computer Equipment										
Accounts Payable										
Notes Payable										
Unearned Day Camp Fees										
Wella Care, Capital										
Wella Care, Drawing										
Day Camp Fees										
Bad Debts Expense										
Rent Expense										
Wages Expense										
Telephone Expense										
Electricity Expense										
Gasoline Expense										
School Supplies Expense										
Advertising Expense										
Toys and Crafts Supplies Expense										
Depreciation Expense - Van										
Depreciation Expense - Computer Eqpt										
Depreciation Expense - Furniture										
Depreciation Expense - Playground Eqpt										
Insurance Expense										
Miscellaneous Expense										

PROBLEM 07 BEAUTIFUL HOLLYWOOD

	TRIAL BALANCE		ADJUSTMENTS		ADJ TRIAL BALANCE		INCOME STATEMENT		BALANCE SHEET	
	DEBIT	CREDIT	DEBIT	CREDIT	DEBIT	CREDIT	DEBIT	CREDIT	DEBIT	CREDIT
Cash										
Office Supplies										
Beauty Supplies										
Prepaid Insurance										
Van										
Accum Depr - Van										
Beauty Parlor Equipment										
Accum Depr - Beauty Parlor Eqpt										
Accounts Payable										
Notes Payable										
Interest Payable										
Wages Payable										
Daia Narra, Capital										
Daia Narra, Drawing										
Service Fees										
Wages Expense										
Telephone Expense										
Gasoline Expense										
Office Supplies Expense										
Beauty Supplies Expense										
Advertising Expense										
Depreciation Expense - Van										
Depreciation Expense - Beauty Parlor Eqpt										
Insurance Expense										
Taxes and Licenses Expense										
Interest Expense										

PROBLEM 08 RELIABLE SECURITY MANAGEMENT SERVICES

	TRIAL BALANCE		ADJUSTMENTS		ADJ TRIAL BALANCE		INCOME STATEMENT		BALANCE SHEET	
	DEBIT	CREDIT	DEBIT	CREDIT	DEBIT	CREDIT	DEBIT	CREDIT	DEBIT	CREDIT
Cash										
Accounts Receivable										
Prepaid Insurance										
Prepaid Rent										
Van										
Accum Depr - Van										
Computer Equipment										
Accum Depr - Computer Eqpt										
Security Services Equipment										
Accum Depr - Security Services Eqpt										
Surveillance Equipment										
Accum Depr - Surveillance Eqpt										
Accounts Payable										
Notes Payable										
Interest Payable										
Reli Able, Capital										
Reli Able, Drawing										
Security Services Fees										
Rent Expense										
Wages Expense										
Telephone Expense										
Electricity Expense										
Gasoline Expense										
Depreciation Expense - Van										
Depreciation Expense - Security Serv Eqpt										
Depreciation Expense - Computer Eqpt										
Depreciation Expense - Surveillance Eqpt										
Van Maintenance Expense										
Insurance Expense										
Taxes and Licenses Expense										
Interest Expense										

CHAPTER 08 ACCOUNTING PROCESS: THE FINANCIAL STATEMENTS

LEARNING OBJECTIVES

L01 Define accounting reports.

L02 Differentiate informal accounting reports from financial statements.

L03 Describe the four financial statements.

L04 Discuss the types of income statement.

L05 Name the equity statements based on the type of business ownership.

L06 Discuss the types of balance sheet.

L07 Discuss the importance of the statement of cash flows.

L08 Describe the operating, investing and financing activities shown in the statement of cash flows.

CHAPTER 08   ACCOUNTING PROCESS: THE FINANCIAL STATEMENTS

ACCOUNTING REPORTS

Accounting reports are used by a business entity to communicate the state of its financial health and the results of its operations to the various users of financial information. They are also used to back-up or provide more detailed information about a particular account being analyzed. Sometimes, management and key officers of businesses require special reports to provide information needed in addressing and resolving operational and financial issues that require decision making actions. Accounting reports are also used to monitor operational and financial performance by comparing actual results with pre-determined budgeted amounts, planned targets and standard rates. Any deviation of the actual results against the predetermined amounts is analyzed and the cause for the deviation is scrutinized. Accounting reports are also used to provide inputs in making financial forecasts and budgets. Standard rates for specific costs, for instance direct labor standard rate in a manufacturing business are also established using actual costs provided in accounting reports.

THE FINANCIAL STATEMENTS

Formal accounting reports are the **financial statements** which consist of the (1) income statement, (2) equity statement and (3) balance sheet. Some businesses include the **statement of cash flows** among its financial statements. These four formal accounting reports are generally used by the external and internal users of financial information, such as the investors, creditors, government, management, etc. in evaluating the financial situation of the business. These parties use the financial reports in making financial decisions related to the business or to their stake in the business. **Informal accounting reports** include all accounting reports other than the financial statements that assist the users of financial information in making decisions.

The financial statements are prepared at the end of the accounting period after the completion of the adjusted trial balance. Usually, the worksheet is prepared in order to facilitate the preparation of the financial statements. The first three financial statements **must be prepared in the proper sequence**. Income statements must be prepared first because the results of operations (net income or net loss) are used as input to the equity statement. The second report, the equity statement is prepared after the income statement and before the balance sheet because the ending capital in the equity statement is used as the ending capital in the balance sheet. To summarize, the income statement provides the net income or net loss that is used in the equity statement, and the equity statement provides the ending capital needed in the balance sheet. The statement of cash flows is prepared as needed.

THE INCOME STATEMENT

The **income statement** identifies the accounting period being covered in the reporting process, therefore, an accounting period can be one month, one quarter, one semester, one year, etc. based on the period reported in the income statement. The **income statement shows the revenues, costs, expenses and the net income or net loss for a given period of time.**

The two types of income statement are the **single-step income statement** and the **multi-step (or multiple-step) income statement.** Generally, the **type of business operation** (service, merchandising and manufacturing) dictates the type of income statement prepared by the business. A **service business** provides service, instead of selling products to its customers. Examples of service businesses are medical office, lawyer's office, dental clinic, janitorial service companies, delivery service companies, etc. The **single-step income statement** is used usually by **service business**; total costs and expenses are deducted from revenues to arrive at the net income or net loss for the period. The **multi-step income statement** is used mostly by **merchandising** and **manufacturing businesses. Merchandising** business buys ready-made products wholesale and sells them to customers. They are not involved in any production or manufacturing activities. **Manufacturing** business converts raw materials into finished products and sells these products to merchandisers. In a multi-step income statement, major elements of revenues, costs and expenses are classified and several steps of computations are done to arrive at the net income or net loss for the period.

SINGLE-STEP INCOME STATEMENT

Prepare the single-step income statement ABC Janitorial Services using the trial balance below.

ABC Janitorial Services
Trial Balance
December 31, 2005

	DEBIT	CREDIT
Cash	25,000	
Accounts Receivable	12,000	
Supplies	2,000	
Prepaid Insurance	2,400	
Computer	12,000	
Accumulated Depreciation – Computer		2,000
Van	25,000	
Accumulated Depreciation – Van		2,500
Accounts Payable		9,000
Wages Payable		1,000
John Smith, Capital		41,600
John Smith, Drawing	5,000	
Revenues		100,000
Supplies Expense	9,000	
Rent Expense	24,000	
Wages Expense	36,000	
Telephone Expense	1,000	
Gasoline Expense	1,500	
Taxes and Licenses Expense	1,200	
	156,100	156,100

ABC Janitorial Services
Income Statement
For one-year ended December 31, 2005

Revenues			$	100,000
Less: Expenses				
Supplies Expense	$	9,000		
Rent Expense		24,000		
Wages Expense		36,000		
Telephone Expense		1,000		
Gasoline Expense		1,500		
Taxes and Licenses Expense		1,200		
Total Expenses				-72,700
Net Income			$	27,300

Note that in the above single-step income statement, all the expenses are itemized and the total expenses amount is simply subtracted from revenues to arrive at net income.

In the single-step and multiple step income statement illustrations, + and - (plus sign and minus sign) are shown to guide the accounting student what mathematical operation to use, but in actual financial statements these mathematical signs are not shown.

MULTIPLE-STEP INCOME STATEMENT

As mentioned earlier, in the multiple-step income statement, several computation steps are performed in order to arrive at net income. Because merchandising and manufacturing business have merchandise inventory both at the beginning and at the end of the accounting period, the cost of goods sold must be computed first and it is subtracted from revenues to arrive at the gross profit. Accounting for merchandising business and the related financial statements of merchandising business are discussed in the chapter on merchandise inventory and merchandising business. The illustration of the multiple-step income statement is shown in this chapter simply to demonstrate the distinction between a single-step income statement and multiple-step income statement.

XYZ Department Stores
Trial Balance
December 31, 2005

	DEBIT	CREDIT
Cash	150,000	
Accounts Receivable	100,000	
Notes Receivable	10,000	
Merchandise Inventory	80,000	
Supplies	5,000	
Prepaid Insurance	3,600	
Store Equipment	70,000	
Accumulated Depreciation – Store Equipment		7,000
Delivery Truck	25,000	
Accumulated Depreciation – Delivery Truck		2,500
Accounts Payable		40,000
Loans Payable		50,000
Richard John, Capital		253,900
Richard John, Drawing	5,000	
Sales		250,000
Sales Returns and Allowances	2,000	
Purchases	50,000	
Purchase Returns and Allowances		5,000
Freight In	3,000	
Gasoline Expense	1,000	
Wages Expense	36,000	
Rent Expense	48,000	
Electricity Expense	3,600	
Telephone Expense	1,200	
Depreciation Expense - Store Equipment	7,000	
Depreciation Expense – Delivery Truck	2,500	
Supplies Expense	3,000	
Interest Revenue		500
Interest Expense	3,000	
	608,900	608,900

The physical inventory count conducted showed that the ending merchandise inventory as of December 31, 2005 is $ 68,000.

XYZ Department Stores
Income Statement
For one year ended December 31, 2005

Sales			$	250,000
Less: Sales Returns and Allowances				-2,000
Net Sales			$	248,000
Less: Cost of Goods Sold				
Merchandise Inventory, beginning		$ 80,000		
Add: Net Purchases				
Purchases	$ 50,000			
Add: Freight In	+3,000			
Total Purchases	$ 53,000			
Less: Purchase Returns & Allowances	-5,000	+48,000		
Cost of Goods Available for Sale		$ 128,000		
Less: Merchandise Inventory, end		-68,000		-60,000
Gross Profit			$	188,000
Less: Operating Expenses				
Gasoline Expense		$ 1,000		
Wages Expense		36,000		
Rent Expense		48,000		
Electricity Expense		3,600		
Telephone Expense		1,200		
Depreciation Expense – Delivery Truck		2,500		
Depreciation Expense – Store Equipment		7,000		
Supplies Expense		3,000		-102,300
Net Income from Operation			$	85,700
Add: Other Revenues				
Interest Revenues				500
Total Income			$	86,200
Less: Other Expenses				
Interest Expense				-3,000
Net Income			$	83,200

Note that in the cost of goods sold section, the beginning merchandise inventory is taken from the trial balance and the ending merchandise inventory is taken from the physical inventory count.

THE EQUITY STATEMENT

The type of **equity statement** prepared for a particular business entity depends on the ownership structure of the business as identified below:

OWNERSHIP STRUCTURE	EQUITY STATEMENT
Sole Proprietorship	Statement of Owner's Equity
Partnership	Statement of Partners Equity
Corporation	Statement of Stockholders Equity

The equity statement shows the changes in the owner's/s' equity (sole proprietor, partners or stockholders as the case maybe), by showing the capital at the beginning of the period, increased by additional investments and net income for the period and decreased by net loss, drawings of owner or partners for a sole proprietorship or partnership respectively, or dividends to stockholders in the case of corporation. The final amount in the equity statement is the capital at the end of the accounting period being reported. For purposes of this chapter, only the statement of owner's equity is discussed. The Statement of Partner's Equity is covered in accounting for partnerships. The Statement of Stockholders' Equity is discussed in accounting for corporations.

The equity statement is prepared **after the income statement and before the balance sheet.** The final amount in the income statement (net income or net loss, as the case maybe) is used in the equity statement while the amount of ending capital computed in the equity statement is used in the balance sheet. The equity statements for ABC Janitorial Services and XYZ Department Stores are shown in the following illustrations.

ABC Janitorial Services
Statement of Owner's Equity
For one year ended December 31, 2005

John Smith, Capital, beginning			$ 41,600
Add: Increase in Capital			
Net Income	$	27,300	
Less: John Smith, Drawing		-5,000	
Increase in Capital			+22,300
John Smith, Capital, end			$ 63,900

XYZ Department Stores
Statement of Owner's Equity
For one year ended December 31, 2005

Richard John, Capital, beginning			$	253,900
Add: Increase in Capital				
Net Income	$	83,200		
Less: Richard John, Drawing		-5,000		
Increase in Capital				+78,200
Richard John, Capital, end			$	332,100

Note that the information and format are basically the same for the above statements of owner's equity for ABC Janitorial Services and XYZ Department Stores. There is no difference between them, even though the income statements for these two businesses look entirely very different from each other.

THE BALANCE SHEET

The **balance sheet shows the assets, liabilities and ending capital and reports on the financial position or financial condition of the business as of a given date.** The balance sheet is a formal presentation of the basic accounting equation, **A = L + OE (Assets = Liabilities plus Owner's Equity).** The two forms of balance sheet are the **report form** and the **account form.** The distinction between the balance sheet forms depends on the presentation of assets, liabilities and owner's ending capital and there is no other difference between them. In the **report form** balance sheet, assets are presented on top of the report and the liabilities and owner's ending capital are shown below the assets. In the **account form** balance sheet, assets are presented on the left side of the report while liabilities and owner's ending capital are presented on the right side of the report.

The **classified balance sheet** classifies or groups together similar accounts based on liquidity or proximity or nearness to cash for assets and based on maturity dates for liabilities. Assets are classified into current assets, temporary investments, long-term investments and long-term assets. Temporary and long-term investments will not be covered in this book as they are appropriately discussed in advanced accounting courses. Liabilities are classified into current liabilities and long-term liabilities.

Operating cycle is the length of time it takes to convert cash back to cash. For a merchandising business, it is the time it takes to purchase merchandise, pay suppliers accounts, sell merchandise and collect customers' accounts. For a service business, one operating cycle is how long it takes to collect accounts receivables from the time the service is rendered. For a manufacturing business, operating cycle is the amount of time required to purchase raw materials, pay suppliers, produce the goods using raw materials, labor and overhead, sell the finished products and collect accounts receivables. The normal operating cycle depends on the type of business operation. Generally, it is shorter than one year for service and merchandising businesses. For manufacturing business, it is generally shorter than one year; however, there are some businesses whose operating cycle is longer than one year, for instance if the product requires more than one year to complete, then the operating cycle for that business is longer than one year. Unless otherwise specified in the problem, assume that the operating cycle, is not longer than one year.

Current assets are cash and non-cash assets that will be converted into cash within one year or one operating cycle whichever is longer. Prepaid expenses that will be consumed within one year or one operating cycle, whichever is longer, are also classified as current assets. Cash, accounts receivable, merchandise inventory, supplies, prepaid expenses such as prepaid insurance, office supplies, notes receivable collectible in one year are examples of current assets.

Long-term assets are assets that are useful to the business for more than one year or one operating cycle, whichever is longer. Long-term assets are also known as (1) plant assets; (2) fixed assets; (3) property, plant and equipment and (4) long-lived assets. Long-term assets are classified into tangible assets, intangible assets and natural resources or wasting assets. **Tangible assets** are long-term assets with physical substance, such as land, building, car, computer, office furniture and fixtures, etc. **Intangible assets** are long-term assets that have no physical substance. These are basically rights that have monetary values such as copyrights, patents, goodwill and trademarks. **Natural resources or wasting assets** are long-term assets that are exhaustible, such as mineral deposits, marble deposits, oil deposits, coal deposits, etc.

Current liabilities are indebtedness or loans due within one year or one operating cycle, whichever is longer from balance sheet date. Accounts payable, notes payable due in one year, unpaid expenses such as unpaid wages, unearned revenues, dividends payable, interest payable are examples of current liabilities. **Long-term liabilities** are indebtedness or loans due after one year or after one operating cycle, whichever is longer, from balance sheet date. Mortgage payable, notes payable due after one year and bonds payable are examples of long-term liabilities. The **current portion** of mortgage payable, notes payable and bonds payable (due within one year or one operating cycle from balance sheet date) is shown in the **current liabilities** section of the balance sheet.

The account form balance sheet is illustrated for ABC Janitorial Services while the report form balance sheet is illustrated for XYZ Department Stores. **Aside from the arrangement of assets, liabilities and ending capital, there is no other difference between these two forms of balance sheet.**

ABC Janitorial Services
Balance Sheet
December 31, 2005

ASSETS			LIABILITIES and CAPITAL		
Current Assets			Current Liabilities		
Cash		$ 25,000	Accounts Payable		$ 9,000
Accounts Receivable		12,000	Wages Payable		1,000
Supplies		2,000			
Prepaid Insurance		2,400	Total Liabilities		$ 10,000
Total Current Assets		$ 41,400			
Long-term Assets			John Smith, Capital		63,900
Computer	$ 12,000				
Less: Accum Depr	2,000	$ 10,000			
Van	$ 25,000				
Less: Accum Depr	2,500	22,500			
Total Long-term Assets		$ 32,500			
Total Assets		$ 73,900	Total Liabilities and Capital		$ 73,900

XYZ Department Stores
Balance Sheet
December 31, 2005

ASSETS

Current Assets				
Cash		$	150,000	
Accounts Receivable			100,000	
Notes Receivable			10,000	
Merchandise Inventory			68,000	
Supplies			5,000	
Prepaid Insurance			3,600	
Total Current Assets				$ 336,600
Long-term Assets				
Store Equipment	$	70,000		
Less: Accumulated Depreciation		7,000	63,000	
Delivery Truck	$	25,000		
Less: Accumulated Depreciation		2,500	22,500	
Total Long-term Assets				85,500
Total Assets				$ 422,100

LIABILITIES & CAPITAL

Current Liabilities		
Accounts Payable		$ 40,000
Long-term Liabilities		
Loans Payable		50,000
Total Liabilities		$ 90,000
Richard John, Capital		332,100
Total Liabilities and Capital		$ 422,100

In the two balance sheets above, total assets equal total liabilities and capital. The total assets of ABC Janitorial Services amount to $73,900, equal to the sum of current assets of $41,400 and long-term assets of $32,500. The total liabilities of $10,000 and ending capital of $63,900 amount to $73,900. The basic accounting equation A = L + OE is reflected in the balance sheet. The same situation is true with XYZ Department Stores. As can be seen from the balance sheet total assets equal the sum of liabilities and capital.

THE STATEMENT OF CASH FLOWS

Cash is a very important and key asset of any business. Since majority of business transactions involve the receipt and payment of cash, a fourth financial statement, the **statement of cash flows** is often added to the three basic financial statements of income statement, equity statement and the balance sheet. FASB (Financial Accounting Standards Board) requires the statement of cash flows as a basic financial statement for corporations. By simply knowing the balance of cash in the balance sheet, a thorough analysis of the cash account can not be made. In evaluating the paying capacity of a business, it is necessary to analyze in detail the cash transactions during the accounting period. Can a profitable business become bankrupt? Many people can not imagine that a profitable business can become bankrupt, but it is possible to happen, if the financial managers of the business do not exercise prudent cash management. The statement of cash flows is useful in providing information if a business can generate enough cash to sustain its operations. It also shows the ability of the business to pay debts and interests to its creditors as they become due. For potential investors, it shows the business' ability to pay cash dividends to stockholders. The effectiveness and efficiency of cash management exercised by the business is reflected in an analysis of the statement of cash flows.

The **statement of cash flows** shows the **inflows and outflows of cash** during the **accounting period. Only cash transactions** are shown in the statement of cash flows. Non-cash transactions are excluded from the statement of cash flows. **Cash inflows** are transactions that generate or increase cash while **cash outflows** are transactions that disburse or decrease cash. In other words, only cash receipts and cash payments are included in the statement of cash flows. In the statement of cash flows, cash transactions are classified into **operating, financing and investing activities.**

Operating activities are transactions that affect the income statement that are necessary to generate income for the business**. Operating activities include transactions that affect revenues, costs and expenses**. Operating activities include the payment of expenses, payment to suppliers for purchase of stock-in-trade and receipt from customers for cash sales and collection of accounts receivable. **Pre-payment of expenses** that will be expensed within one year or the purchase of current assets, such as office supplies that will be used in one year is also classified as operating activities The **payment of interest** expense is classified as operating activity because interest expense is shown in the income statement, even though the receipt of loan proceeds and the payment of the loan are classified as financing activities. Likewise, **interest revenues/income and dividend revenues/income** are considered cash inflows from operating activities even though the investments in stocks and other marketable securities are classified as investing activities.

Financing activities are transactions that involve increasing cash through borrowings (obtaining loan from creditors or issuing certificates of indebtedness such as bonds) or obtaining investments from the owners or stockholders. Cash outflows in financing activities include payment of loans to creditors, redemption of bonds issued, re-purchase of company stocks (called treasury stocks), and payment of owner's cash withdrawal or cash dividends to stockholders. Note that the receipt of dividend income is an inflow from operating activities but the payment of dividends to stockholders is an outflow from financing activities. **Financing**

activities include cash transactions with the creditors or stockholders or the owner/s of the business.

Investing activities are transactions that involve the purchase and sale of long-term assets, extending long-term non-trade loans to debtors and collecting the same, and purchase and sale of other companies' stocks and bonds intended as long-term investments, which are not marketable securities or cash equivalents (very liquid, readily convertible to cash).

There are two methods of computing cash flows from operating activities. Under the **direct method**, operating disbursements are simply deducted from operating receipts or collections to arrive at the net cash flow from operating activities. Under the **indirect method**, net income computed under the accrual accounting is adjusted to reflect only cash receipts and disbursements. For purposes of this book, only the direct method will be covered. The indirect method is a topic appropriately covered in advanced accounting courses.

ILLUSTRATION PROBLEM

Consider the following transactions of Efficient Services and prepare the statement of cash flows for the month of December, 2005.

Dec	01 2005	Received $150,000 investment from Clark Kent to start Efficient Services. Issued official receipt (OR) 001.
	02	Issued check (CK) 001 for office supplies, $3000.
	03	Bought computer equipment from Best Buy, $15,000. Issued CK 002 for $3,000 down payment. Balance is on account.
	06	Bought delivery van from A-J Car Dealership, $25,000. Issued CK 003 for $2,000 down payment. Balance is on account.
	07	Paid one year rent, $3,000. Issued CK 004.
	08	Performed services for cash, $5,000. Issued OR 002 and sales invoice (SI) 001.
	09	Performed services, $10,000. Issued OR 003 for the $4,000 down payment and SI 002 for the full amount. Balance is on account.
	13	Obtained bank loan, $50,000. Issued promissory note (PN) 001.
	14	Paid $300 for van maintenance. Issued CK 005.
	15	Paid wages, $3,000. Issued CK 006.

16	Performed services, $20,000. Issued OR 004 for the $4,000 down payment and SI 003 for the full amount. Balance is on account.
17	Issued OR 005 for $6,000 collected from customers for previous services.
17	Bought $10,000 IBM stocks as long-term investments. Issued CK 007.
18	Issued CK 008 as payment for telephone expense, $400.
19	Issued CK 009 as payment for electricity expense, $600.
20	Received cash dividends from IBM, $1,000. Prepared OR 006.
20	Issued CK 010 partial payment to Best Buy, $6,000 (see Dec 03).
21	Issued CK 011 payment to A-J Dealership, $5,000 (see Dec 06).
22	Issued CK 012 to Clark Kent for cash withdrawal, $4,000.
23	Collected $2,000 from customers on account. Issued OR 007.
28	Paid entertainment expense, $400. Issued CK 013.
30	Paid wages, $5,000. Issued CK 014.

The T account for the cash account for the above transactions is shown below.

CASH

Date	Debit	Date	Credit
12/01	150,000	12/02	3,000
12/08	5,000	12/03	3,000
12/09	4,000	12/06	2,000
12/13	50,000	12/07	3,000
12/16	4,000	12/14	300
12/17	6,000	12/15	3,000
12/21	1,000	12/18	10,000
12/25	2,000	12/19	400
		12/20	600
		12/22	6,000
		12/23	5,000
		12/24	4,000
		12/28	400
		12/30	5,000

Debit Footing 222,000
Less: Credit Footing -45,700
Balance 176,300

Credit Footing 45,700

Fundamentals of Accounting

Efficient Services
Statement of Cash Flows
For one month ended December 31, 2005

Cash Flows from Operating Activities			
Collections from customers	$ 21,000		
Receipt of dividends from IBM	1,000		
Total Cash Inflow from Operating Activities	$ 22,000		
Purchase of supplies	$ (3,000)		
Payment of rent	(3,000)		
Payment for van maintenance	(300)		
Payment of wages	(8,000)		
Payment of telephone expense	(400)		
Payment of electricity	(600)		
Total Cash Outflow from Operating Activities		(15,700)	
Net Cash Provided by Operating Activities		$ 6,300	
Cash Flows from Investing Activities			
Purchase of computer	$ (9,000)		
Purchase of delivery van	(7,000)		
Purchase of IBM stocks	(10,000)		
Net Cash Used for Investing Activities		(26,000)	
Cash Flows from Financing Activities			
Investment from owner	$ 150,000		
Proceeds of bank loan	50,000		
Total Cash Inflow from Financing Activities	$ 200,000		
Owner withdrawal	(4,000)		
Net Cash Provided by Financing Activities		196,000	
Net Increase in Cash		$ 176,300	
Cash Balance, Nov. 30, 2005		0	
Cash Balance, December 31, 2005		$ 176,300	

NOTE: Collections from customers (12/8 $5,000; 12/9 $4,000; 12/16 $4,000; 12/17 $6,000; 12/25 $2,000 total $21,000)

Payment of wages (12/15 $3,000; 12/30 $5,000 total $8,000)

Transactions that reduce cash are shown in parenthesis.

ACCOUNTING REPORTS IN ADDITION TO FINANCIAL STATEMENTS

Aside from the financial statements, there are numerous accounting reports, mostly used by internal users of financial information, namely the company officers, employees such as the accountants, budget analysts, financial analyst, cost analysts, tax analysts, etc. in order to make in-depth analyses of various items or accounts reported in the financial statements. Some of these reports can be classified as (1) accounting process reports such as the worksheet, trial balance, adjusted trial balance, post closing trial balance which are prepared as an integral part of the accounting process, (2) account analysis reports such as bank reconciliation statement for cash in bank; aging analysis and collection reports for accounts receivables; schedule of accounts payable; etc., (3) reports to provide information to improve the efficiency of business operations such as cost comparisons between standard costs, budgeted costs and actual costs and (4) special purpose reports which are prepared as needed to provide answers to specific situations such as salaries and wages and benefits costs analyses during collective bargaining contract negotiations. Some of these reports, such as the accounting process reports identified will be covered in later chapters in this book, but others are appropriately covered in higher accounting courses.

ILLUSTRATION PROBLEM: THE INCOME STATEMENT, STATEMENT OF OWNER'S EQUITY AND THE BALANCE SHEET

Let us use the worksheet of Efficient Services prepared in Chapter 7 to illustrate the preparation of the income statement, statement of owner's equity and balance sheet.

The income statement column of the worksheet provides the information used in the preparation of the income statement. Revenues, expenses and net income are shown in the income statement. In a single-step income statement, total expenses are subtracted from revenues to arrive at net income. In a multi-step income statement, total operating expenses are subtracted from revenues to arrive at net operating income (or net income from operations) and other expenses, such as interest expense are subtracted from net operating income to arrive at net income. Regardless of the type of income statement prepared the final net income is the same for both types of income statement.

The statement of owner's equity is prepared after the income statement. Remember that the three financial statements must be prepared in the correct sequence (1) income statement, (2) statement of owner's equity and (3) balance sheet. The beginning capital is the balance of the capital account in the balance sheet column. Compute the increase in capital by subtracting drawing from net income (from the income statement). The difference between the net income and the drawing is the increase or decrease in capital. If net income is greater than drawing there is an increase in capital; if net income is smaller than drawing, there is a decrease in capital. In the case of Efficient Services, net income is $23,400 and drawing is $4,000, so there is an increase of capital amounting to $19,400 ($23,400-4,000). The increase in capital is then added to the beginning capital to arrive at the ending capital. The ending capital is then carried over to the balance sheet. If the owner made additional investment during the period, the additional investment is added to net income before deducting the drawing account to arrive at the increase in capital.

The last financial statement prepared is the balance sheet. As discussed earlier there are two ways of preparing a balance sheet, namely (1) the account form and the (2) report form. The only difference between these two types of balance sheet is in the presentation of the assets, liabilities and owner's equity. In the account form balance sheet, assets are shown on the left side and the liabilities and owner's equity are shown on the right side of the report. In the report form balance sheet, assets are shown on top of the report while liabilities and owners equity are presented below the assets.

The multi-step income statement for Efficient Services is shown below:

EFFICIENT SERVICES
INCOME STATEMENT
FOR ONE MONTH ENDED DECEMBER 31, 2005

Revenues		35,000
Less: Operating Expenses		
Wages Expense	8,000	
Telephone Expense	400	
Electricity Expense	600	
Entertainment Expense	400	
Van Maintenance Expense	300	
Bad Debts Expense	350	
Rent Expense	250	
Depreciation Expense - Delivery Van	250	
Depreciation Expense - Computer Equipment	250	
Office Supplies Expense	500	
Total Operating Expenses		11,300
Net Operating Income		23,700
Less: Other Expenses		
Interest Expense		300
Net Income		23,400

The single-step income statement for Efficient Services is shown below:

EFFICIENT SERVICES
INCOME STATEMENT
FOR ONE MONTH ENDED DECEMBER 31, 2005

Revenues		35,000
Less: Expenses		
Wages Expense	8,000	
Telephone Expense	400	
Electricity Expense	600	
Entertainment Expense	400	
Van Maintenance Expense	300	
Bad Debts Expense	350	
Rent Expense	250	
Depreciation Expense - Delivery Van	250	
Depreciation Expense - Computer Equipment	250	
Office Supplies Expense	500	
Interest Expense	300	
Total Expense		11,600
Net Income		23,400

Take note that the net income is carried over in the statement of owner's equity; that is why, the income statement must be prepared before the statement of owner's equity.

The statement of owner's equity for Efficient Services is shown below:

EFFICIENT SERVICES
STATEMENT OF OWNER'S EQUITY
FOR ONE MONTH ENDED DECEMEBER 31, 2005

Clark Kent, Capital, beginning			$ 150,000
Add: Increase in Capital			
Net Income	$	23,400	
Less: Clark Kent, Drawing		4,000	
Increase in Capital			19,400
Clark Kent, Capital, end			$ 169,400

Note that the capital at the end, the final amount in the statement of owner's equity is carried over to the balance sheet; that is why, the statement of owner's equity is prepared ahead of the balance sheet.

The report form balance for Efficient Services is shown below:

EFFICIENT SERVICES
BALANCE SHEET
DECEMBER 31, 2005

ASSETS

CURRENT ASSETS
Cash		185,300	
Accounts Receivable	14,000		
Less: Allowance for Bad Debts	350	13,650	
Office Supplies		2,500	
Prepaid Rent		2,750	
TOTAL CURRENT ASSETS			204,200

LONG TERM ASSETS
Delivery Van	25,000		
Less: Accumulated Depreciation	250	24,750	
Computer Equipment	15,000		
Less: Accumulated Depreciation	250	14,750	
TOTAL LONG TERM ASSETS			39,500

TOTAL ASSETS   243,700

LIABILITIES AND OWNER'S EQUITY

CURRENT LIABILITIES
Accounts Payable	24,000	
Interest Payable	300	
TOTAL CURRENT LIABILITIES		24,300

LONG TERM LIABILITIES
Loans Payable	50,000

TOTAL LIABILITIES   74,300

OWNER'S EQUITY
Clark Kent Capital	169,400

TOTAL LIABILITIES AND OWNER'S EQUITY   243,700

The account form balance sheet for Efficient Services is shown below:

EFFICIENT SERVICES
BALANCE SHEET
DECEMBER 31, 2005

ASSETS				LIABILITIES AND OWNER'S EQUITY			
CURRENT ASSETS				CURRENT LIABILITIES			
Cash		185,300		Accounts Payable		24,000	
Accounts Receivable	14,000			Interest Payable		300	
Less: Allowance for Bad Debts	350	13,650		TOTAL CURRENT LIABILITIES			24,300
Office Supplies		2,500					
Prepaid Rent		2,750		LONG TERM LIABILITIES			
TOTAL CURRENT ASSETS			204,200	Loans Payable			50,000
LONG TERM ASSETS							
Delivery Van	25,000			TOTAL LIABILITIES			74,300
Less: Accumulated Depreciation	250	24,750					
Computer Equipment	15,000			OWNER'S EQUITY			
Less: Accumulated Depreciation	250	14,750		Clark Kent Capital			169,400
TOTAL LONG TERM ASSETS			39,500				
TOTAL ASSETS			243,700	TOTAL LIABILITIES AND OWNER'S EQUITY			243,700

CHAPTER 08   ACCOUNTING PROCESS: THE FINANCIAL STATEMENTS

REVIEW QUESTIONS

1. What are accounting reports?

2. Differentiate formal accounting reports from informal accounting reports.

3. What are financial statements?

4. Describe the income statement and discuss its importance.

5. Describe the equity statement and discuss its importance.

6. Describe the balance sheet and discuss its importance.

7. Describe the statement of cash flows and discuss its importance.

8. Can a profitable company become bankrupt?

9. Discuss the two types of income statement.

10. Discuss the two types of balance sheet.

11. Discuss the three types of equity statement.

12. Why is it important that the income statement, equity statement and balance sheet be prepared in the correct sequence?

CHAPTER 08 ACCOUNTING PROCESS: THE FINANCIAL STATEMENTS

REVIEW EXAMINATION

TRUE or FALSE: *WRITE TRUE or FALSE IN THE SPACE PROVIDED.*

_____ 1. Financing activities in the statement of cash flows are transactions that involve increasing cash through borrowings (obtaining loan from creditors or issuing certificates of indebtedness such as bonds) or obtaining investments from the owners or stockholders.

_____ 2. Cash inflows in financing activities include payment of loans to creditors, redemption of bonds issued, re-purchase of company stocks (called treasury stocks), and payment of owner's cash withdrawal or cash dividends to stockholders.

_____ 3. Operating activities include cash transactions with the creditors or stockholders or the owner/s of the business.

_____ 4. Informal accounting reports are the financial statements which consist of the (1) income statement, (2) equity statement and (3) balance sheet.

_____ 5. Some businesses include the statement of cash flows among its financial statements.

_____ 6. Formal accounting reports include all accounting reports other than the financial statements that assist the users of financial information in making decisions.

_____ 7. The financial statements are prepared at the end of the accounting period after the completion of the adjusted trial balance.

_____ 8. Usually, the worksheet is prepared in order to facilitate the preparation of the financial statements.

_____ 9. The first three financial statements must be prepared in the proper sequence.

_____ 10. The balance sheet provides the net income or net loss that is used in the equity statement.

_____ 11. The equity statement provides the ending capital needed in the balance sheet.

_____ 12. The balance sheet identifies the accounting period being covered in the reporting process.

Fundamentals of Accounting

_____ 13. The statement of owner's equity shows the revenues, costs, expenses and the results of operations which may either be a net income or net loss for a given period of time.

_____ 14. In the account form balance sheet, assets are presented on the left side of the report while liabilities and owner's ending capital are presented on the right side of the report.

_____ 15. The classified balance sheet classifies or groups together similar accounts based on liquidity or proximity or nearness to cash for assets and based on maturity dates for liabilities.

_____ 16. Accounting period is the length of time it takes to convert cash back to cash.

_____ 17. Current assets are cash and non-cash assets that will be converted into cash within one year or one operating cycle whichever is longer.

_____ 18. Prepaid expenses that will be consumed within one year or one operating cycle, whichever is longer, are also classified as long-term assets.

_____ 19. Cash, accounts receivable, merchandise inventory, supplies, prepaid expenses such as prepaid insurance, office supplies, notes receivable collectible in one year are examples of long term investments.

_____ 20. Current liabilities are indebtedness or loans due within one year or one operating cycle, whichever is longer from balance sheet date.

_____ 21. Accounts payable, notes payable due in one year, unpaid expenses such as unpaid wages, unearned revenues, dividends payable, interest payable are examples of current liabilities.

_____ 22. Long-term liabilities are indebtedness or loans due after one year or after one operating cycle, whichever is longer, from balance sheet date.

_____ 23. The current portion of mortgage payable, notes payable and bonds payable (due within one year or one operating cycle from balance sheet date) is shown in the long-term liabilities section of the balance sheet.

_____ 24. Aside from the arrangement of assets, liabilities and ending capital, there is no other difference between these two forms of balance sheets.

_____ 25. The statement of cash flows is often added to the three basic financial statements.

273

_____ 26. Long-term assets are assets that are useful to the business for more than one year or one operating cycle, whichever is longer.

_____ 27. The statement of cash flows shows the inflows and outflows of cash for the accounting period.

_____ 28. Only non-cash transactions are shown in the statement of cash flows.

_____ 29. Cash outflows are transactions that generate or increase cash.

_____ 30. Cash receipts and cash payments are included in the statement of cash flows.

COMPLETION: *WRITE THE ANSWER IN THE SPACE PROVIDED.*

1. Formal accounting reports are the _____ which consist of the (1) income statement, (2) equity statement and (3) balance sheet.

2. Some businesses include the _____ among its financial statements.

3. Informal accounting reports include all accounting reports other than the _____ that assist the users of financial information in making decisions.

4. The financial statements are prepared at the end of the accounting period after the completion of the _____ trial balance.

5. Usually, the _____ is prepared in order to facilitate the preparation of the financial statements.

6. The first three financial statements must be prepared in the _____ sequence.

7. The income statement provides the _____ or _____ that is used in the equity statement.

8. The equity statement provides the ending capital needed in the _____.

9. The two types of income statement are the _____ and the _____.

10. A service business sells _____ instead of tangible products to its customers.

11. The single-step income statement is used usually by _____ business.

12. The multi-step income statement is used mostly by _____ and _____ businesses.

13. _____ business converts raw materials into finished products and sells these products to merchandisers.

14. In the _____ income statement, several computation steps are performed in order to arrive at net income.

15. The type of equity statement prepared for a particular business entity depends on the _____ structure of the business.

16. _____ activities are transactions that involve the purchase and sale of long-term assets, extending long-term non-trade loans to debtors and collecting the same, and purchase and sale of other companies' stocks and bonds intended as long-term investments, which are not marketable securities or cash equivalents.

17. _____ business buys ready-made products wholesale and sells them to customers.

18. The_____ identifies the accounting period being covered in the reporting process.

19. The _____ shows the revenues, costs, expenses and the results of operations which may either be a net income or net loss for a given period of time.

20. Under the _____ method of reporting cash flows from operating activities, operating disbursements are simply deducted from operating receipts or collections to arrive at the net cash flow from operating activities.

21. Under the _____ method of reporting cash flows from operating activities, net income computed under the accrual accounting is adjusted to reflect only cash receipts and disbursements.

22. In the _____ balance sheet, assets are presented on the left side of the report while liabilities and owner's ending capital are presented on the right side of the report.

23. The _____ classifies or groups together similar accounts based on liquidity or proximity or nearness to cash for assets and based on maturity dates for liabilities.

24. _____ cycle is the length of time it takes to convert cash back to cash.

25. _____ assets are cash and non-cash assets that will be converted into cash within one year or one operating cycle whichever is longer.

26. _____ assets are assets that are useful to the business for more than one year or one operating cycle, whichever is longer.

27. _____ assets are long-term assets with physical substance such as land, building, car, computer, office furniture and fixtures, etc.

28. _____ assets are long-term assets that are basically rights that have monetary values such as copyrights, patents, goodwill and trademarks.

29. The _____ shows the inflows and outflows of cash for the accounting period.

30. Only _____ transactions are shown in the statement of cash flows.

31. Cash _____ are transactions that generate or increase cash.

32. Cash _____ are transactions that disburse or decrease cash.

32. _____ activities are transactions that affect the income statement that are necessary to generate income for the business.

33. _____ expenses that will be consumed within one year or one operating cycle, whichever is longer are also classified as current assets.

34. Cash, accounts receivable, merchandise inventory, supplies, prepaid expenses such as prepaid insurance, office supplies, notes receivable collectible in one year are examples of _____ assets.

35. Natural resources or wasting assets are long-term assets that are _____, such as mineral deposits, marble deposits, oil deposits, coal deposits, etc.

36. Pre-payment of expenses that will be expensed within one year or the purchase of current assets, such as office supplies that will be used in one year is also classified as _____ activities.

37. The payment of _____ expense is classified as operating activity because it is shown in the income statement, even though the receipt of loan proceeds and the payment of the loan are classified as financing activities.

38. The receipt of interest income and dividend income are considered cash inflows from _____ activities even though the investments in stocks and other marketable securities are classified as _____ activities.

40. The _____ statement shows the changes in the owner's/s' equity.

41. The equity statement is prepared after the _____ and before the _____.

42. The _____ is useful in providing information if a business can generate enough cash to sustain its operations.

43. The balance sheet shows the _____, _____ and _____ and reports on the _____ of the business as of a given date.

44. The balance sheet is a formal presentation of the _____.

45. The two forms of balance sheet are the _____ form and the _____ form.

46. _____ activities are transactions that involve increasing cash through borrowings or obtaining investments from the owners or stockholders.

47. Cash outflows in _____ activities include payment of loans to creditors, redemption of bonds issued, re-purchase of company stocks and payment of owner's cash withdrawal or cash dividends to stockholders.

48. Financing activities include cash transactions with the _____ or _____.

49. In the _____ form balance sheet, assets are presented on top of the report and the liabilities and owner's ending capital are shown below the assets.

50. If net income is greater than drawing there is _____ in capital; if net income is smaller than drawing, there is _____ in capital.

EXERCISES

1. Use the trial balance below, to compute the following:

   a. total expenses
   b. net income
   c. total current assets
   d. total assets
   e. total liabilities
   f. owner's capital, beginning
   g. owner's capital, end
   h. increase in capital
   i. total long-term assets
   j. total liabilities and owner's equity

MOIRA ANNE DANCING SCHOOL
TRIAL BALANCE
DECEMBER 31, 2005

	DEBIT	CREDIT
Cash	149,500	
Accounts Receivable	15,000	
Office Supplies	1,000	
Land	150,000	
Building	200,000	
Accumulated Depreciation – Building		20,000
Dance Equipment	100,000	
Accumulated Depreciation – Dance Equipment		10,000
Accounts Payable		35,000
Notes Payable		15,000
Interest Payable		1,000
Mortgage Payable		200,000
Moira Anne, Capital		243,500
Moira Anne Drawing	5,000	
Revenues		195,000
Office Supplies Expense	2,000	
Wages Expense	60,000	
Depreciation Expense – Building	10,000	
Depreciation Expense – Dance Equipment	5,000	
Electricity Expense	3,600	
Telephone Expense	2,400	
Heating Expense	7,500	
Miscellaneous Expenses	1,500	
Interest Expense	7,000	
	719,500	719,500

Fundamentals of Accounting

2. Classify the following cash activities into operating activities, investing activities or financing activities. Identify the transaction as cash inflow or cash outflow

    a. Owner invested $200,000 into the business.

    b. Obtained bank loan, $50,000.

    c. Owner withdrew cash for personal use, $10,000.

    d. Paid rent, $2,000.

    e. Bought car, $20,000.

    f. Collected customer accounts, $20,000.

    g. Paid accounts payable to suppliers, $12,000.

    h. Received cash dividends from investments in stocks, $7,000.

    i. Paid bank loan, $30,000.

    j. Paid interest on bank loan, $3,000.

3. Fill in the blanks the required information.

    a. If total expenses = $188,000 and net income is $48,000, then revenues = _____.

    b. If total expenses = $188,000 and net loss = $48,000, then revenues = _____.

    c. If beginning capital = $45,000; ending capital = $78,000 and drawing = $3,000 then net income = _____.

    d. If ending capital is $45,000; beginning capital = $78,000, there is a _____ in capital of _____.

    e. If increase in capital = $67,000 and net income is $75,000, then drawing = _____.

    f. If decrease in capital is $5,000 and drawing = $2,000, then net loss = _____.

g. If total assets = $100,000; total liabilities = $30,000, then owner's equity = _____.

h. If total liabilities = $50,000; owner's equity = $45,000, then total assets = _____.

i. If total expenses = $37,000; net loss = $9,000, then revenues = _____.

j. If total assets = $199,000; long-term assets = $89,000, then current assets = _____.

PROBLEMS

1. Statement of Cash Flows

Prepare the Statement of Cash Flows for the following businesses using the transactions in Chapter 2.

01	Global Delivery Services
02	Garden Landscaping & Pool Services
03	Grade A Plus Tutorial Services
04	Jolie Kids Day Care Services
05	James Deane Tours
06	Have Fun Day Camp
07	Beautiful Hollywood
08	Reliable Security Management Services

2. Income Statement, Statement of Owner's Equity and Balance Sheet

Prepare the income statement, statement of owner's equity and balance sheet for the above businesses using the income statement and balance sheet columns of the worksheet prepared in Chapter 7.

CHAPTER 09 ACCOUNTING PROCESS: THE CLOSING ENTRIES AND THE POST CLOSING TRIAL BALANCE

LEARNING OBJECTIVES

L01   Define closing entries.

L02   Discuss the purpose of recording closing entries.

L03   Identify the two types of accounts.

L04   Describe and give examples of nominal accounts.

L05   Describe and give examples of permanent accounts.

L06   Discuss the role of the Income and Expense Summary account.

L07   Identify and describe the four closing entries.

L08   Describe the post closing trial balance.

CHAPTER 09 ACCOUNTING PROCESS: THE CLOSING ENTRIES AND THE POST CLOSING TRIAL BALANCE

THE CLOSING ENTRIES

Closing entries are accounting entries prepared at the end of the accounting period, after the preparation of the financial statements in order to zero out the balance of nominal or temporary accounts, namely, revenues, costs, expenses (income statement accounts) and drawing. Closing entries are recorded in the general journal and posted to the general ledger to prepare the accounts for the next accounting period. **Note that not all accounts are closed. Real accounts**, also known as **permanent or balance sheet accounts** such as assets, liabilities and capital accounts are not closed. The **balance of nominal accounts are not carried over to the next accounting period, that is why these accounts are closed at the end of the accounting period.** The balance of permanent accounts is carried over to the next accounting period. Nominal accounts with debit balance are closed by crediting each account for the balance amount and debiting Income and Expense Summary for the total of the credited amounts. Nominal accounts with credit balance are closed by debiting each account for the balance amount and crediting Income and Expense Summary for the total of the debited amounts. After the nominal accounts are closed, the remaining balance of Income and Expense Summary is closed to Capital. Finally, the balance of drawing account is closed to Capital.

During the closing process, Income and Expense Summary, a new temporary account is introduced. The four types of closing entries are:

1. Close credit balance accounts to Income and Expense Summary
2. Close debit balance accounts to Income and Expense Summary
3. Close Income and Expense Summary to Capital
4. Close Drawing to Capital

Take note that the Income and Expense Summary is also closed during the closing process.

Under the periodic system of accounting for merchandise inventory, the beginning merchandise inventory account, although an asset is also closed. The beginning merchandise inventory is closed by debiting Income and Expense Summary and crediting the beginning balance of merchandise inventory. The ending merchandise inventory is established by debiting the ending balance of merchandise inventory and crediting Income and Expense Summary. The closing process for merchandising business is covered in accounting for merchandise inventory and merchandising business.

The four closing entries are shown below:

PURPOSE	CLOSING ENTRY
1. Close credit balance accounts to Income and Expense Summary	Debit *each* credit balance account Credit the sum of all credit balance accounts to Income and Expense Summary
2. Close debit balance accounts to Income and Expense Summary	Debit the sum of all debit balance accounts to Income and Expense Summary Credit *each* debit balance account
3. Close Income and Expense Summary to Capital	If the resulting balance of Income and Expense Summary from 1 and 2 above is *debit* *(total debit per item 2 is greater than total credit per item 1), the business operation resulted in net loss* Debit Capital Credit Income and Expense Summary If the resulting balance of Income and Expense Summary from 1 and 2 above is *credit* *(total credit per item 1 is greater than total debit per item 2), the business operation resulted in net income* Debit Income and Expense Summary Credit Capital
4. Close Drawing to Capital	Debit Capital Credit Drawing

THE POST CLOSING TRIAL BALANCE

The last step in the accounting process done for the current accounting period is the preparation of the post closing trial balance, also called the after closing trial balance. As the name suggests, it is prepared after the recording of the closing entries in the general journal and posting them in the general ledger. Since the balances of temporary or nominal accounts are zeroed out during the closing process, only the real or permanent accounts are shown in the post closing trial balance. Therefore, only the balance sheet accounts, namely, assets, liabilities and capital are carried over to the next accounting period. The post closing trial balance shows the account titles for asset, liability and capital with their corresponding balances. The amounts in the post closing trial balance will serve as the beginning balance for assets, liabilities and capital for the next accounting period. Just like the ordinary trial balance, the total debit must equal the total credit.

ILLUSTRATION PROBLEM

REQUIRED: (1) Prepare the closing entries for Best Deal Tutorial using the completed worksheet for one year ended December 31, 2005.

(2) Prepare the post closing trial balance as of December 31, 2005.

BEST DEAL TUTORIAL
Worksheet
For the year ended December 31, 2005

ACCOUNT TITLE	TRIAL BALANCE DEBIT	TRIAL BALANCE CREDIT	ADJUSTMENTS DEBIT	ADJUSTMENTS CREDIT	ADJUSTED TRIAL BALANCE DEBIT	ADJUSTED TRIAL BALANCE CREDIT	INCOME STATEMENT DEBIT	INCOME STATEMENT CREDIT	BALANCE SHEET DEBIT	BALANCE SHEET CREDIT
Cash	155,900				155,900				155,900	
Accounts Receivable	14,000				14,000				14,000	
Allowance for Bad Debts				02) 1,400		1,400				1,400
Office Supplies	3,000			01) 2,500	500				500	
Prepaid Insurance	2,400			03) 1,200	1,200				1,200	
Notes Receivable	5,000				5,000				5,000	
Interest Receivable			04) 27		27				27	
Land	50,000				50,000				50,000	
Building	150,000				150,000				150,000	
Accum. Depreciation – Building				05) 7,000		7,000				7,000
Computer	15,000				15,000				15,000	
Accum. Depreciation – Computer				06) 3,000		3,000				3,000
Delivery Van	25,000				25,000				25,000	
Accum. Depreciation - Delivery Van				07) 200		200				200
Accounts Payable		24,000				24,000				24,000
Wages Payable				08) 1,600		1,600				1,600
Unearned Rental Revenues		12,000	10) 3,000			9,000				9,000
Interest Payable				09) 6,000		6,000				6,000
Loans Payable		50,000				50,000				50,000
Clark Kent, Capital		250,000				250,000				250,000
Clark Kent, Drawing	4,000				4,000				4,000	
Revenues		140,000				140,000		140,000		
Bad Debts Expense			02) 1,400		1,400		1,400			
Gasoline Expense	300				300		300			
Wages Expense	48,000		08) 1,600		49,600		49,600			
Telephone Expense	1,400				1,400		1,400			
Taxes and Licenses Expense	400				400		400			
Electricity Expense	1,600				1,600		1,600			
Office Supplies Expense			01) 2,500		2,500		2,500			
Insurance Expense			03) 1,200		1,200		1,200			
Depreciation Expense – Building			05) 7,000		7,000		7,000			
Depreciation Expense – Computer			06) 3,000		3,000		3,000			
Depreciation Expense - Delivery Van			07) 200		200		200			
Interest Revenues				04) 27		27		27		
Earned Rental Revenues				10) 3,000		3,000		3,000		
Interest Expense			09) 6,000		6,000		6,000			
	476,000	476,000	25,927	25,927	495,227	495,227	74,600	143,027	420,627	352,200
NET INCOME							68,427			68,427
							143,027	143,027	420,627	420,627

285

BEST DEAL TUTORIAL SERVICES CLOSING ENTRIES

Date	Description	Debit	Credit
2005			
Dec 31	Revenues	140,000	
	Interest Revenues	27	
	Earned Rental Revenues	3,000	
	Income and Expense Summary		143,027
	close credit balance accounts		
	Income and Expense Summary	74,600	
	Bad Debts Expense		1,400
	Gasoline Expense		300
	Wages Expense		49,600
	Telephone Expense		1,400
	Taxes and Licenses Expense		400
	Electricity Expense		1,600
	Office Supplies Expense		2,500
	Insurance Expense		1,200
	Depreciation Expense – Building		7,000
	Depreciation Expense – Computer		3,000
	Depreciation Expense – Delivery Van		200
	Interest Expense		6,000
	close debit balance accounts		
	Income and Expense Summary	68,427	
	Clark Kent, Capital		68,427
	close income and expense summary		
	Cark Kent, Capital	4,000	
	Cark Kent, Drawing		4,000
	close drawing		

Best Deal Tutorial Services
Post Closing Trial Balance
December 31, 2005

	DEBIT	CREDIT
Cash	155,900	
Accounts Receivable	14,000	
Allowance for Bad Debts		1,400
Office Supplies	500	
Prepaid Insurance	1,200	
Notes Receivable	5,000	
Interest Receivable	27	
Land	50,000	
Building	150,000	
Accumulated Depreciation – Building		7,000
Computer	15,000	
Accumulated Depreciation – Computer		3,000
Delivery Van	25,000	
Accumulated Depreciation – Delivery Van		200
Accounts Payable		24,000
Wages Payable		1,600
Unearned Rental Revenues		9,000
Loans Payable		50,000
Clark Kent, Capital		314,427
	416,627	416,627

CHAPTER 09   ACCOUNTING PROCESS: THE CLOSING ENTRIES AND THE POST CLOSING TRIAL BALANCE

REVIEW QUESTIONS

1. What are closing entries? Why are they prepared?

2. What are nominal accounts? What are the other names of nominal accounts?

3. What are permanent accounts? What are the other names of permanent accounts?

4. Explain the purpose of the Income and Expense Summary account.

5. What are the four types of closing entries? Give the closing entry for each type.

6. Describe the post closing trial balance.

7. What accounts are shown in the post closing trial balance?

CHAPTER 09 ACCOUNTING PROCESS: THE CLOSING ENTRIES AND THE POST CLOSING TRIAL BALANCE

REVIEW EXAMINATION

TRUE or FALSE: *WRITE TRUE or FALSE IN THE SPACE PROVIDED.*

_____ 1. Closing entries are journal entries prepared at the beginning of the accounting period, after the preparation of the financial statements in order to zero out the balance of nominal or temporary accounts.

_____ 2. Revenues, costs, expenses and drawing are examples of permanent accounts.

_____ 3. Closing entries are recorded in the general journal and posted to the general ledger to prepare the accounts for the next accounting period.

_____ 4. All accounts are closed.

_____ 5. The balance of nominal accounts are not carried over to the next accounting period, that is why these accounts are closed at the end of the accounting period.

_____ 6. Nominal accounts with debit balance are closed by crediting the account for the balance amount and debiting Income and Expense Summary.

_____ 7. Closing entries are recorded in the general journal and posted to the general ledger to prepare the accounts for the next accounting period.

_____ 8. Nominal accounts with credit balance are closed by crediting the account for the balance amount and debiting Income and Expense Summary.

_____ 9. Real accounts, also known as permanent or balance sheet accounts such as assets, liabilities and capital accounts are not closed.

_____ 10. The balance of Income and Expense Summary is closed to drawing.

_____ 11. The balance of drawing account is closed to capital.

_____ 12. The balance of permanent accounts is carried over to the next accounting period.

_____ 13. During the closing process, Income and Expense Summary, a new temporary account is introduced.

_____ 14. Income and Expense Summary is also closed during the closing process.

_____ 15. If after closing the debit and credit balances of nominal accounts, the resulting balance of Income and Expense Summary is a debit balance, the business operation resulted in net loss.

_____ 16. The business operation resulted in net income if the Income and Expense Summary showed a credit balance after closing the nominal accounts with debit and credit balances.

_____ 17. To close drawing account, debit drawing and credit capital.

_____ 18. To close the Income and Expense Summary when the business incurred a net loss, debit Income and Expense Summary and credit capital.

_____ 19. To close the resulting credit balance of Income and Expense Summary, debit Income and Expense Summary and credit capital.

_____ 20. The balance of Income and expense Summary is carried over to the next accounting period.

COMPLETION: *WRITE THE ANSWER IN THE SPACE PROVIDED.*

1. Closing entries are recorded in the _____ and posted to the _____ .

2. Closing entries are recorded to _____ the accounts for the next accounting period.

3. Only _____ accounts are closed.

4. Real accounts, also known as permanent or balance sheet accounts such as _____, _____ and _____ not closed.

5. The balance of permanent accounts is _____ to the next accounting period.

6. Income statement accounts with _____ balance are closed by crediting the account for the balance amount and debiting Income and Expense Summary.

7. Income statement accounts with credit balance are closed by _____ the account for the balance amount and _____ Income and Expense Summary.

8. The balance of Income and Expense Summary is closed to _____ .

9. The balance of drawing account is closed to _____ .

10. Closing entries are journal entries prepared at the end of the accounting period, after the preparation of the financial statements in order to _____ the balance of nominal or temporary accounts.

11. Revenues, costs, expenses drawing accounts are examples of _____ accounts.

12. The balance of _____ accounts are not carried over to the next accounting period.

13. _____ accounts are closed at the end of the accounting period.

14. During the closing process, _____, a new temporary account is introduced.

15. Income and Expense Summary is _____ during the closing process.

16. If the resulting balance of Income and Expense is debit, the business operation resulted in _____.

17. If the resulting balance of Income and Expense is credit, the business operation resulted in _____.

19. To close drawing account, _____ capital and _____ drawing.

20. To close the debit balance of Income and Expense Summary debit _____ credit _____.

PROBLEMS

I. Use the income statements and statements of owner's equity prepared in Chapter 08 to prepare the closing entries for the following businesses:

	BUSINESSES	ACCOUNTING PERIOD ENDED
1.	Global Delivery Services	June 30, 2006
2.	Garden Landscaping & Pool Services	December 31, 2005
3.	Grade A Plus Tutorial Services	October 31, 2005
4.	Jolie Kids Day Care Services	September 30, 2005
5.	James Deane Tours	June 30, 2005
6.	Have Fun Day Camp	December 31, 2005
7.	Beautiful Hollywood	March 31, 2006
8.	Reliable Security Management Services	May 31, 2002

Use the general journal form provided.

II. Use the balance sheet prepared in Chapter 8 to prepare the post closing trial balance for the above businesses.

GENERAL JOURNAL

PAGE _____

DATE	DOC REF	ACCT CODE	DESCRIPTION	POST REF	DEBIT	CREDIT

GENERAL JOURNAL

PAGE

DATE	DOC REF	ACCT CODE	DESCRIPTION	POST REF	DEBIT	CREDIT

Fundamentals of Accounting

GENERAL JOURNAL

PAGE _____

DATE	DOC REF	ACCT CODE	DESCRIPTION	POST REF	DEBIT	CREDIT

GENERAL JOURNAL

PAGE

DATE	DOC REF	ACCT CODE	DESCRIPTION	POST REF	DEBIT	CREDIT

Fundamentals of Accounting

GENERAL JOURNAL

PAGE

DATE	DOC REF	ACCT CODE	DESCRIPTION	POST REF	DEBIT	CREDIT

GENERAL JOURNAL

PAGE

DATE	DOC REF	ACCT CODE	DESCRIPTION	POST REF	DEBIT	CREDIT

POST CLOSING TRIAL BALANCE
AS OF _____

ACCOUNT TITLE	DEBIT	CREDIT

POST CLOSING TRIAL BALANCE
AS OF _____

ACCOUNT TITLE	DEBIT	CREDIT

POST CLOSING TRIAL BALANCE
AS OF _____

ACCOUNT TITLE	DEBIT	CREDIT

POST CLOSING TRIAL BALANCE
AS OF _____

ACCOUNT TITLE	DEBIT	CREDIT

POST CLOSING TRIAL BALANCE
AS OF _____

ACCOUNT TITLE	DEBIT	CREDIT

POST CLOSING TRIAL BALANCE
AS OF _____

ACCOUNT TITLE	DEBIT	CREDIT

POST CLOSING TRIAL BALANCE
AS OF _____

ACCOUNT TITLE	DEBIT	CREDIT

POST CLOSING TRIAL BALANCE
AS OF _____

ACCOUNT TITLE	DEBIT	CREDIT

CHAPTER 10 ACCOUNTING PROCESS: THE REVERSING ENTRIES

LEARNING OBJECTIVES

L01 Define reversing entries.

L02 Explain the purpose of reversing entries.

L03 Identify the adjusting entries that must be reversed.

CHAPTER 10   ACCOUNTING PROCESS: THE REVERSING ENTRIES

REVERSING ENTRIES

Reversing entries are accounting entries recorded in the general journal on the **first day of the next accounting period before any transactions for the next accounting period are recorded** in order to **reverse adjustments or adjusting entries** that increase assets or liabilities. Note that not all adjusting entries are reversed. To reverse an entry simply means to debit the account credited and credit the account debited in the original adjusting entry. In other words, do the opposite of what was done in the original adjusting entry. Reversing entries are prepared to simplify the recording of transactions and to adhere to the accounting principle of consistency.

The following adjusting entries are reversed:

1. prepaid expenses using the expense method

2. unearned revenues using the revenue method

3. accrual of revenues and receivables

4. accrual of expenses and payables

Accounting for Prepaid Expense Using the Expense Method

Upon pre-payment of the expense, a journal entry is prepared to debit the expense account and credit cash. At the end of the accounting period, an adjusting entry is prepared debiting an asset for the unexpired or unused portion of the expense and crediting the expense account, to recognize the asset for the unused or unexpired portion. After posting the adjusting entry to the expense account, the balance of the expense account is the used or expired portion. At the beginning of the next accounting period, the adjusting entry is reversed, by simply debiting the expense account and crediting the asset account in the adjusting entry. The reversing entry makes the balance of the prepaid expense equal to zero and establishes the balance of the expense account equal to the unused or unexpired portion. Remember that after the adjusting entries are prepared the expense account is closed to Income and Expense Summary to complete the accounting process.

ILLUSTRATION:

On October 1, 2005, ABC Janitorial Services issued check 9327 to pay for one year advanced rent amounting to $24,000. ABC uses the calendar year as its accounting year and the expense method in accounting for prepaid expenses.

Required: Prepare   (1)   general journal entry on October 1, 2005.
(2)   adjusting entry (ADJ001) on December 31, 2005.
(3)   closing entry (CLS001) on December 31, 2005.
(4)   reversing entry (REV001) on January 1, 2006.

ANALYSIS:

Monthly rent is $2,000 ($24,000/12). Expired rent for three months (Oct-Dec) amounts to $6,000 (3 x $2,000). Unexpired rent for nine months (Jan to Sept 2006) is $18,000 (9 x $2,000).

GENERAL JOURNAL

DATE	DOC REF	DESCRIPTION	DEBIT	CREDIT
Oct 01 05	CK9327	Rent Expense Cash one year advanced rent	24,000	24,000
Dec 31 05	ADJ001	Prepaid Rent Rent Expense unexpired rent (Jan to Sept 2006)	18,000	18,000
	CLS001	Income and Expense Summary Rent Expense close rent expense	6,000	6,000
Jan 01 06	REV001	Rent Expense Prepaid Rent reverse ADJ001	18,000	18,000

The T accounts for Rent Expense and Prepaid Rent are shown below:

```
           RENT EXPENSE                        PREPAID RENT
  10/01 GJ   24,000 | 12/31 ADJ  18,000   12/31 ADJ  18,000 |
  12/31 BAL   6,000 |                     12/31 BAL  18,000 |
                    | 12/31 CLS   6,000                     | 01/01 REV  18,000
  12/31 BAL   ZERO
  01/01 REV  18,000

  01/01 BAL  18,000                        01/01 BAL  ZERO
```

To understand the entries, the T accounts demonstrate in detail the postings made to Prepaid Rent and Rent Expense. The T accounts show that the accounting principle of consistency is satisfied by the preparation of the reversing entry. If the reversing entry is not recorded, prepaid rent will have a balance and rent expense will have a zero balance and this violates the accounting principle of consistency because ABC will be shifting from expense method to asset method of recording prepaid expenses for no apparent reason.

Note that in the closing entry CLS001, Rent Expense is credited by $6,000 (debited on Oct 01 for $24,000 and credited on Dec 31 for $18,000), the actual amount of expired rent for three months in 2005 (Oct to Dec 2005).

Accounting for Unearned Revenues Using the Revenue Method

Upon the advanced collection of the revenues, a general journal entry is made to debit cash and credit the revenues account (for example subscriptions revenues, ticket sales revenues, rent revenues, etc.). At the end of the accounting period, the unearned portion of the revenues account is recognized as a liability by crediting the unearned portion and debiting the revenues account for the same amount. After posting the adjusting entry, the balance of the revenues account is the portion already earned and this amount is closed to Income and Expense Summary during the closing process. At the start of the next accounting period, a reversing entry is made debiting the unearned revenue account and crediting the revenues account. The reversing entry will zero out unearned revenues.

ILLUSTRATION:

On September 1, 2005 Brentwood Fitness Center (BFC) sold 1,000 annual memberships at $300 each. BFC issued official receipts 4378 to 4678. Members are allowed unlimited use of all facilities from September 1, 2005 to August 31, 2006. BFC uses the calendar year as its accounting year and records unearned revenues using the revenue method.

Required: Prepare
(1) general journal entry on September 1, 2005.
(2) adjusting entry (ADJ001) on December 31, 2005.
(3) closing entry (CLS001) on December 31, 2005.
(4) reversing entry (REV001) on January 1, 2006.

ANALYSIS:

Monthly dues amount to $25 ($300/12) per member. Earned revenues for four months (Sep to Dec 05) is $100 (4 x $25) per member, total earned revenues amount to $100,000 ($100 x 1,000 members). Total unearned revenues for eight months (Jan to Aug 06) amount to $200,000 ($200 x 1,000 members).

GENERAL JOURNAL

DATE	DOC REF	DESCRIPTION	DEBIT	CREDIT
Sep 01 05	OR4378 to 4678	Cash Membership Revenues one year membership dues ($300 x 1,000)	300,000	300,000
Dec 31 05	ADJ001	Membership Revenues Unearned Membership Revenues unearned revenues (Jan to Aug 2006)	200,000	200,000
	CLS001	Membership Revenues Income and Expense Summary close membership revenues	100,000	100,000
Jan 01 06	REV001	Unearned Membership Revenues Membership Revenues reverse ADJ001	200,000	200,000

The above entries are posted in the T account for Membership Revenues and Unearned Membership Revenues.

MEMBERSHIP REVENUES		UNEARNED MEMBERSHIP REVENUES	
12/31 ADJ 200,000	09/01 GJ 300,000	01/01 REV 200,000	12/31 ADJ 200,000
12/31 CLS 100,000	12/31 BAL 100,000		12/31 BAL 200,000
	12/31 BAL ZERO		
	01/01 REV 200,000	01/01 BAL ZERO	
	01/01 BAL 200,000		

Accounting for Accrual of Revenues and Receivables

Accrued revenues are revenues already earned but not yet collected as of the end of the accounting period. Since these are already earned but remains uncollected, the business must record an asset to recognize that it has a right to collect from its customers/debtors. At the end of the accounting period, an adjusting entry is made debiting a receivable account and crediting the revenues account Typical example of accrued revenues are interest revenues due on notes receivable, rental revenues for landlords, retainer fees of professionals such as lawyer's, etc. At the start of the next accounting period, the adjusting entry is reversed by debiting the revenues account and crediting the receivable account.

ILLUSTRATION

On November 1, 2005, Moira Anne Law Offices (MALO) received a promissory note (PN005) from one of its clients. The principal of the note is $100,000, interest rate is 6% and term is 360 days due on Oct 27, 2006. MALO uses the calendar year as its accounting year.

Required: Prepare
(1) general journal entry on November 1, 2005.
(2) adjusting entry (ADJ001) on December 31, 2005.
(3) closing entry (CLS001) on December 31, 2005.
(4) reversing entry (REV001) on January 1, 2006.
(5) general journal entry to record collection of the note on maturity date. OR5678 is issued.

ANALYSIS:

Interest revenues are earned for 60 days from November 1 to December 31, 2005. The term of the note is 360 days; so it is not yet due as of December 31. Interest revenues for 60 days amount to $1,000 ($100,000 x 6% x 60/360). Total interest revenues for 360 days amount to $6,000 ($100,000 x 6% x 360/360). Total cash collected at maturity date is $106,000, the sum of principal and total interest revenues ($100,000 + $6,000).

GENERAL JOURNAL

DATE	DOC REF	DESCRIPTION	DEBIT	CREDIT
Nov 01 05	PN005	Notes Receivable	100,000	
		Legal Fees		100,000
		note from client 6% 360 days		
Dec 31 05	ADJ001	Interest Receivable	1,000	
		Interest Revenues		1,000
		interest for 60 days (Nov 1 to Dec 31)		
	CLS001	Interest Revenues	1,000	
		Income and Expense Summary		1,000
		close interest income		
Jan 01 06	REV001	Interest Revenues	1,000	
		Interest Receivable		1,000
		reverse ADJ001		
Oct 27 06	OR5678	Cash	106,000	
		Notes Receivable		100,000
		Interest Revenues		6,000
		PN001 collected		

Before the closing entry on Dec 31, 2005, the balance of Interest Receivable is $1,000 and Interest Revenues amount to $1,000.

The reversing entry on January 1, 2006 debiting interest revenues by $1,000 will result in correctly reflecting only $5,000 interest revenues earned in 2006 ($1,000 was already earned in 2005). If the reversing entry was not made on January 1, 2006 when the collection of the note is made at maturity date, interest revenues will be overstated by $1,000 in 2006. The postings to the T accounts below demonstrate the effect of the transactions to interest receivable and interest revenues.

INTEREST RECEIVABLE		INTEREST REVENUES	
12/31 ADJ 1,000			12/31 ADJ 1,000
		12/31 CLS 1,000	
	01/01 REV 1,000	01/01 REV 1,000	10/27 6,000
BAL ZERO			BAL 5,000

Accounting for Accrual of Expenses and Payables

Accrued expenses are expenses that are already incurred but remain unpaid as at the end of the accounting period. Since these are already incurred even though still unpaid, the business must record a liability to recognize that it has an obligation to pay its creditors. At the end of the accounting period, an adjusting entry is made debiting an expense account and crediting a liability account Typical example of accrued expenses are accrued wages, accrued interest notes payable, accrued rent, accrued income tax payable, etc. At the start of the next accounting period, the adjusting entry is reversed by debiting the liability account and crediting the expense account.

ILLUSTRATION

In the earlier illustration on accrued revenues above, the client Shirley Clinic issued the promissory note to Moira Anne Law Offices on November 1, 2005. Principal is $100,000; interest rate is 6% and term is 360 days, due on October 27, 2006. Shirley Clinic uses the calendar year as its accounting year.

Required: Prepare the following entries in the books of Shirley Clinic:

  (1) general journal entry on November 1, 2005.
  (2) adjusting entry (ADJ001) on December 31, 2005.
  (3) closing entry (CLS001) on December 31, 2005.
  (4) reversing entry (REV001) on January 1, 2006.
  (5) general journal entry to record payment of the note at maturity date. OR5678 was received.

ANALYSIS:

Interest expense is accrued for 60 days from November 1 to December 31, 2005. The term of the note is 360 days; so it is not yet due as of December 31. Interest expense for 60 days amounts to $1,000 ($100,000 x 6% x 60/360). Total interest expense for 360 days amounts to $6,000 ($100,000 x 6% x 360/360). Total cash paid at maturity date is $106,000, the sum of principal and total interest income ($100,000 + $6,000).

GENERAL JOURNAL

DATE	DOC REF	DESCRIPTION	DEBIT	CREDIT
Nov 01 05	PN005	Legal Expenses	100,000	
		Notes Payable		100,000
		note issued 6% 360 days		
Dec 31 05	ADJ001	Interest Expense	1,000	
		Interest Payable		1,000
		interest for 60 days (Nov 1 to Dec 31)		
	CLS001	Income and Expense Summary	1,000	
		Interest Expense		1,000
		close interest expense		
Jan 01 06	REV001	Interest Payable	1,000	
		Interest Expense		1,000
		reverse ADJ001		
Oct 27 06	OR5678	Notes Payable	100,000	
		Interest Expense	6,000	
		Cash		106,000
		PN001 paid		

The T accounts below show that the interest expense for 2006 is only $5,000 and not $6,000. If the reversing entry was not made, the interest expense will be overstated by $1,000 in 2006, which was amount in the adjusting entry for accrued interest expense in 2005.

INTEREST PAYABLE		INTEREST EXPENSE	
	12/31 ADJ 1,000	12/31 ADJ 1,000	
			12/31 CLS 1,000
01/01 REV 1,000			01/01 REV 1,000
BAL ZERO		10/27 6,000	
		BAL 5,000	

CHAPTER 10 ACCOUNTING PROCESS: THE REVERSING ENTRIES

REVIEW QUESTIONS

1. What are reversing entries?

2. Why are reversing entries necessary?

3. Identify and describe the four adjusting entries that must be reversed.

CHAPTER 10   ACCOUNTING PROCESS: THE REVERSING ENTRIES

REVIEW EXAMINATION

TRUE or FALSE: *WRITE* **TRUE** or **FALSE** *IN THE SPACE PROVIDED.*

_____ 1. Adjusting entries are recorded in the general journal on the first day of the next accounting period before any transactions for the next accounting period are recorded.

_____ 2. All adjusting entries are reversed.

_____ 3. Adjusting entries to account for prepaid expenses using the asset method are reversed.

_____ 4. Under the asset method of accounting for prepaid expenses, upon prepayment of an expense, a journal entry is prepared debiting the expense account and crediting cash.

_____ 5. Under the expense method of accounting for prepaid expenses, at the end of the accounting period, an adjusting entry is prepared debiting an asset for the unexpired or unused portion and crediting the expense account.

_____ 6. After the adjusting entries are prepared the expenses are closed to Income and Expense Summary.

_____ 7. To reverse an entry simply means to debit the account credited and credit the account debited in the original adjusting entry.

_____ 8. Reversing entries are prepared to simplify the recording of transactions and to adhere to the accounting principle of consistency.

_____ 9. Adjusting entries recording unearned revenues using the liability method are reversed.

_____ 10. Under the revenue method of accounting for unearned revenues, upon the advanced collection of revenues, a general journal entry is made to debit cash and credit the revenues account.

_____ 11. Accrued revenues are revenues already earned and already collected as of the end of the accounting period.

_____ 12. Typical examples of accrued expenses are interest income due on notes receivable, rental revenues for landlords, retainer fees of professionals.

_____ 13. Adjusting entries recording accrual of revenues and receivables are reversed.

_____ 14. Accrued expenses are expenses that are already incurred but remain unpaid as at the end of the accounting period.

_____ 15. Reversing entries are prepared to adhere to the accounting principle of consistency.

COMPLETION: *WRITE THE ANSWER IN THE SPACE PROVIDED.*

1. _____ entries are recorded in the general journal on the first day of the next accounting period before any transactions for the next accounting period are recorded in order to reverse some adjusting entries.

2. Adjusting entries that increase _____ or _____ are reversed.

3. Not all _____ entries are reversed.

4. Reversing entries are prepared to _____ the recording of transactions and to adhere to the accounting principle of _____.

5. The four adjusting entries that must be reversed are _____, _____, _____ and _____.

6. Under the expense method of recording pre-payment of expense, a journal entry is prepared to debit the _____ account and credit _____.

7. Under the expense method of accounting for prepaid expenses, at the end of the accounting period, an adjusting entry is prepared debiting an _____ for the unexpired or unused portion of the expense and crediting the _____ account.

8. During the closing process, expenses and revenues are closed to _____ account.

9. To reverse an entry simply means to _____ the account credited and _____ the account debited in the original adjusting entry.

10. Under the revenue method of accounting for unearned revenues, upon the advanced collection of the revenues, a general journal entry is made to debit _____ and credit the _____ account.

11. Accrued revenues are revenues already _____ but not yet _____ as of the end of the accounting period.

12. Typical examples of _____ are interest income due on notes receivable, rental revenues for landlords, retainer fees of professionals, already earned but not yet collected.

13. Accrued expenses are expenses that are already _____ but remain _____ as at the end of the accounting period.

14. Accrued expenses are recognized in the books by debiting the _____ account and crediting the _____ account.

15. Since _____ expenses are already incurred even though still unpaid, the business must record a liability to recognize that it has an obligation to pay its creditors.

EXERCISES: Use the general journal form provided.

I. Write **R** in the space before each item if the adjusting entry is to be reversed and **N** if it is not to be reversed.

			DEBIT	CREDIT
1.	_____	Bad Debts Expense	1,000	
		Allowance for Bad Debts		1,000
		bad debts expense		
2.	_____	Depreciation Expense – Car	3,000	
		Accumulated Depreciation – Car		3,000
		depreciation expense		
3.	_____	Wages Expense	2,500	
		Wages Payable		2,500
		accrued wages		
4.	_____	Rent Expense	7,000	
		Prepaid Rent		7,000
		expired rent		
5.	_____	Prepaid Rent	8,000	
		Rent Expense		8,000
		unexpired rent		
6.	_____	Unearned Magazine Subscriptions	5,000	
		Magazine Subscriptions Revenues		5,000
		earned subscription revenues		
7.	_____	Season Theatre Revenues	9,000	
		Unearned Season Theatre Revenues		9,000
		unearned season theatre revenues		

8.	_____	Interest Receivable	4,700	
		Interest Income		4,700
		accrued interest		
9.	_____	Interest Expense	3,800	
		Interest Payable		3,800
		accrued interest		
10.	_____	Office Supplies Expense		
		Office Supplies		
		used office supplies		

II. Prepare the reversing entries for the adjusting entries in I above that need to be reversed.

PROBLEMS

Use the adjusting entries prepared in Chapter 6, to prepare the reversing entries on the first day of the next accounting period for the following businesses:

  01. Global Delivery Services
  02 Garden Landscaping and Pool Services
  03 Grade A Plus Tutorial Services
  04 Jolie Kids Day Care Services
  05 James Deane Tours
  06 Have Fun Day Camp
  07 Beautiful Hollywood
  08 Reliable Security Management Services

Use the general journal form provided.

GENERAL JOURNAL

PAGE

DATE	DOC REF	ACCT CODE	DESCRIPTION	POST REF	DEBIT	CREDIT

GENERAL JOURNAL

PAGE _____

DATE	DOC REF	ACCT CODE	DESCRIPTION	POST REF	DEBIT	CREDIT

GENERAL JOURNAL

PAGE

DATE	DOC REF	ACCT CODE	DESCRIPTION	POST REF	DEBIT	CREDIT

GENERAL JOURNAL

PAGE _____

DATE	DOC REF	ACCT CODE	DESCRIPTION	POST REF	DEBIT	CREDIT

GENERAL JOURNAL

PAGE

DATE	DOC REF	ACCT CODE	DESCRIPTION	POST REF	DEBIT	CREDIT

GENERAL JOURNAL

PAGE

DATE	DOC REF	ACCT CODE	DESCRIPTION	POST REF	DEBIT	CREDIT

GENERAL JOURNAL

PAGE

DATE	DOC REF	ACCT CODE	DESCRIPTION	POST REF	DEBIT	CREDIT

GENERAL JOURNAL

PAGE

DATE	DOC REF	ACCT CODE	DESCRIPTION	POST REF	DEBIT	CREDIT

CHAPTER 11 — FINANCIAL STATEMENTS ANALYSIS

LEARNING OBJECTIVES

L01 Describe the factors used in assessing company performance.

L02 Discuss why business ethics is given much attention in the 21st century.

L03 Discuss the importance of corporate responsibility in business.

L04 Describe the relevant sources of information used in evaluating company performance.

L05 Discuss the importance of financial statement analysis.

L06 Identify and describe the different methods used in financial statements analysis.

L07 Describe how to use trend analysis, vertical analysis and horizontal analysis.

L08 Discuss financial statements component percentages analysis.

L09 Discuss the liquidity, profitability and solvency financial ratios.

CHAPTER 11   FINANCIAL STATEMENTS ANALYSIS

ASSESSING COMPANY PERFORMANCE

Businesses prepare financial statements in order to satisfy the information needs of various users of financial information. The usefulness of financial statements is served only when they are analyzed. Without analysis, the financial information in financial statements is simply a list of account titles and their corresponding balances. In assessing company performance, the decision maker must make qualitative and quantitative evaluation. The decision maker must be well informed not only about the specific company but also about so many other considerations about the business world in general. Qualitative evaluation pertains to matters that are not strictly financial in nature such as assessing the company environment by ascertaining its strengths, weaknesses, opportunities and threats. Qualitative evaluation includes looking at the relative presence of the company in the market, its market share, whether its actions influence the direction of the industry, the strength of its brand name, its reputation, goodwill, integrity in the business community, its business ethics practices, its corporate responsibility projects. The industry where the company belongs is also a factor in assessing future direction and financial performance. For instance, after the tragedy of September 11, 2001 and the outbreak of the Iraq war in 2003, companies belonging to defense and security industries performed very well despite the downturn in the economy after the 911 tragedy; whereas the airline industry and the hospitality industry suffered major setbacks. Companies in the biometric industry that produce scanning equipment are expected to profit from the strict security measures that are implemented in airports worldwide. On the other hand airlines who pay for the costs of stricter security measures feel the burden on their bottom line. The defense industry is another beneficiary of the 911 tragedy and the war on terror because they need to supply the arms and equipment requirements in combating terrorism. Sometimes, an opportunity for one industry becomes a threat to another. The location where the business operates is also a factor in assessing the company. Companies located in areas where there is peace and order concerns spend a lot more for security, insurance and other incidental costs that are not major considerations for businesses located in more stable environment. A company's competitive edge is a also a gauge used in assessing company performance. Over the years, the auto industry was dominated by American companies, such as General Motors, Ford Motors and Chrysler. They were the biggest auto makers and they led the industry. However during the start of the 21st century, Japan has positioned itself quite aggressively and seized the opportunity during the time that the US auto giants were suffering from a lot of financial, economic and operational problems. The US auto makers lost their competitive advantage and suffered billions of dollars in losses. Companies do not always stay at the forefront of their industry if they lose their competitive advantage. Currently Toyota Motors has displaced General Motors as the world's the number one auto maker.

In addition to assessing the overall business environment, decision makers now scrutinize the business ethics practices of companies. **Business ethics** refers to the standards of moral conduct in business; doing what is right under the circumstances. Corporations practicing ethical standards of conduct are preferred over those that have reputations of being unethical. The tobacco industry suffered the negative consequences of concealing the bad effects of nicotine to peoples' health. On the other hand, Johnson & Johnson earned the admiration of the public when it withdrew all Tylenol products from store shelves worldwide after it was found out that some bottles in a drugstore in the United States were tampered and tainted with cyanide poison. Despite the enormous cost of the Tylenol withdrawal, Johnson & Johnson gave higher importance to its customers than the adverse effect on its income. This incident has resulted in a very positive way for Johnson & Johnson and the consuming public as well because it gave birth to tamper-proof drug packaging. The corporate scandals committed by top executives at the end of the 20th century to the early years of the 21st century have affected the impression that the investing public has on corporate executives and thereby also adversely affected the attractiveness of stock investments. To protect the investing public, the US Congress passed the Sarbanes-Oxley Act of 2002. The Securities and Exchange Commission imposed stricter corporate reporting requirements. The investing public now scrutinizes the stock option package for major executives, as it was identified as one of the reasons for some of the lapses in applying generally accepted accounting principles and fraudulent financial statements reporting. The business ethics practices, internal controls, company integrity and top executive character are now being examined carefully before investors and creditors risk their investments in companies. Although the wrongdoings were committed only by a handful few, the corporate scandals have tarnished the high degree of trust and confidence that the investing public used to place on corporate executives.

Corporate responsibility is also a major consideration in assessing company performance. **Corporate responsibility** pertains to how businesses give back to the community. It involves corporate philanthropy or corporate giving. Many big corporations are always ready to donate funds and resources where their help is needed. Many corporations give funds to charitable institutions that aim to control the spread of AIDS particularly in Africa. Drug companies manufacturing AIDS medications offer cheaper AIDS drugs for African patients. During disasters and calamities, such as the hurricane Katrina that happened in New Orleans in 2005 and the Asian tsunami in 2004 for instance, corporations are always ready to make contributions towards the relief of disaster victims and the rehabilitation of destroyed infrastructures. The donations to victims of the 911 tragedy reached billions of dollars from individual and business donors. Many corporations sponsor social responsibility projects benefiting specific sectors of the society. McDonalds run the McDonalds House of Charity to provide shelter to families of sick children while they undergo medical treatment away from home. Corporate responsibility also involves activities that preserve and conserve the environment. How businesses treat nature is now a consideration in assessing business performance. If an oil company spills oil into the ocean it is expected to clean the polluted waters because it is toxic to the marine plants and animals. Companies are very careful that they do not contribute to the pollution of the environment. The auto industry must make sure that vehicles that they produce comply with legally acceptable emission standards. Timber lands are being reforested by companies that cut trees for their raw materials. Disposal by companies of hazardous and toxic waste is now vigilantly guarded by concerned population. Companies do not want to invite negative publicity resulting from irresponsible behavior. Social responsibility projects benefit society in general and at the same time create a favorable corporate image to its sponsors.

Quantitative evaluation involves the analysis and relationships of the financial information and disclosures reflected in the financial statements. As mentioned earlier, the financial statements are meaningless, without an analysis of its components. There are several methods used in analyzing financial statements. Trend analysis, vertical and horizontal analysis, industry bench marks and financial ratios are used in quantitative evaluation of financial statements.

SOURCES OF FINANCIAL INFORMATION

In evaluating companies, information is obtained from internal and external sources. Information from internal sources are those originating from the company being evaluated while external sources of information are provided by outside parties. With the advancement in information technology, it is now a lot easier to research anything; companies' profiles, historical financial information, products and services, business plans, etc are all available in websites accessible through the internet. The annual report of companies issued during the annual stockholders' meeting provides a lot of useful financial and non-financial information. The management report section of the annual report explains management decisions and actions, opportunities, challenges and other significant aspects of the company operations. Disclosures in the financial statements are additional information that can be used in the financial evaluation of the company. In addition to the annual report, companies make periodic announcements to the print and broadcast media concerning their financial and operational performance. External information can be obtained from news articles about the company, usually covered by business magazines, newspapers, bulletins from financial services firms such as the Dun and Bradstreet and Morningstar that rates the stock market performance of various company stocks. Business magazines such as the Business Week, Fortune and Forbes publish an annual report on the rankings of corporations based on certain financial criteria, such as sales, net income, total assets, etc. A word of caution in obtaining company information is advised; insider trading, getting information from sources not available to other prudent investors is illegal and punishable by law. Many financial advisers, stock brokers and even investors were prosecuted, fined and jailed for engaging in insider trading.

The decision maker must exhaust all available information from all sources and use these in making qualitative and quantitative evaluations of company performance. The decision that he makes depends on the analysis that he undertakes. Investment decisions can be very costly if he erred in his judgment because his analysis is faulty in the first place.

METHODS USED IN FINANCIAL STATEMENTS ANALYSIS

Several methods are used in analyzing financial statements. **Trend analysis** involves using past and current financial information in predicting probable future outcomes. If conditions remain relatively stable, past performance is an effective means of forecasting future performance. **Vertical analysis** involves analyzing the financial information pertaining to one accounting period and evaluating one item relative to another item in the same financial statement. In making the income statement evaluation, all items in the income statement are related to net sales, which is given a percentage equivalent of 100% and in the computation of the item percentage, the numerator is the item being evaluated and the denominator is always the net sales amount. The result is multiplied by 100 to convert it to per cent. For the balance sheet vertical analysis, total assets is given the percentage equivalent of 100% and in the computation of the item percentage, the numerator is the item being evaluated and the denominator is the total assets amount. The result is multiplied by 100 to convert it to per cent. For example, in the year 2005, total operating expenses is analyzed and compared with sales amount, in order to see if gross profit margin established is enough to cover operating expenses. If total operating expenses is $150,000 and net sales amount to $450,000; then the operating expenses percentage relative to net sales is 33.33% ($150,000/$450,000 x 100). This means that 33.33% of sales is allocated to the payment of operating expenses. Therefore, gross profit margin must be higher than 33.33% to generate net income to the owners. **Horizontal analysis** involves analyzing the same financial information pertaining to several accounting periods to establish the growth trends of that specific financial information. The earliest year is used as the starting point in establishing the base year. Horizontal analysis requires comparative financial statements. **Comparative financial statements** are financial statements that present financial information covering more than one accounting period; at least two accounting periods' financial information are presented in the financial statements. For example sales for a period of five years from 2000 to 2005 are evaluated with 2000 sales as the base year and growth trends are established using 2000 as the base year. The dollar amount change is computed by subtracting the base year amount from the year being evaluated. The dollar amount change is then divided by the base year amount multiplied by 100 to arrive at the percentage change from the base year. The financial statements show the dollar amounts for the years being evaluated and the base year, the dollar amount change and the % change. Sometimes, the growth trend is computed from year to year, not from the earliest base year but using last year as the base year such that the base year moves from year to year. In making a financial analysis of 5 year data from 2000 to 2005, the base year for 2002 is 2001; for 2003 the base year is 2002; for 2004 the base year is 2003, etc.

Component percentages analysis is used when financial statement information are presented in percentages, to help in comparing the same company's financial performance from one period to another. Component percentages analysis is also used to facilitate the comparison of companies of different sizes. The financial statements that show component percentages, instead of absolute dollar amounts are known as **common-size financial statements.** For the income statement, net sales is assigned the equivalent of 100% and the component percentage of each income statement item is computed by dividing the dollar amount of the specific item by the net sales amount and the result is multiplied by 100 to convert it to per cent. For the balance sheet, total assets is assigned the equivalent of 100% and the component percentage of each balance sheet item is computed by dividing the dollar amount of the specific item by the total assets amount and the result is multiplied by 100 to convert it to per cent.

Financial ratios are essential yardsticks used in financial statement analysis. Financial ratios measure the **short term liquidity, long-term solvency and profitability** of businesses. Among the various users of financial information, the owners/equity investors and the creditors are the user groups who rely heavily on financial ratios before rendering financial decisions. Although creditors and owners/equity investors both intend to preserve their investments in the business, their financial interests in the company vary. Creditors want to be assured that they will be paid when it is time to collect maturing liabilities of their debtors. Creditors are interested in the short term liquidity and long term solvency of their debtors. On the other hand, owners/equity investors are more interested in the profitability as well as long-term solvency of the business. Owners/equity investors expect income returns as well as value growth from their investments. Owners/equity investors want to make sure that they are investing in profitable ventures that will provide them with their income expectations through dividends and that if they decide to sell their investments they will be able to make a profit by selling their investments at a higher price than what they originally paid. Business profitability builds the value of the business and a company that continuously makes profit sustains its long term existence.

Short term liquidity is the short term staying power of the business; it is the ability of the business to pay currently maturing obligations; those that are due within one year from balance sheet date. A company may have so much asset to cover all its liabilities but if the assets are considered as non-liquid assets, the interests of short term creditors are prejudiced if cash is unavailable when the short term liabilities become due. Prudent financial managers must always make sure that maturing obligations are paid on time. Creditors are not willing to extend loans to non-paying or late paying customers. Once a business entity mismanages its cash, its credit rating suffers and it encounters difficulties in raising capital. If this happens, it becomes a high credit risk and if creditors extend credit to the business, it is at a much higher interest rate. Financing costs become more expensive. Short term liquidity ratios reflect that there are enough current assets to cover maturing short term liabilities at maturity date. **Working capital** is the difference between current assets and current liabilities. It is the amount available to fund the operations of the business after current liabilities are paid; it is the amount earmarked to pay for purchases of merchandise inventory for a merchandising business and raw materials for a manufacturing business and pay for all the expenses of the business. **Current ratio** is the most popular short term liquidity ratio. Current ratio is the relationship of current assets to current liabilities and it is computed by dividing total current assets by total current liabilities. In actual business practice, it is common to set a bench mark of 2:1 ($2 current assets for every $1 current liabilities). However, this bench mark may not be applicable to all industries. The higher the current ratio, the more favorable it is for short term creditors. **Quick ratio** or **acid test ratio** is a more stringent measurement of short term liquidity. The numerator includes only cash, marketable securities and accounts receivable. These are assets that are very easily convertible into cash. Merchandise inventory and prepaid expenses are excluded from the numerator. The numerator is divided by the total current liabilities to arrive at the quick ratio. Liquidity is also affected by how fast accounts receivables are collected and how fast merchandise inventories are sold. Companies want to collect credit sales and convert accounts receivable to cash as soon as possible. The efficiency of the collection department is measured by the accounts receivable turnover ratio and the number of days sales in receivables. **Accounts receivable turnover ratio** is computed by dividing net credit sales by the average accounts receivable. Average accounts receivable is equal to the sum of accounts receivable at the beginning and accounts receivable at the end of the period, divided by 2 ((accounts receivable, beginning + accounts receivable, end) / 2). The accounts receivable turnover ratio indicates the number of times during the period the company was able to roll over its accounts receivable and convert them back to credit sales. Number of days sales in receivable reflects how long the receivables remain uncollected and outstanding; it is also called average collection period in days. **Days sales in receivable** is computed by dividing 365 days by the accounts receivable turnover ratio. Companies want to have their accounts receivable at the lowest possible level; **the higher the accounts receivable turnover ratio the better it is**. The number of days sales in receivable is indirectly related to accounts receivable turnover. A lower accounts receivable turnover ratio results in higher days sales in receivable and vice-versa. Companies want to sell their merchandise as fast as they can. The efficiency of the sales department is measured by computing the merchandise inventory turnover ratio and the days sales in inventory. The inventory turnover ratio indicates the number of times during the period that the company was able to roll over its inventory and convert it back to cost of goods sold. The days sales in inventory shows the average number of days it takes to convert merchandise inventory to cost of goods sold, effectively, the average number of days it takes to sell merchandise inventory. **Inventory turnover ratio** is equal to cost of goods sold divided by average merchandise inventory. Average merchandise inventory is equal to the sum of merchandise inventory at the beginning and merchandise inventory at the end, divided by 2 ((merchandise inventory, beginning + merchandise inventory, end) / 2). **Days sales in inventory** is equal to 365 days divided by the inventory turnover ratio. **A high inventory turnover ratio** indicates good sales performance, meaning merchandise inventory are converted to cost of goods sold, effectively to sales at a fast pace. The inventory turnover ratio is indirectly related to days sales in inventory. A higher inventory turnover ratio results in lower days sales in inventory and vice-versa. **Cash-to-cash operating cycle** reflects the number of days it takes for the business to convert cash back to cash and it is the sum of days sales in receivable and days sales in inventory.

Solvency is the long-term staying power of the business; it is the ability of the business to obtain sufficient cash to pay long-term debts at maturity date. Long-term debts are obligations that mature beyond one year from balance sheet date. Owners/equity investors and creditors are both concerned about the solvency of the business. They are interested in ascertaining the degree of insolvency risk and profit stability. A business that becomes insolvent will not be able to pay its maturing obligations to the creditors and fail to pay income returns and provide investment growth to it owners/equity investors. Businesses that have proportionately higher liabilities in relation to owners' equity have a lot of pressure to pay interests and therefore have greater chances of suffering losses. **Total debts to total assets ratio** show the share of the creditors to the total assets of the business. Owners must have more stake than creditors in the assets of the business. If creditors have greater claim on the assets, it is a sign of poor financial health on the part of the business. Total debts to total assets ratio is computed by dividing total liabilities to total assets. It is the goal of businesses to have low total debts to total assets ratio; it means that the owners have more claims to the assets of the business than creditors. **Total debts to total equity ratio** shows the relationship between the claim of the creditors to the claim of the owners/equity investors in the business; it is computed by dividing total liabilities by total owners' equity. **Interest coverage ratio** is a measurement of how many times interest expenses will be covered sufficiently by operating income (net income before interest and taxes). Many companies establish interest coverage ratio of 5 times; but again bench marks do not apply uniformly to all companies. Interest coverage ratio is equal to net income before interest and taxes divided by interest expense.

Profitability is the ability of the business to make profits continuously. Owners/equity investors are focused on a company's profitability. If a business continuously suffers losses there is a high risk that it will not be able to operate over time because its working capital will eventually dry up. In due time it will close down and owners/equity investors will also lose their investments. **Gross profit ratio or gross profit margin** is the relationship between gross profit and net sales and it reflects what part of net sales is allocated to gross profit. Gross profit ratio is equal to gross profit divided by net sales. **ROE or Return on equity (stockholders' equity for corporations)** is the relationship between net income and owner's equity and it shows the amount of owners' equity needed to generate net income. ROE is equal to net income divided by average owners' equity. Average owners' equity is equal to (owners' equity, beginning + owners' equity, end) / 2. A high ROE is a good indicator of profitability. **Return on sales (ROS) or net profit margin ratio** is the relationship between net income and net sales and it shows the portion of net sales that goes to net income. ROS is equal to net income divided by net sales. **Return on assets (ROA)** is the relationship between net income and total assets and it shows the level of total assets needed to generate net income. ROA is equal to net income divided by average total assets. Average total assets is equal to (total assets, beginning + total assets, end) / 2. **Asset turnover ratio** is the relationship between net sales and total assets and it shows the level of total assets needed to generate sales for the period. Asset turnover ratio is equal to net sales divided by average total assets.

Aside from these financial ratios there are other ratios that are intentionally left out in this chapter. These ratios, such as earnings per share (EPS) price-earnings, dividend yield and dividend payout are covered in the chapter on corporate capitalization.

EVALUATION OF FINANCIAL RATIOS

In order to evaluate the significance of calculated financial ratios they must be related or compared to other ratios. The calculated ratios can be compared to (1) the company's own historical ratios over a specific period of time; (2) rules of thumb established by the accounting profession or the business community and (3) ratios of other companies belonging to the same industry. The calculated ratios are merely numbers and without comparing them with other ratios, they are meaningless. For instance, comparing the current year's ratios with the company's own ratios in the past years will show if the company is performing better or worse than its track record. Bench marks or rules of thumb are useful in assessing if the company is doing at par with established acceptable standards. It is possible that the company is improving over the years but comparing its ratios with the bench marks might reflect that it is still far off from satisfying the established bench marks. It is also good to compare the company's financial ratios with the ratios of other companies in the same industry because the company will be able to gauge how it measures up with its competitors. Any business operation must always be ahead of its competitors in order to maintain its competitive advantage and an effective strategy is always to be informed about ones competitors. In order to effectively evaluate the financial ratios, decision makers must use the three comparisons in conjunction with each other. Using just one method of comparison is unwise and the decision maker might err in his judgment because his evaluation is based on limited information.

SUMMARY OF FINANCIAL RATIOS and FORMULA

LIQUIDITY

1.	Working Capital	Current assets – current liabilities
2.	Current ratio	Current assets / current liabilities
3.	Quick or acid test ratio	(Cash + marketable securities + accounts receivable) / current liabilities
4.	Accounts receivable turnover	Net credit sales / average accounts receivable*
5.	Days sales in receivable	365 / accounts receivable turnover
6.	Inventory turnover	Cost of goods sold / average merchandise inventory*
7.	Days sales in inventory	365 / inventory turnover ratio
8.	Cash-to-cash operating cycle	Days sales in receivable + days sales in inventory

SOLVENCY

1.	Total debts to total assets ratio	Total liabilities / total assets
2.	Total debts to total equity ratio	Total liabilities / owners' equity
3.	Interest coverage ratio	Net operating income / interest expense

PROFITABILITY

1.	Gross profit ratio	Gross profit / net sales
2.	Return on owners' equity ratio	Net income / average owners' equity*
3.	Return on sales ratio	Net income / net sales
4.	Return on assets ratio	Net income / average total assets*
5.	Asset turnover ratio	Net sales / average total assets*

* Average = (beginning balance + ending balance) / 2

ILLUSTRATION PROBLEMS: Use the comparative income statement and balance sheet of Erica Moira Boutique to analyze the financial statements using the methods identified.

ERICA MOIRA BOUTIQUE
COMPARATIVE INCOME STATEMENTS
FOR YEARS ENDED DECEMBER 31, 2005 AND 2006

	2,006	2,005
Sales	998,000	875,000
Less: Cost of Goods Sold		
Merchandise Inventory, January 1	127,700	149,800
Add: Purchases	560,100	452,900
Goods Available for Sale	687,800	602,700
Less: Merchandise Inventory, December 31	169,800	127,700
Cost of Goods Sold	518,000	475,000
Gross Profit	480,000	400,000
Less: Operating Expenses		
Bad Debts Expense	27,000	13,500
Store Supplies Expense	5,200	5,000
Wages Expense	109,000	99,000
Rent Expense	52,800	48,000
Gas & Electricity Expense	11,300	10,900
Telephone Expense	8,000	8,600
Transportation Expense	9,800	8,000
Depreciation Expense - Truck	4,000	4,000
Depreciation Expense - Store Equipment	12,000	12,000
Advertising Expense	8,700	7,200
Taxes & Licenses Expense	3,000	3,000
Insurance Expense	2,200	1,800
Total Operating Expenses	253,000	221,000
Income from Operations	227,000	179,000
Add: Other Revenues		
Interest Revenues	5,000	3,000
Total Income	232,000	182,000
Less: Other Expenses		
Interest Expense	7,000	2,000
Net Income	225,000	180,000

ERICA MOIRA BOUTIQUE
COMPARATIVE BALANCE SHEET
AS OF DECEMBER 31, 2005 AND 2006

	2006	2005
ASSETS		
CURRENT ASSETS		
Cash	357,600	305,200
Marketable Securities	43,000	43,000
Accounts Receivable, net	429,000	289,000
Prepaid Expenses	1,100	1,100
Merchandise Inventory	169,800	127,700
Store Supplies	12,000	15,000
TOTAL CURRENT ASSETS	1,012,500	781,000
LONG-TERM ASSETS		
Truck, net	64,000	68,000
Store Equipment, net	136,000	148,000
TOTAL LONG-TERM ASSETS	200,000	216,000
TOTAL ASSETS	1,212,500	997,000
LIABILITIES AND OWNER'S EQUITY		
CURRENT LIABILITIES		
Accounts Payable	206,500	156,500
Notes Payable, current	50,000	50,000
Wages Payable	8,500	8,500
Interest Payable	10,000	5,000
TOTAL CURRENT LIABILITIES	275,000	220,000
LONG-TERM LIABILITIES		
Notes Payable, non-current	200,000	250,000
TOTAL LIABILITIES	475,000	470,000
Erica Moira, Capital	737,500	527,500
TOTAL LIABILITIES AND OWNER'S EQUITY	1,212,500	997,500

ILLUSTRATION PROBLEM: VERTICAL ANALYSIS

REQUIRED: Analyze the comparative financial statements of Erica Moira Boutique using vertical analysis. Interpret the significance of the percentages calculated.

ERICA MOIRA BOUTIQUE
COMPARATIVE INCOME STATEMENTS
FOR YEARS ENDED DECEMBER 31, 2005 AND 2006

	2,006		2,005	
Sales	998,000	100.00%	875,000	100.00%
Less: Cost of Goods Sold				
Merchandise Inventory, January 1	127,700		149,800	
Add: Purchases	560,100		452,900	
Goods Available for Sale	687,800		602,700	
Less: Merchandise Inventory, December 31	169,800		127,700	
Cost of Goods Sold	518,000	51.90%	475,000	54.29%
Gross Profit	480,000	48.10%	400,000	45.71%
Less: Operating Expenses				
Bad Debts Expense	27,000	2.71%	13,500	1.54%
Store Supplies Expense	5,200	0.52%	5,000	0.57%
Wages Expense	109,000	10.92%	99,000	11.31%
Rent Expense	52,800	5.29%	48,000	5.49%
Gas & Electricity Expense	11,300	1.13%	10,900	1.25%
Telephone Expense	8,000	0.80%	8,600	0.98%
Transportation Expense	9,800	0.98%	8,000	0.91%
Depreciation Expense - Truck	4,000	0.40%	4,000	0.46%
Depreciation Expense - Store Equipment	12,000	1.20%	12,000	1.37%
Advertising Expense	8,700	0.87%	7,200	0.82%
Taxes & Licenses Expense	3,000	0.30%	3,000	0.34%
Insurance Expense	2,200	0.22%	1,800	0.21%
Total Operating Expenses	253,000	25.35%	221,000	25.26%
Income from Operations	227,000	22.75%	179,000	20.46%
Add: Other Revenues				
Interest Revenues	5,000	0.50%	3,000	0.34%
Total Income	232,000	23.25%	182,000	20.80%
Less: Other Expenses				
Interest Expense	7,000	0.70%	2,000	0.23%
Net Income	225,000	22.55%	180,000	20.57%

ERICA MOIRA BOUTIQUE
COMPARATIVE BALANCE SHEET
AS OF DECEMBER 31, 2005 AND 2006

	2006		2005	
ASSETS				
CURRENT ASSETS				
Cash	357,600	29.49%	305,200	30.61%
Marketable Securities	43,000	3.55%	43,000	4.31%
Accounts Receivable, net	429,000	35.38%	289,000	28.99%
Prepaid Expenses	1,100	0.09%	1,100	0.11%
Merchandise Inventory	169,800	14.00%	127,700	12.81%
Store Supplies	12,000	0.99%	15,000	1.50%
TOTAL CURRENT ASSETS	1,012,500	83.51%	781,000	78.34%
LONG-TERM ASSETS				
Truck, net	64,000	5.28%	68,000	6.82%
Store Equipment, net	136,000	11.22%	148,000	14.84%
TOTAL LONG-TERM ASSETS	200,000	16.49%	216,000	21.66%
TOTAL ASSETS	1,212,500	100.00%	997,000	100.00%
LIABILITIES AND OWNER'S EQUITY				
CURRENT LIABILITIES				
Accounts Payable	206,500	17.03%	156,500	15.70%
Notes Payable, current	50,000	4.12%	50,000	5.02%
Wages Payable	8,500	0.70%	8,500	0.85%
Interest Payable	10,000	0.82%	5,000	0.50%
TOTAL CURRENT LIABILITIES	275,000	22.68%	220,000	22.07%
LONG-TERM LIABILITIES				
Notes Payable, non-current	200,000	16.49%	250,000	25.08%
TOTAL LIABILITIES	475,000	39.18%	470,000	47.14%
Erica Moira, Capital	737,500	60.82%	527,500	52.91%
TOTAL LIABILITIES AND OWNER'S EQUITY	1,212,500	100.00%	997,500	100.00%

NOTE: To calculate the percentage for each item, compute the percentage of each income statement item relative to net sales by dividing the income statement item amount by net sales. Compute the percentage of each balance sheet item relative to total assets by dividing the balance sheet item amount by total assets.

INTERPRETATION OF VERTICAL ANALYSIS

INCOME STATEMENT: Net sales amounted to $875,000 in 2005 and $998,000 in 2006. In 2005, cost of goods sold amounting to $400,000 is 54.29% of net sales giving a gross profit of $400,000 equal to 45.71% of net sales. Operating expenses of $221,000 accounted to 25.26% of net sales. Interest revenues and interest expenses are less than 1% of net sales. Net income of $180,000 is 20.57% of net sales. In 2006, there is an improvement in gross profit to 48.10% from 45.71% in 2005. The percentage of cost of goods sold relative to net sales is reduced by about 3% from 54.29% to 51.90% resulting in 2.39% improvement in gross profit from 45.71% to 48.10%. Interest items now make up more than 1 % of net sales. Net income relative to net sales showed a 1.98% improvement from 20.57% in 2005 to 22.55% in 2006.

BALANCE SHEET: In 2005, total current assets relative to total assets amounted to $781,000, equivalent to 78.34%. Cash (30.61%) and accounts receivable (28.99%) are the major components of total current assets. Long-term assets account for 21.66% of total assets, equivalent to $216,000. Current liabilities amount to 22.07%; long-term liabilities amount to 25.08% and capital is 52.91% of total assets. In 2006, there was more than 5% improvement in current assets relative to total assets, from 78.34% in 2005 to 83.51% in 2006. Total current liabilities maintained its percentage relationship to total assets while long-term liabilities showed a marked reduction of 8.59% to total assets, from $250,000 to $200,000; there was a $50,000 payment made to lower long-term liabilities. Effectively, the total liabilities in 2006 relative to total assets were down by 7.96%. There was a marked improvement in capital relative to total assets in 2006 by 7.91%.

ILLUSTRATION PROBLEM: HORIZONTAL ANALYSIS

REQUIRED: Analyze the comparative financial statements of Erica Moira Boutique using horizontal analysis. Interpret the significance of the percentages calculated.

ERICA MOIRA BOUTIQUE
COMPARATIVE INCOME STATEMENTS
FOR YEARS ENDED DECEMBER 31, 2005 AND 2006

	2,006	2,005	CHANGE	% CHANGE
Sales	998,000	875,000	123,000	14.06%
Less: Cost of Goods Sold				
Merchandise Inventory, January 1	127,700	149,800		
Add: Purchases	560,100	452,900		
Goods Available for Sale	687,800	602,700		
Less: Merchandise Inventory, December 31	169,800	127,700		
Cost of Goods Sold	518,000	475,000	43,000	9.05%
			0	
Gross Profit	480,000	400,000	80,000	20.00%
Less: Operating Expenses				
Bad Debts Expense	27,000	13,500	13,500	100.00%
Store Supplies Expense	5,200	5,000	200	4.00%
Wages Expense	109,000	99,000	10,000	10.10%
Rent Expense	52,800	48,000	4,800	10.00%
Gas & Electricity Expense	11,300	10,900	400	3.67%
Telephone Expense	8,000	8,600	-600	-6.98%
Transportation Expense	9,800	8,000	1,800	22.50%
Depreciation Expense - Truck	4,000	4,000		
Depreciation Expense - Store Equipment	12,000	12,000		
Advertising Expense	8,700	7,200	1,500	20.83%
Taxes & Licenses Expense	3,000	3,000		
Insurance Expense	2,200	1,800	400	22.22%
Total Operating Expenses	253,000	221,000	32,000	14.48%
Income from Operations	227,000	179,000	48,000	26.82%
Add: Other Revenues				
Interest Revenues	5,000	3,000	2,000	66.67%
Total Income	232,000	182,000	50,000	27.47%
Less: Other Expenses				
Interest Expense	7,000	2,000	5,000	250.00%
Net Income	225,000	180,000	45,000	25.00%

ERICA MOIRA BOUTIQUE
COMPARATIVE BALANCE SHEET
AS OF DECEMBER 31, 2005 AND 2006

	2006	2005	CHANGE	% CHANGE
ASSETS				
CURRENT ASSETS				
Cash	357,600	305,200	52,400	17.17%
Marketable Securities	43,000	43,000		
Accounts Receivable, net	429,000	289,000	140,000	48.44%
Prepaid Expenses	1,100	1,100		
Merchandise Inventory	169,800	127,700	42,100	32.97%
Store Supplies	12,000	15,000	-3,000	-20.00%
TOTAL CURRENT ASSETS	1,012,500	781,000	231,500	29.64%
LONG-TERM ASSETS				
Truck, net	64,000	68,000	-4,000	-5.88%
Store Equipment, net	136,000	148,000	-12,000	-8.11%
TOTAL LONG-TERM ASSETS	200,000	216,000	-16,000	-7.41%
TOTAL ASSETS	1,212,500	997,000	215,500	21.61%
LIABILITIES AND OWNER'S EQUITY				
CURRENT LIABILITIES				
Accounts Payable	206,500	156,500	50,000	31.95%
Notes Payable, current	50,000	50,000		
Wages Payable	8,500	8,500		
Interest Payable	10,000	5,000	5,000	100.00%
TOTAL CURRENT LIABILITIES	275,000	220,000	55,000	25.00%
LONG-TERM LIABILITIES				
Notes Payable, non-current	200,000	250,000	-50,000	-20.00%
TOTAL LIABILITIES	475,000	470,000	5,000	1.06%
Erica Moira, Capital	737,500	527,500	210,000	39.81%
TOTAL LIABILITIES AND OWNER'S EQUITY	1,212,500	997,500	215,000	21.55%

NOTE: For each line item compute the amount of change from 2005 to 2006 and divide the computed amount of change by the 2005 base year amount to get the % change from 2005 to 2006.

INTERPRETATION OF HORIZONTAL ANALYSIS

INCOME STATEMENT: Net sales grew by 14.06% in 2006 from $875.000 in 2005 to $998,000 in 2006. Cost of goods sold increased at a lower pace than net sales by 9.05% from $475,000 to $518,000. Gross profit improved by 20% from $400,000 to $480,000. Total operating expenses increased by 14.48% from $221,000 to $253,000. The increase of 100% in bad debts expense is to be noted because it can be a warning that the company is experiencing collection problems, maybe a sign of forthcoming economic downturn. The 250% significant increase in interest expense from $2,000 to $7,000 is attributable to the fact that the long-term note was obtained sometime in 2005, so only partial annual interest was incurred; in 2006, annual interest is charged on the long term notes payable. Net income increased by $45,000 or 25% from $180,000 in 2005 to $225,000 in 2006.

BALANCE SHEET: Total assets registered a 29.64% improvement from $781,000 to $1,012,500. However, there is a marked build up of accounts receivable, increasing by 48.44% amounting to $140,000, from $289,000 to $429,000. A review of credit and collection policies is in order to remedy the situation. Total assets increased by $215,500, equivalent to 21.61%. The increase in total liabilities is insignificant at 1.06% while capital increase significantly by $$210,000 or 39.81%.

ILLUSTRATION PROBLEM: COMPONENT PERCENTAGES ANALYSIS

REQUIRED: Analyze the comparative financial statements of Erica Moira Boutique using horizontal analysis. Interpret the significance of the percentages calculated.

ERICA MOIRA BOUTIQUE
COMPARATIVE INCOME STATEMENTS
FOR YEARS ENDED DECEMBER 31, 2005 AND 2006

	2,006	2,005
Sales	100.00%	100.00%
Less: Cost of Goods Sold		
Merchandise Inventory, January 1		
Add: Purchases		
Goods Available for Sale		
Less: Merchandise Inventory, December 31		
Cost of Goods Sold	51.90%	54.29%
Gross Profit	48.10%	45.71%
Less: Operating Expenses		
Bad Debts Expense	2.71%	1.54%
Store Supplies Expense	0.52%	0.57%
Wages Expense	10.92%	11.31%
Rent Expense	5.29%	5.49%
Gas & Electricity Expense	1.13%	1.25%
Telephone Expense	0.80%	0.98%
Transportation Expense	0.98%	0.91%
Depreciation Expense - Truck	0.40%	0.46%
Depreciation Expense - Store Equipment	1.20%	1.37%
Advertising Expense	0.87%	0.82%
Taxes & Licenses Expense	0.30%	0.34%
Insurance Expense	0.22%	0.21%
Total Operating Expenses	25.35%	25.26%
Income from Operations	22.75%	20.46%
Add: Other Revenues		
Interest Revenues	0.50%	0.34%
Total Income	23.25%	20.80%
Less: Other Expenses		
Interest Expense	0.70%	0.23%
Net Income	22.55%	20.57%

ERICA MOIRA BOUTIQUE
COMPARATIVE BALANCE SHEET
AS OF DECEMBER 31, 2005 AND 2006

	2006	2005
ASSETS		
CURRENT ASSETS		
Cash	29.49%	30.61%
Marketable Securities	3.55%	4.31%
Accounts Receivable, net	35.38%	28.99%
Prepaid Expenses	0.09%	0.11%
Merchandise Inventory	14.00%	12.81%
Store Supplies	0.99%	1.50%
TOTAL CURRENT ASSETS	83.51%	78.34%
LONG-TERM ASSETS		
Truck, net	5.28%	6.82%
Store Equipment, net	11.22%	14.84%
TOTAL LONG-TERM ASSETS	16.49%	21.66%
TOTAL ASSETS	100.00%	100.00%
LIABILITIES AND OWNER'S EQUITY		
CURRENT LIABILITIES		
Accounts Payable	17.03%	15.70%
Notes Payable, current	4.12%	5.02%
Wages Payable	0.70%	0.85%
Interest Payable	0.82%	0.50%
TOTAL CURRENT LIABILITIES	22.68%	22.07%
LONG-TERM LIABILITIES		
Notes Payable, non-current	16.49%	25.08%
TOTAL LIABILITIES	39.18%	47.14%
Erica Moira, Capital	60.82%	52.91%
TOTAL LIABILITIES AND OWNER'S EQUITY	100.00%	100.00%

For one accounting period, say 2005, compute the percentage of each income statement item relative to net sales by dividing the income statement item amount by net sales. Compute the percentage of each balance sheet item relative to total assets by dividing the balance sheet item amount by total assets. Only the percentages are shown.

INTERPRETATION: COMPONENT PERCENTAGES ANALYSIS

No dollar amounts are shown in the solution, so only the percentages are interpreted as to how income statement items relate to net sales and balance sheet items relate to total assets.

INCOME STATEMENT: In 2005, cost of goods sold is 54.29% and gross profit is 45.71% of net sales. Perhaps the company was able to source their purchases at lower prices because cost of goods sold improved to 51.90% (lower cost of goods sold is an improvement) and gross profit increased to 48.10% of net sales. Operating expenses relative to net sales for both years remained relatively stable at 25.26% and 25.35% respectively. Net income for 2005 is 20.57% of net sales while in 2006 it is 22.55%.

BALANCE SHEET: Total current assets relative to total assets registered a 5.17% improvement from 78.34% in 2005 to 83.51% in 2006. Again, a close scrutiny must be made about the build up in accounts receivable from 28.99% to 35.38% of total assets. Total current liabilities relative to total assets remain relatively stable at 22.07% and 22.68% respectively. Capital relative to total assets resulted in marked improvement at 52.91% in 2005 and 60.82% in 2006.

Fundamentals of Accounting

ILLUSTRATION PROBLEM: FINANCIAL RATIOS

Required: Use the comparative income statement and balance sheet of Erica Moira Boutique and compute the following ratios for 2005 and 2006. Net credit sales in 2005 amount to $525,000; net credit sales in 2006 amount to $848,300. The following are balances of selected items on December 31, 2004:

Accounts Receivable, net	$ 200,000
Total Assets	800,000
Total Liabilities	370,000
Erica Moira Capital	430,000

1. Liquidity ratios
    a) Working capital
    b) Current ratio
    c) Acid test ratio
    d) Accounts receivable turnover ratio
    e) Days sales in receivable
    f) Merchandise inventory turnover
    g) Days sales in inventory
    h) Cash-to-cash operating cycle

2. Solvency ratios
    a) Total debts to total assets ratio
    b) Total debts to total equity ratio
    c) Interest coverage ratio

3. Profitability ratios
    a) Gross Profit Ratio
    b) Return on owners' equity
    c) Return on sales
    d) Return on assets
    e) Asset turnover ratio

FINANCIAL RATIOS:	ERICA MOIRA BOUTIQUE			
LIQUIDITY RATIOS	2006 COMPUTATION	2006 RATIO	2005 COMPUTATION	2005 RATIO
Working capital	1,012,000 - 275,000	737,000.00	781,000 - 220,000	561,000.00
Current ratio	1,012,000 / 275,000	3.68	781,000 / 220,000	3.55
Acid test ratio	(357,600 + 43,000 + 429,000) / 275,000	3.02	(305,200 + 43,000 + 289,000) / 220,000	2.90
Accounts receivable turnover	848,300 / ((429,000 + 289,000) / 2)	2.36	525,000 / ((200,000 + 289,000) / 2)	2.15
Days sales in receivable	365 / 2.36	154.66	365 / 2.15	169.77
Inventory turnover	518,000 / ((127,700 + 169,000) / 2)	3.49	475,000 / ((149,800 + 127,700) / 2)	3.42
Days sales in inventory	365 / 3.49	104.58	365 / 3.42	106.73
Cash-to-cash operating cycle	154.66 + 104.58	259.24	169.77 + 106.73	276.50
SOLVENCY RATIOS				
Total debts to total assets	475,000 / 1,212,500	0.39	470,000 / 997,000	0.47
Total debts to total equity	475,000 / 737,500	0.64	470,000 / 527,500	0.89
Interest coverage	227,000 / 7,000	32.43	179,000 / 2,000	89.50
PROFITABILITY				
Gross profit	480,000 / 998,000	0.48	400,000 / 875,000	0.46
Return on owners' equity	225,000 / ((737,500 + 527,500) / 2)	0.36	180,000 / ((527,500 + 430,000) / 2)	0.38
Return on sales	225,000 / 998,000	0.23	180,000 / 875,000	0.21
Return on assets	225,000 / ((1,212,500 + 997,000) / 2)	0.20	180,000 / ((997,000 + 800000) / 2)	0.20
Asset turnover	998,000 / ((1,212,500 + 997,000) / 2)	0.90	875,000 / ((997,000 + 800000) / 2)	0.97

This is
blank page

CHAPTER 11 — FINANCIAL STATEMENTS ANALYSIS

REVIEW QUESTIONS

1. What are some of the factors used in assessing overall company performance?

2. Differentiate qualitative from quantitative evaluation.

3. Discuss the importance of corporate responsibility in business.

4. Why is business ethics given a lot of importance in the 21st century?

5. What are external sources of information? Give examples.

6. What are internal sources of information? Give examples.

7. Why is it important to analyze financial statements?

8. What are the different methods used in financial statement analysis?

9. Differentiate vertical analysis from horizontal analysis.

10. Why are equity investors and creditors interested in the liquidity, solvency and profitability of business?

11. Describe the liquidity ratios.

12. Describe the solvency ratios.

13. Describe the profitability ratios.

14. Why is it necessary to compare the computed ratios to the company's own historical ratios? to rule of thumb ratios? to ratios of other companies in the same industry?

CHAPTER 11   FINANCIAL STATEMENTS ANALYSIS

REVIEW EXAMINATION

TRUE or FALSE: *WRITE TRUE or FALSE IN THE SPACE PROVIDED.*

_____ 1. The usefulness of financial statements is served only when they are analyzed.

_____ 2. Quantitative evaluation pertains to matters that are not strictly financial in nature such as assessing the company environment by ascertaining its strengths, weaknesses, opportunities and threats.

_____ 3. Corporate responsibility refers to the standards of moral conduct in business; doing what is right under the circumstances.

_____ 4. Social responsibility projects benefit society in general and at the same time create a favorable corporate image to its sponsors.

_____ 5. The decision maker must exhaust all available information from all sources and use these in making qualitative and quantitative evaluations of company performance.

_____ 6. Information provided from external sources are those originating from the company being evaluated while internal sources of information are provided by outside parties.

_____ 7. Comparative financial statements are financial statements that present financial information covering more than one accounting period;

_____ 8. Vertical analysis is used when financial statement information are presented in percentages, to help in comparing the same company's financial performance from one period to another.

_____ 9. Business ethics pertains to how businesses give back to the community.

_____ 10. Horizontal analysis involves analyzing the same financial information pertaining to several accounting periods to establish the growth trends of that specific financial information.

_____ 11. Current ratio is a more stringent measurement of short term liquidity because the numerator includes only cash, marketable securities and accounts receivable.

_____ 12. Vertical analysis involves analyzing the financial information pertaining to one accounting period and evaluating one item relative to another item in the same financial statement.

_____ 13. In making the income statement evaluation using vertical analysis, all items in the income statement are related to net sales, which is given a percentage equivalent of 100%

_____ 14. The financial statements that show component percentages, instead of absolute dollar amounts are known as common-size financial statements.

_____ 15. Financial ratios measure the short term liquidity, long-term solvency and profitability of businesses.

_____ 16. Financial ratios involve using past and current financial information in predicting probable future outcomes.

_____ 17. Creditors want to be assured that they will be paid when it is time to collect maturing liabilities of their debtors.

_____ 18. Owners/equity investors want to make sure that they are investing in profitable ventures that will provide them with their income expectations through dividends and that if they decide to sell their investments they will be able to make a profit by selling their investments at a higher price than what they originally paid.

_____ 19. Profitability is the short term staying power of the business; it is the ability of the business to pay currently maturing obligations

_____ 20. Solvency is the difference between current assets and current liabilities.

COMPLETION: *WRITE THE ANSWER IN THE SPACE PROVIDED.*

1. _____ is the relationship between net income and total assets.

2. _____ is equal to net income divided by average owners' equity.

3. _____ is the relationship between gross profit and net sales and it reflects what part of net sales is allocated to gross profit.

4. _____ is the ability of the business to make profits continuously.

5. Interest coverage ratio is a measurement of how many times interest expenses will be covered sufficiently by _____.

6. Total debts to total assets ratio show the share of the _____ to the total assets of the business.

7. _____ the long-term staying power of the business.

8. Solvency is the ability of the business to obtain sufficient cash to pay _____ at maturity date.

9. Long-term debts are obligations that mature beyond _____ from balance sheet date.

10. _____ reflects the number of days it takes for the business to convert cash back to cash and it is the sum of days sales in receivable and days sales in inventory.

11. The number of days sales in receivable is _____ related to accounts receivable turnover.

12. In the computation of the acid test ratio, the numerator includes only _____, _____ and _____.

13. _____ is the ability of the business to pay currently maturing obligations

14. _____ want to be assured that they will be paid when it is time to collect maturing liabilities of their debtors.

15. The financial statements that show component percentages, instead of absolute dollar amounts are known as _____ financial statements.

16. In the vertical analysis income statement evaluation, all items in the income statement are related to _____, which is given a percentage equivalent of 100%.

17. Financial ratios measure the _____, _____ and _____ of businesses.

18. _____ financial statements are financial statements that present financial information covering more than one accounting period.

19. _____ evaluation pertains to matters that are not strictly financial in nature such as assessing the company environment by ascertaining its strengths, weaknesses, opportunities and threats.

20. _____ refers to the standards of moral conduct in business.

PROBLEMS:

Use the comparative income statement and balance sheet of Donna Anne Enterprises shown below. In addition, use the information in 2005 to calculate the financial ratios. Prepare the following:

1. Horizontal analysis

2. Vertical analysis for 2005 and 2006.

3. Component percentages for 2005 and 2006.

4. Financial ratios

	2006	2005
Credit sales	$ 700,000	$ 500,000
Accounts receivable, beginning		80,000
Total assets, beginning		500,000
Total liabilities, beginning		200,000
Total owners' equity, beginning		300,000

Compute the following financial ratios:

a) current ratio

b) acid test ratio

c) working capital

d) accounts receivable turnover

e) days sales in receivable

f) Inventory turnover

g) days sales in inventory

h) total debts to total assets

i) return on owners' equity

j) asset turnover

DONNA ANNE ENTERPRISES
COMPARATIVE INCOME STATEMENT
FOR THE YEARS ENDED DECEMBER 31, 2005 AND 2006

	2,006	2,005
Sales	998,000	888,000
Less: Cost of Goods Sold		
Merchandise Inventory, January 1	187,300	247,500
Add: Purchases	500,500	358,900
Goods Available for Sale	687,800	606,400
Less: Merchandise Inventory, December 31	319,000	187,300
Cost of Goods Sold	368,800	419,100
Gross Profit	629,200	468,900
Less: Operating Expenses		
Bad Debts Expense	24,000	8,700
Store Supplies Expense	5,200	5,000
Wages Expense	90,000	75,000
Rent Expense	42,000	36,000
Gas & Electricity Expense	12,000	6,000
Telephone Expense	7,000	3,600
Transportation Expense	9,800	8,000
Depreciation Expense - Truck	4,000	4,000
Depreciation Expense - Store Equipment	12,000	12,000
Advertising Expense	8,700	4,200
Taxes & Licenses Expense	3,000	3,000
Insurance Expense	2,200	1,800
Total Operating Expenses	219,900	167,300
Income from Operations	409,300	301,600
Add: Other Revenues		
Interest Revenues	5,000	3,000
Total Income	414,300	304,600
Less: Other Expenses		
Interest Expense	4,000	2,000
Net Income	410,300	302,600

DONNA ANNE ENTERPRISES
COMPARATIVE BALANCE SHEET
AS OF DECEMBER 31, 2005 AND 2006

	2006	2005
ASSETS		
CURRENT ASSETS		
Cash	328,200	245,000
Marketable Securities	23,000	23,000
Accounts Receivable, net	129,000	89,000
Prepaid Expenses	1,100	2,100
Merchandise Inventory	319,000	187,300
Store Supplies	12,800	8,700
TOTAL CURRENT ASSETS	813,100	555,100
LONG-TERM ASSETS		
Truck, net	64,000	68,000
Store Equipment, net	136,000	148,000
TOTAL LONG-TERM ASSETS	200,000	216,000
TOTAL ASSETS	1,013,100	771,100
LIABILITIES AND OWNER'S EQUITY		
CURRENT LIABILITIES		
Accounts Payable	168,700	116,300
Notes Payable, current	50,000	50,000
Wages Payable	3,000	2,500
Interest Payable	7,000	5,000
TOTAL CURRENT LIABILITIES	228,700	173,800
LONG-TERM LIABILITIES		
Notes Payable, non-current	200,000	250,000
TOTAL LIABILITIES	428,700	423,800
Donna Anne, Capital	584,400	347,300
TOTAL LIABILITIES AND OWNER'S EQUITY	1,013,100	771,100

QUICK REFERENCE GUIDE - CHAPTER HIGHLIGHTS

CHAPTER 01   THE ACCOUNTING PROFESSION

Accounting is the art of collecting, analyzing, recording and posting, summarizing and reporting financial transactions in a significant and orderly manner to provide useful information essential to decision making.

Bookkeeping is the recording phase of the accounting process. It involves recording accounting journal entries in the general journal and posting these general journal entries in the general ledger.

Auditing (sometimes referred to as public accounting) involves the application of generally accepted auditing standards, methods, testing and procedures in order to determine that business entities adhere to generally accepted accounting principles in the preparation of their financial statements The auditor, specifically, the **certified public accountant (CPA)** after conducting a thorough audit, issues an audit report whereby he expresses an opinion whether the financial statements present fairly the results of operation and financial condition of the business in accordance with generally accepted accounting principles (GAAPs) that are consistently applied.

The **FASB (Financial Accounting Standards Board)** issues pronouncements on generally accepted accounting principles. It is essential that certain principles are followed by accountants in order to maintain the integrity, reliability and fairness of financial statements.

The principle of **going concern** stipulates that the business entity will continue its normal operations and will not terminate its business operations.

The principle of **separate business entity** states that the business entity has a personality separate and distinct from its owners. All business transactions are analyzed and recorded from the point of view of the business, not from the point of view of the owner.

The principle of **consistency** states that accounting principles, rules, methods and procedures must be applied in the same manner from year to year in order to enhance the comparability and maintain the integrity of financial statement.

The principle of **full disclosure** provides that accounting information and other relevant information must be identified and explained in the financial statements so that the financial statements will provide better information and will not be misleading to the users of the financial information.

The principle of **materiality** is closely related to the full disclosure principle. According to the principle of materiality, businesses are obligated to disclose in their financial statements significant or material information that might affect the judgment of a reasonably informed person in making a decision that might be influenced by knowing or not knowing the material information.

The principle of **matching of costs and revenues** provides that revenues must be recorded in the same accounting period or over the same periods as expenses, costs or expenditures are spent or will provide the benefits, to earn the revenues.

The principle of **monetary measurement** means that money is the most appropriate unit of measure used in recording financial transactions and reporting financial statements.

The **realization** principle identifies that changes in assets, liabilities, revenues, costs, capital and expenses should not be recognized until the change is definitely certain and that the change is measurable in monetary terms to justify the recognition in the books of accounts.

CHAPTER 02   THE ACCOUNTING EQUATIONS

The **basic accounting equation** is expressed as $A = L + OE$. A stands for assets, L stands for liabilities and OE stands for owner's equity. The basic accounting equation serves as the foundation in analyzing business transactions. However, only the **three basic accounting elements** are expressed in the basic accounting equation. To make it easier for accounting students to analyze accounting transactions, the expanded accounting equation is introduced.

The **expanded accounting equation** is expressed as $A = L + C + R - E - D$. In addition to the basic accounting elements, assets and liabilities, the third basic accounting element, the owner/s' equity is expanded to include C for capital, R for revenues, E for expenses and D for drawing (for sole proprietorship and partnership) or dividends (for corporation).

Assets are (1) anything that the business owns such as cash, land, building, car, office equipment, computer, etc. (2) rights that are convertible into cash or another form of asset such as accounts receivable (the business has a right to collect the receivable from customer if it performs a service or sells merchandise and the customer did not pay cash at the time of purchase), patents (rights granted to inventor of products or technology), copyrights (rights granted to authors, musicians, composers, singers, painters, artists, sculptors, etc.); (3) prepaid expenses such as when the business makes a payment for car insurance covering a period of one year or makes advanced payment for one-year rent.

Current assets are cash and non-cash assets that will be converted into cash or will be consumed, used or expired within one year or one operating cycle whichever is longer. Cash, accounts receivable, merchandise inventory, supplies, prepaid expenses such as prepaid insurance, office supplies, notes receivable collectible in one year are examples of current assets.

Long-term assets are assets that are useful to the business for more than one year or one operating cycle, whichever is longer. Long-term assets are also known as (1) plant assets; (2) fixed assets; (3) property, plant and equipment and (4) long-lived assets.

Liabilities are the debts (indebtedness, loans or payables) of business, anything that it owes. Liabilities are classified based on their maturity period; **current liabilities** mature within one year or one operating cycle whichever is longer, whereas **long-term liabilities** have maturity dates beyond one year or one operating cycle whichever is longer.

Owner's Equity is the claim of the owner/s in the assets of the business. There are two parties who have legal rights to the assets of the business; the owners and the creditors. The creditors' claims are represented by the liabilities while the claims of the owner/s are represented by the owner/s' equity. In the expanded accounting equation, owner/s' equity is expressed as **C + R – E – D.**

Capital is the balance of the original investment of the owner/s increased by the cumulative owner/s' additional investments and net income and decreased by the cumulative net losses and owner/s' drawings or withdrawals (dividends for corporations).

Revenues represent the total amount of products or services billed to customers.

Expenses are the costs and charges that the business incurs to earn the revenues. The most common expenses are rent expense, utilities expense, wages expense, transportation expense, supplies expense, delivery expense, travel expense, gasoline expense, telephone expense, taxes and licenses expense, depreciation expense, insurance expense, miscellaneous expense, interest expense, etc.

The pillar of the basic foundation of accounting knowledge rests on a very good understanding of the accounting elements. **It is very important to know all the six accounting elements because the rules of debit and credit which are used in the analysis of transactions, recording in the general journal, posting in the general ledger are based on the accounting element affected by the transaction. Likewise, in the preparation of financial statements, the accounting elements also dictate the financial information shown in each particular financial statement.**

In analyzing transactions, recording in the general journal and posting to the general ledger, the rules of debits and credits are used to identify the necessary action (debit or credit) to the affected accounts. The **rules of debits and credits are based on the affected accounting elements.** In the preparation of financial statements items shown in each financial statement are also based on the accounting elements, meaning, **accounting elements are exclusively shown in specific financial statements, except for ending capital that is reported in both the equity statement and the balance sheet.**

CHAPTER 03   ACCOUNTING PROCESS: ANALYZING TRANSACTIONS

A **business transaction** is any event or happening measured in terms of money that has an affect on the financial condition or results of operations of a business entity. Each business transaction results in balanced effect to at least two accounts.

Analyzing is the process of evaluating the effects of business transactions on the accounting elements. Analyzing is the first step in the accounting process. It is very important because if the analysis of transactions is incorrect, wrong journal entries will be recorded in the general journal and this error will be carried over to the financial statements. It is therefore imperative that the correct transaction analysis be made in order to arrive at accurate financial reports.

According to the accounting principle of **separate business entity, the business entity is separate and distinct from its owners**. The business entity and its owners are two separate personalities, distinct and different from each other. **Transactions must be analyzed from the point of view of the business entity** and not from the point of view of the owners.

Transactions happen continuously and repetitiously as the business entity goes through its usual operations. Every day, business entities pay expenses, purchase assets, perform services, sell products, borrow money and incur liabilities, collect receivables, pay liabilities, allow owners to withdraw funds for personal use, etc. The same transactions happen throughout the life of the business and the same transactions are analyzed, recorded, reported and interpreted in the accounting process.

Accounting is precise and specific. For a unique transaction, the same analysis is done, and the same general journal entry is made in the accounting records.

In the process of analyzing transactions, the **rules of debit and credit** dictate the action to take, based on the effect of the transaction on the accounting elements, as shown in the expanded accounting equation, $A = L + C + R - E - D$.

- A for Assets, anything that the business owns
- L for Liabilities, anything that the business owes
- C for Capital, the claim of the owner/s in the assets of the business
- R for Revenues, the amount charged by the business to its customers for services performed or products sold (effectively increases owner's equity)
- E for expenses, the amount spent by the business to earn the revenues (effectively decreases owner's equity)
- D for Drawing (for sole proprietorship and partnership) or Dividends (for corporation), owner's withdrawal of assets, usually cash for personal use (effectively decreases owner's equity)

Capital, revenues, expenses and drawing/dividends are components of owner's equity.

In accounting, **debit simply means the left side of the account** and **credit simply means the right side of the account. There should be no other meaning to be associated with debit and credit.**

The **rules of debit and credit** identify the action to take (debit or credit) to specific accounts based on the effect (increase or decrease) of the transaction to the accounting elements. The rules of debit and credit are directly related to the expanded accounting equation. Both of them are based on the accounting elements. The expanded accounting equation is expressed as $A = L + C + R - E - D$. In algebra, the expanded accounting equation can also be expressed as $A + E + D = L + C + R$. The accounting elements on the left side of this derived equation, **assets, expenses and drawing/dividends follow the same debit and credit rule** and the accounting elements on the right side of this derived equation, **liabilities, capital and revenues follow the same debit** and credit rule. The **debit and credit rule for the assets, expenses and drawing/dividends is the opposite of the debit and credit rule for liabilities, capital and revenues.**

The rules of debit and credit for each accounting elements are shown below:

ACTION (DEBIT OR CREDIT)	EFFECT ON ACCOUNTING ELEMENT
DEBIT	INCREASES in ASSETS
CREDIT	DECREASES IN ASSETS
DEBIT	INCREASES in EXPENSES
CREDIT	DECREASES IN EXPENSES
DEBIT	INCREASES in DRAWING/DIVIDENDS
CREDIT	DECREASES IN DRAWING/DIVIDENDS
CREDIT	INCREASES in LIABILITIES
DEBIT	DECREASES IN LIABILITIES
CREDIT	INCREASES in CAPITAL
DEBIT	DECREASES IN CAPITAL
CREDIT	INCREASES in REVENUES
DEBIT	DECREASES IN REVENUES

The following illustration summarizes the rules of debit and credit.

ASSETS, EXPENSES and DRAWING		LIABILITIES, CAPITAL and REVENUES	
DEBIT	CREDIT	DEBIT	CREDIT
INCREASES	DECREASES	DECREASES	INCREASES

The **normal balance** of accounts is the **increased side** of the account. **Debit is the increased side of assets, expenses and drawing. Credit is the increased side of liabilities, capital and revenues.** Therefore, **debit balance is the normal balance of assets, expenses and drawing/dividends and credit balance is the normal balance of liabilities, capital and revenues.** It is important to know the normal balance of accounts because this knowledge will be helpful in analyzing transactions, recording general journal entries, posting to the general ledger and preparing accounting reports.

According to the **double entry accounting system (also called the dual accounting system), a business transaction affects at least two accounts and the debit and credit amounts recorded for the affected accounts must be balanced. A transaction can affect more than two accounts.**

Business entities develop a **chart of accounts, a list of account titles with their corresponding account codes that the business will use in recording and posting in the books of accounts and in reporting in the financial statements. The purpose of the chart of accounts is to make sure that the same account title and account codes are used for the same transaction in order to have uniformity in recording the same transactions**. Since there are many internal and external users of financial information shown in the financial statements of the business, it is therefore important to use standardized account titles so that there is consistency in the recording of specific transactions and reporting the same in the financial statements. In recording transactions, the **account titles as shown exactly in the chart of accounts must be used.**

Account codes are assigned based on the accounting elements. The prefix or the first digit in the account code identifies the accounting element of the account and the next 2 or 3 digits (small businesses usually have fewer accounts than larger businesses, so small businesses usually have 3 digit account codes and large businesses have 4 digit account codes) **is the sequence or order number of the account in the accounting element. Businesses assign the sequence number in the order that the accounts are presented in the financial statements.**

Devices or tools are used to facilitate analyzing transactions. The transaction analysis chart is a preliminary analysis of transactions and shows the following information:

Date of transaction
Accounting element (asset, liability, capital, revenues, expense, drawing or dividend)
Account title (as shown in the chart of accounts)
Effect (increase or decrease)
Action (debit or credit)
Debit amount
Credit amount

The heading of the transaction analysis chart shows the name of the business on the first line, the title of the report (transaction analysis chart) on the second line and the period covered on the third line. In processing each transaction, all debits must be written before the credits. A blank or space line separates each transaction. At the end of the report, total debit column must equal total credit column.

The **T account** is an accounting device that facilitates the analysis of transactions. It is called the T account because it is in the form of the letter T. A **T account has three parts, namely, the account title or account name, the debit side on the left side and the credit side on the right side. One T account is created for every account title.**

A transaction affecting the particular account title is posted either in the debit side or the credit side of the T account. In posting transactions to the T account it is advisable to indicate the date on the left side of each posted amount. It is easier to trace errors later if the postings are cross referenced by date.

Footing is the process of computing the total of each side of the T account by adding all the amounts on each side. Therefore since there are two sides to a T account, a **T account can have**

one or two footings, the **debit footing** and the **credit footing**. Footing is computed only if there are more than one amount posted on the side of the account, if there is only one amount posted, there is no need to compute the footing.

Balancing is the process of computing the balance or net amount of an account by getting the difference between the debit footing and the credit footing. **There is no need to compute the balance if an account has only one footing, the footing is already the balance of the account. The balance of an account is computed by deducting the smaller footing from the larger footing and the resulting balance is placed on the side with the larger footing.**

CHAPTER 04   ACCOUNTING PROCESS: THE BOOKS OF ACCOUNTS

The **accounting cycle** involves a series of activities undertaken during the accounting period to process business transactions and produce financial statements. The **accounting period** or **reporting period** is the period (can be one month, one quarter, six months, one year, etc.) covered in the heading of the income statement. An **accounting year** is any twelve-month period. An accounting year can be a calendar year or a fiscal year. A **calendar year** follows the calendar; it starts on January 1 and ends on December 31. A **fiscal year** is any twelve-month period that does not start on January 1.

The steps undertaken during the accounting cycle comprise the **accounting process**. The accounting process has three basic phases, the input, the processing and the output. The inputs in the accounting process are the source documents which support the business transactions. The processing phase involves analyzing the effects of the transaction in the accounting elements and recording them in the books of accounts. In the output phase (sometimes called the reporting phase), financial statements, namely, the income statement, equity statement, balance and statement of cash flows are produced. The steps in the accounting process are grouped into three major classifications, those that are done (1) during the current accounting period to record and post transactions as they happen, (2) at the end of the current accounting period to summarize and report financial statements and (3) at the beginning of the next accounting period to simplify the accounting process.

The steps in the accounting process are shown below:

I.   During the current accounting period

        1. Analyzing business transactions
        2. Journalizing (recording) accounting entries in the general journal
        3. Posting (classifying) to the general ledger

II. At the end of the current accounting period

        4. Preparing (summarizing) the trial balance
        5. Preparing and recording the adjusting entries in the general journal and posting them to the general ledger
        6. Preparing the worksheet

7. Preparing the adjusted trial balance
8. Preparing the financial statements (income statement, equity statement, balance sheet and statement of cash flows)
9. Preparing and recording the closing entries in the general journal and posting them to the general ledger
10. Preparing the post-closing trial balance (also called after closing trial balance)

III. At the start of the next accounting period

11. Preparing and recording reversing entries in the general journal and posting them in the general ledger

There are two general books of accounts in accounting. These are the **general journal** and the **general ledger**.

The **general journal** is called the **book of original entry** because it is the **first formal record** of accounting transactions. **Journalizing**, which is the **recording phase** of accounting is the process of recording business transactions in the general journal in **chronological order** as they happen. Using the information obtained from source documents, transactions are analyzed and their effects in the accounting elements are recorded in the general journal through the general journal entries. **For every transaction, a general journal entry is prepared. Each general journal entry must have at least one debit account and one credit account and the total of the debit amount/s must equal the total of the credit amount/s.** A *simple entry* is a journal entry that has one debit and one credit, only two accounts are affected by the transaction. A *compound entry* **is a journal entry that has more than one debit and/or credit, 3 or more accounts are affected by the transaction.**

The general journal is actually a thick book with several pages that are sequentially pre-numbered and each page contains the following columns of information:

Date
Document Reference
Account Code
Description
Posting Reference
Debit Amount
Credit Amount

Accounting entries are classified into several types based on the transactions that they document, the timing when they are recorded and the objective that they attain. In addition, accounting entries are also classified based on the number of accounts affected by the transaction.

General journal entries are recorded **chronologically in the general journal during the accounting period as the transactions occur**. Source documents, such as sales invoices, official receipts, checks, etc. are used to provide information in the preparation of general journal entries.

Adjusting entries or adjustments are recorded in the general journal at the **end of the accounting period after the trial balance is prepared** in order to reflect the correct balances of accounts that are affected by the adjustments. After all adjustments are posted to the general ledger, an **adjusted trial balance** is prepared which serves as the basis in the preparation of the **financial statements.**

Financial statements are formal accounting reports that include the (1) **income statement,** (2) **equity statement (statement of owner's equity for single proprietorship; statement of partner's equity for partnership; statement of retained earnings and stockholders' equity for corporation)** and (3) **balance sheet.** Some businesses include the **statement of cash flows** in their financial statements.

Closing entries are recorded in the general journal at the **end of the accounting period after the financial statements are prepared in order to zero out the balances of temporary** or **nominal** accounts. Temporary or nominal accounts include (1) **revenues** (such as sales, service fees, interest revenues, rental revenues, etc.), (2) **costs and expenses** (such as purchases, salaries expense, rent expense, depreciation expense, telephone expense, etc.) and (3) **drawing** (single proprietorship and partnership) or **dividends** (corporation). Notice that these accounts, **revenues, costs, expenses and drawing or dividends are sometimes called temporary equity accounts because they are closed to the permanent equity account capital (single proprietorship and partnership) or retained earnings (corporation)** The balances of temporary accounts are zeroed out at end of the current accounting period so that they will not be carried over in the next accounting period.

Correcting entries are recorded **any time** in the general journal and posted to the general ledger in order to **correct accounting entries that were previously recorded erroneously.** Correcting entries should be recorded **as soon as the error is identified.**

Memorandum or memo entries are made only as notation in the general journal to describe certain transactions that need to be documented, which do not affect the balances of accounts and therefore no debit or credit account and amount are recorded in the general journal. An example of a memo entry is the declaration of stock dividends or stock splits for corporations.

Reversing entries are recorded in the general journal on the **first day of the next accounting period before any transactions for the next accounting period are recorded** in order to **reverse the adjustments or adjusting entries that increase assets or liabilities.** Not all adjusting entries are reversed.

Accounting entries can also be classified based on the number of account titles affected by the transaction. A **simple entry** is an accounting entry that affects only one debit account title and one credit account title; only two accounts are affected. A **compound entry** is an accounting entry that affects more than two account titles; three or more accounts are affected.

The general ledger is called the **book of final entry** because it is the last book of accounts that reflect the effect of business transactions on the accounting elements. **Posting or classifying** is the process of transcribing or transferring information from the general journal to the general ledger. Each account in the general journal entry is posted in the general ledger in the same order that they appear in the general journal, however, accounting information are presented in the general ledger arranged **by account code according to the chart of accounts.**

Just like the general journal, the general ledger is a book of many pages that are sequentially **pre-numbered.** A page in the general ledger contains the following columns:

GENERAL LEDGER

PAGE:_____

ACCOUNT CODE: _____   TITLE: _____

DATE	DESCRIPTION	POST REF	TRANSACTION DEBIT	CREDIT	BALANCE DEBIT	CREDIT

The above columns contain the following information:

DATE: date of the transaction copied from the general journal

DESCRIPTION: explanation of the transaction copied from the last line of the general journal entry in the general journal

POST REF: constant letters GJ nnn; GJ means general journal and nnn is the page number of the general journal where the general journal entry is recorded

TRANSACTION DEBIT AMOUNT: copy the debit amount from the general journal

TRANSACTION CREDIT AMOUNT: copy the credit amount from the general journal

BALANCE DEBIT AMOUNT: debit balance is computed by adding the last debit balance to the debit transaction amount OR subtracting the credit transaction amount from the previous debit balance

BALANCE CREDIT AMOUNT: credit balance is computed by adding the last credit balance to the credit transaction amount OR subtracting the debit transaction amount from the previous credit balance

For **every posting** in the general ledger a **running balance of the account is always computed.**

Cross-referencing facilitates the process of matching the general journal entry in the general journal to the posting in the general ledger through the page numbers reflected in the posting reference of both books of accounts. By writing the GL page number in the general journal, the accountant is guided that the particular general journal entry has been posted and therefore, it will not be posted more than once. It is easier to trace errors (for instance, trial balance is out of balance) in accounting records if both books of accounts are cross-referenced.

After posting an entry in the general ledger, the *post reference column in the general journal must be filled in with the page number of the general ledger where the entry is posted*. Filling in the post reference column of the general journal indicates that the entry has been posted to the general ledger.

The *T account* is referred to as a simplified version of the general ledger.

CHAPTER 05   ACCOUNTING PROCESS: THE TRIAL BALANCE

The summarizing process is the first in a series of steps done at the end of the accounting period. During the summarizing process, the **trial balance is prepared using the ending account balances in the general ledger. The trial balance** is an accounting report prepared at the end of the accounting period that shows the account titles and their corresponding balances with the total debit column amount equal to the total credit column amount. The trial balance shows the equality of debit total and credit total.

The heading of the trial balance shows the name of the business on the first line, the title of the report (trial balance) on the second line and the date of the trial balance on the third line. To prepare the trial balance, simply copy the account titles and the corresponding balances from the general ledger. Add the amounts in the debit and credit columns. The total for both columns must equal. **Accounts with zero balances are not shown in the trial balance.** So even if there are so many accounts in the chart of accounts, only the ones with balances are reflected in the trial balance.

At the end of the accounting period, three types of trial balance are prepared, based on the timing when they are done. The three types of trial balance are:

1. The **trial balance** is prepared after all general journal entries are posted to the general ledger. The preparation of the trial balance is the first step done at the end of accounting period. The trial balance provides the initial balance in the worksheet.

2. The **adjusted trial balance** is prepared after all adjusting entries/adjustments are recorded in the general journal and posted in the general ledger, incorporating the effect of the adjustments in the affected accounts. The adjusted trial balance provides the information used in the preparation of the financial statements (the income statement, equity statement, balance sheet and statement of cash flows).

3. The **post closing trial balance also called the after closing trial balance** is prepared after all closing entries are recorded in the general journal and posted in the general

ledger. It contains only balance sheet or permanent accounts (assets, liabilities and capital). The post closing trial balance provides the beginning balance of the accounts for the next accounting period.

CHAPTER 06 ACCOUNTING PROCESS: THE ADJUSTING ENTRIES

Adjusting entries or adjustments are recorded at the end of the accounting period after the trial balance, but before the financial statements are prepared in order to reflect the correct balance of accounts. If adjusting entries are not made, the balance of some accounts will be overstated while the balance of some accounts will be understated.

The matching of costs and revenues principle states that costs and expenses must be recorded in the same accounting period that the related revenues are recorded. For example, bad debts expense for uncollectible accounts receivable are recorded in the same accounting period when the credit was extended to the customer for products sold or services rendered.

Under the **cost recovery principle**, certain purchases of goods or services or prepayments of expenses in the current period, the benefits of which are applicable to future periods (like the payment of one-year insurance premium) are initially recorded as assets. When these goods, services or prepaid expenses are used, consumed or expired as time passes by, then these assets are reduced and correspondingly transferred to the appropriate expense accounts. For example, businesses usually buy office supplies in bulk, to be consumed for several months. At the time of purchase, an asset account, Office Supplies is debited. As the office supplies are consumed, no accounting entries are recorded; it will be impractical and time consuming to make an accounting entry every time ball pens, copy papers, paper clips, staples, etc. are consumed. The accounting practice is to count the office supplies at the end of the accounting period and allocate the cost corresponding to the office supplies on hand. The difference between the available office supplies (beginning balance of office supplies plus purchases of office supplies during the period) and the ending balance of office supplies resulting from the inventory count is considered as the office supplies consumed. The office supplies consumed is then transferred from the asset Office Supplies to an expense account Office Supplies Expense.

Expressed or explicit transactions are the routinary, ordinary and repetitious transactions that occur during the ordinary course of business. These transactions are supported by source documents. **In recording expressed transactions, the information used is definite and specific, and the actual amounts, not estimates are used because they come from the source documents that serve as the evidence of the business transaction.**

Implied or implicit transactions are incidents or events, such as the passage of time, that are not recorded during the course of ordinary business, but are accounted only at the end of the accounting period as adjusting entries or adjustments. Examples of implied transactions are the recording of depreciation expense for long-term assets, bad debts expense for uncollectible accounts, the transfer from asset to expense of expired insurance, office supplies used, used rent, used interest, etc. Unlike the actual amount used in the recording of expressed transactions, **the amount recorded for implied transactions are derived from calculations, not directly as indicated in the source documents.** Sometimes, the amounts are based on estimates using the historical experience of the business, such as the recording of depreciation expense and bad debts expense. **It must be remembered however that before an implied transaction can happen, it is preceded by a related expressed transaction.** Before the implied transaction of recording depreciation expense can be made, an expressed transaction, the purchase of asset must happen beforehand. The recording of bad debts expense is preceded by the recording of accounts receivable for the performance of services on account or sale of products on account. The recording of office supplies expense is preceded by the purchase of office supplies.

Under the **cash basis of accounting, transactions are recorded only when cash is received or when cash is paid.** In other words, when services are rendered on account or when a product is sold on account, or when an asset is bought on account, these transactions are not reflected in the accounting records, because no cash is received or paid. Effectively, under the cash basis of accounting, there are no liability accounts and no receivable accounts. The **cash basis violates the matching of costs and revenues principle of accounting. The cost recovery principle of recording expenses is also violated by the cash basis.** The cash basis results in incomplete records of business transactions and it is therefore very difficult to reconcile non-cash transactions as they are not even recorded. **Under the cash basis of accounting, no adjusting entries are recorded at the end of the accounting period.** The cash basis results in incomplete accounting records and consequently if users of financial statements will use financial statements produced under the cash basis, it is very likely that they will make erroneous decisions.

The deficiencies of the cash basis of accounting are corrected by the accrual basis. Under the **accrual basis, the effects of all transactions on the financial statements are recognized, even though no cash is received or no cash is paid.** Revenues are recorded when they are earned or rendered whether or not cash is received. Expenses are recorded when they are incurred, whether or not cash is paid. For example, if the business renders services on account, Accounts Receivable is debited and Revenues is credited. Under the cash basis of accounting, this transaction will not be recorded because no cash was received. If the business has an outstanding loans payable, and the monthly interest payments are paid every 15th of the month, the month-end financial statements must reflect the effect of an adjusting entry debiting Interest Expense and crediting Interest Payable for the accrual of the half-month interest from the 16th to month-end, even though it has not yet paid said interest at month-end. **Under the accrual basis, adjusting entries are recorded at the end of the accounting period to reflect the correct balance of accounts.**

Prepaid expenses are expenses paid in advance, the benefit, use or consumption of which is chargeable to the current period and to future accounting period/s after the payment was made. Prepaid expenses are classified as current assets if they will benefit the business for a period of one year or less; if the benefit is for more than one year, then they are shown in the balance sheet as current assets for the portion good for one year and long term assets for the portion beyond one year. There are two ways to account for prepaid expenses, namely:

    A.   **Asset method: Upon payment, an asset account, such as Prepaid Expense** (ex. Prepaid Insurance or Office Supplies) **is debited and Cash is credited. When adjusting entries are made at the end of the accounting period, the portion of the asset Prepaid Expense that expired/used/consumed from the date of payment up to the end of the accounting period is expensed and must be recorded as debit to an expense account (ex. Supplies Expense or Insurance Expense). The **reduction in the asset Prepaid Expense is recorded as credit to Prepaid Expense**, such as Prepaid Insurance or Office Supplies.

B. **Expense Method: Upon payment, an expense account** (ex. Insurance Expense or Supplies Expense) **is debited and Cash is credited. When adjusting entries are made at the end of the accounting period, the portion NOT YET expired/used/consumed is an asset and must be recorded as debit to Prepaid Expense** (ex. Office Supplies or Prepaid Insurance). The **unexpired or unused portion is a reduction from the expense account and is recorded as a credit to the appropriate expense account**, such as Office Supplies Expense or Insurance Expense.

At the end of the accounting period, it is very likely that there are some expenses that the business already incurred, although, they are not yet paid in cash. These expenses are called **accrued expenses (also called unpaid expenses).** At the end of the accounting period, accrued expenses must be recorded because if they are left unrecorded, the corresponding expense item will be understated, resulting in overstatement of net income. Since accrued expenses are not yet due for payment, a liability account must be recorded to recognize that the business has an obligation to pay the accrued expenses on due date. If accrued liabilities are not recorded at the end of the accounting period, the total liabilities of the business will be understated. Many businesses use the word **accrued** before the liability account title to distinguish accrued liability (used only in adjusting entries) from ordinary liability. However, it is also acceptable simply to use directly the liability account, without using the word accrued. What is important is to record the accrued expenses and the corresponding liability at the end of the accounting period.

The adjusting entry to record accrued expense is to **debit the expense account and credit the accrued liability account.**

Accrued revenues are revenues already earned but have not yet been collected at the end of the accounting period. Accrued revenues give rise to accrued receivables. Accrued revenues are recorded at the end of the accounting period in order to reflect the correct balance of the revenues of the business. If accrued revenues are not recorded then the revenues of the business will be understated resulting in understatement of net income in the income statement and understatement of the owner's equity account in the balance sheet. Since accrued revenues are not yet due for collection, an asset account, accrued receivable is recorded in order to recognize that the business has a right to collect from a customer for services already rendered or an implicit transaction already happened, such as the passage of time in the case of notes receivable.

The adjusting entry to record the accrual of unrecorded revenues is to debit the asset account accrued receivable and credit revenues.

Unearned revenues (also called deferred credit or deferred revenues) are revenues collected in advance even though they are not yet earned. In other words, the business already collected cash before it performed the services or sold the product to its customers. **Unearned revenues**

are classified as current liabilities because the business is obligated to perform a service or sell a product in the future in exchange for the cash that it collected in advance. Typical examples of unearned revenues are collecting advanced subscription payment for magazines or newspapers, selling season tickets to sports events, collecting advanced rent from tenants, restaurants collecting deposits for reservations, lottery ticket receipts good for several drawings collected in advance, etc. It is important to record properly what portion of customer advances have been earned, which should be appropriately recorded as revenues and what portion is unearned which should be appropriately recorded as liability.

The two methods of accounting for unearned revenues are the liability method and the revenue method.

(1) Under **the liability method**, at the time of the collection of the advanced payment, a liability account, unearned revenues is credited and asset cash is debited for the same amount. At the end of the year, an adjusting entry is recorded whereby the earned portion is credited to earned revenues and the liability account unearned revenues is debited for the same amount.

(2) Under the **revenue method**, a revenue account is credited at the time of the collection of the advanced payment and asset cash is debited for the same amount. At the end of the year, an adjusting entry is recorded whereby the unearned portion is credited to a liability account, unearned revenues and the revenue account is debited for the same amount.

Depreciation is the cost allocation of long-term tangible assets over its useful life. Long-term assets are also called (1) plant assets, (2) fixed assets, (3) property plant and equipment and (4) long-lived assets. These are assets that serve the business for many years. Long term assets are classified into tangible assets (such as land, building, office equipment, delivery equipment, trucks, van, etc.), intangible assets (such as copyrights, patents, goodwill, trademarks, etc.) and wasting assets or natural resources (such as gold mine, oil deposits, marble deposits, diamond mines, etc.).

Tangible long term assets are assets that have physical substance. These are assets that are sensible to the senses (can be seen, heard, touched, etc.). When a long term asset is acquired, its cost (also called acquisition cost) is recorded as debit to the corresponding asset account and reflected in the balance sheet. As the long term asset is used in the business, the cost applicable to the period that the asset was used is charged to expense, by transferring the allocated cost portion from asset to expense. This is in compliance with the principle of matching of cost and revenues. As long as the asset is used to produce revenues, the portion of the asset used to earn the revenues is allocated to expense. If depreciation expense is not recorded, the book value of the asset will remain the same, hence will be overstated. As the asset is depreciated, its book value diminishes over time. Sometimes, obsolescence or the state at which the asset loses its usefulness also demands that the asset be depreciated. In addition, mere passage of time also reduces the book value of the asset.

The **book value** is the undepreciated cost of the asset and it is equal to cost minus accumulated depreciation. **Accumulated depreciation (also called allowance for depreciation)** is the depreciated cost of the asset, which is the cumulative total of the depreciation expenses over the years from the first year that the asset was placed in production. Accumulated depreciation is a contra asset account and it is presented in the balance sheet as a deduction from the related asset account.

When a long-term asset is acquired, the business *estimates* the useful life of the asset. **Useful life** is the number of years that the business will use the asset; it is the number of years that the asset will be productive. Sometimes, useful life is expressed as the number of units of product that the asset will produce. For a fabric making machine, useful life is expressed in the number of yards of cloth that the machine will produce. For transportation equipment, useful life is sometimes expressed as the number of miles that the vehicle will cover over its life.

At the time of asset acquisition, the business also *estimates* the **salvage value (also called residual value or scrap value or disposal value)** of the asset. **Salvage value** is the amount that the business will receive when the asset is disposed or sold at the end of its useful life, when it is fully depreciated.

The **straight line depreciation method** assumes that assets are depreciated based on a uniform depreciation rate every year; the annual depreciation expense is fixed, constant and the same throughout the useful life of the asset. Depreciation rate is equal to 1 divided by the useful life of the asset. If the useful life is 10 years, then the depreciation rate is 10% (1/10). The **depreciable cost of an asset is equal to cost minus salvage value.**

Two ways to compute the annual depreciation expense using the straight line method are shown below:

(1) Annual depreciation expense = (Cost minus salvage value) x 1/useful life
   Note that cost minus salvage value is the depreciable cost of the asset and 1/useful life is the depreciation rate

(2) Annual depreciation expense = (Cost minus salvage value) / useful life
   Again, in the above formula, the numerator is the depreciable cost of the asset.

The same amount of annual depreciation expense will result using either one of the above formula.

CHAPTER 07   ACCOUNTING PROCESS: THE WORKSHEET

At the end of the accounting period, the worksheet is prepared to facilitate the preparation of the financial statements. The worksheet is an accounting device or tool, not an accounting report. It contains the account titles and 5 pairs of debit and credit money columns for trial balance, adjustments, adjusted trial balance, income statement and balance sheet. The account titles are shown in the order that they appear in the chart of accounts, i.e. assets, liabilities, owner's equity, revenues, costs and expenses.

The **first pair of money column** shows the trial balance and serves as the beginning balance used in the worksheet.

The **second pair of money column** shows the adjustments or adjusting entries that affect accounts that need to be adjusted at the end of the accounting period. Adjustments must be made for some accounts because the balances of these accounts will be overstated or understated if the adjustments are not made.

The **third pair of money column** shows the adjusted trial balance, which reflects the accurate balances of the accounts, with the effect of adjustments already effected in the balances. In the adjusted trial balance money columns, the accounts affected by the adjustments will show a different balance from the trial balance amount, whereas accounts not affected by the adjustments will show the same balance as the trial balance amount because the trial balance amounts are simply extended or copied to the appropriate column in the adjusted trial balance. The total debit and total credit must equal for the trial balance, adjustments and the adjusted trial balance, the first three pairs of money columns.

The **fourth pair of money column** shows the balance of income statement accounts. The balances of revenues, costs and expenses in the adjusted trial balance are simply extended or copied to the income statement column. The total debit and total credit in the income statement column are not equal. The difference between the debit total and credit total is the result of operations for the period. If the total debit is larger than the total credit, the difference is the net loss of the business and if the total credit is larger than the total debit, the difference is the net income for the period.

The **last pair of money column** shows the balance of balance sheet accounts. The balances of assets, liabilities and equity accounts are copied to the balance sheet column. Just like in the income statement column, the total debit and total credit in the balance sheet column are not equal. The difference between the total debit and total credit in the balance sheet column must equal the difference between the total debit and total credit in the income statement column. This difference must be added to the column with the smaller amount for both the income statement and balance sheet columns, and when this difference (net income or net loss) is added to the column with the smaller amount then the debit total and credit total for the income statement and balance sheet columns will equal. It is only after adding the net income or net loss to the money columns with smaller amount that the total debit and total credit of the income statement and balance sheet will equal.

CHAPTER 08   ACCOUNTING PROCESS: THE FINANCIAL STATEMENTS

Accounting reports are used by a business entity to communicate the state of its financial health and the results of its operations to the various users of financial information. They are also used to back-up or provide more detailed information about a particular account being analyzed. Sometimes, management and key officers of businesses require special reports to provide information needed in addressing and resolving operational and financial issues that require decision making actions. Accounting reports are also used to monitor operational and financial performance by comparing actual results with pre-determined budgeted amounts, planned targets and standard rates. Any deviation of the actual results against the predetermined amounts is analyzed and the cause for the deviation is scrutinized. Accounting reports are also used to provide inputs in making financial forecasts and budgets. Standard rates for specific costs, for instance direct labor standard rate in a manufacturing business are also established using actual costs provided in accounting reports.

Formal accounting reports are the **financial statements** which consist of the (1) income statement, (2) equity statement and (3) balance sheet. Some businesses include the **statement of cash flows** among its financial statements. These four formal accounting reports are generally used by the external and internal users of financial information, such as the investors, creditors, government, management, etc. in evaluating the financial situation of the business. These parties use the financial reports in making financial decisions related to the business or to their stake in the business. **Informal accounting reports** include all accounting reports other than the financial statements that assist the users of financial information in making decisions.

The financial statements are prepared at the end of the accounting period after the completion of the adjusted trial balance. Usually, the worksheet is prepared in order to facilitate the preparation of the financial statements. The first three financial statements **must be prepared in the proper sequence**. Income statements must be prepared first because the results of operations (net income or net loss) are used as input to the equity statement. The second report, the equity statement is prepared after the income statement and before the balance sheet because the ending capital in the equity statement is used as the ending capital in the balance sheet. To summarize, the income statement provides the net income or net loss that is used in the equity statement, and the equity statement provides the ending capital needed in the balance sheet. The statement of cash flows is prepared as needed.

The **income statement** identifies the accounting period being covered in the reporting process, therefore, an accounting period can be one month, one quarter, one semester, one year, etc. based on the period reported in the income statement. The **income statement shows the revenues, costs, expenses and the net income or net loss for a given period of time.**

The type of **equity statement** prepared for a particular business entity depends on the ownership structure of the business as identified below:

OWNERSHIP STRUCTURE	EQUITY STATEMENT
Sole Proprietorship	Statement of Owner's Equity
Partnership	Statement of Partners Equity
Corporation	Statement of Stockholders Equity

The **equity statement shows the changes in the owner's/s' equity (sole proprietor, partners or stockholders as the case maybe),** by showing the capital at the beginning of the period, increased by additional investments and net income for the period and decreased by net loss, drawings of owner or partners for a sole proprietorship or partnership respectively, or dividends to stockholders in the case of corporation. The final amount in the equity statement is the capital at the end of the accounting period being reported.

The equity statement is prepared **after the income statement and before the balance sheet.** The final amount in the income statement (net income or net loss, as the case maybe) is used in the equity statement while the amount of ending capital computed in the equity statement is used in the balance sheet.

The **balance sheet shows the assets, liabilities and ending capital and reports on the financial position or financial condition of the business as of a given date.** The balance sheet is a formal presentation of the basic accounting equation, **A = L + OE (Assets = Liabilities plus Owner's Equity).** The two forms of balance sheet are the **report form** and the **account form.** The distinction between the balance sheet forms depends on the presentation of assets, liabilities and owner's ending capital and there is no other difference between them. In the **report form** balance sheet, assets are presented on top of the report and the liabilities and owner's ending capital are shown below the assets. In the **account form** balance sheet, assets are presented on the left side of the report while liabilities and owner's ending capital are presented on the right side of the report.

Cash is a very important and key asset of any business. Since majority of business transactions involve the receipt and payment of cash, a fourth financial statement, the **statement of cash flows** is often added to the three basic financial statements of income statement, equity statement and the balance sheet. FASB (Financial Accounting Standards Board) requires the statement of cash flows as a basic financial statement for corporations. By simply knowing the balance of cash in the balance sheet, a thorough analysis of the cash account can not be made. In evaluating the paying capacity of a business, it is necessary to analyze in detail the cash transactions during the accounting period. The **statement of cash flows** shows the **inflows and outflows of cash** during the **accounting period. Only cash transactions** are shown in the statement of cash flows. Non-cash transactions are excluded from the statement of cash flows. **Cash inflows** are transactions that generate or increase cash while **cash outflows** are transactions that disburse or decrease cash. In other words, only cash receipts and cash payments are included in the statement of cash flows. In the statement of cash flows, cash transactions are classified into **operating, financing and investing activities.**

Operating activities are transactions that affect the income statement that are necessary to generate income for the business. **Operating activities include transactions that affect revenues, costs and expenses.** Operating activities include the payment of expenses, payment to suppliers for purchase of stock-in-trade and receipt from customers for cash sales and collection of accounts receivable. **Financing activities** are transactions that involve increasing cash through borrowings (obtaining loan from creditors or issuing certificates of indebtedness such as bonds) or obtaining investments from the owners or stockholders. Cash outflows in financing activities include payment of loans to creditors, redemption of bonds issued, re-purchase of company stocks (called treasury stocks), and payment of owner's cash withdrawal or cash dividends to stockholders. Note that the receipt of dividend income is an inflow from operating activities but the payment of dividends to stockholders is an outflow from financing activities. **Financing activities** include cash transactions with the creditors or stockholders or the owner/s of the business.

Investing activities are transactions that involve the purchase and sale of long-term assets, extending long-term non-trade loans to debtors and collecting the same, and purchase and sale of other companies' stocks and bonds intended as long-term investments, which are not marketable securities or cash equivalents (very liquid, readily convertible to cash).

There are two methods of computing cash flows from operating activities. Under the **direct method**, operating disbursements are simply deducted from operating receipts or collections to arrive at the net cash flow from operating activities. Under the **indirect method**, net income computed under the accrual accounting is adjusted to reflect only cash receipts and disbursements.

CHAPTER 09   ACCOUNTING PROCESS: THE CLOSING ENTRIES AND THE POST CLOSING TRIAL BALANCE

Closing entries are accounting entries prepared at the end of the accounting period, after the preparation of the financial statements in order to zero out the balance of nominal or temporary accounts, namely, revenues, costs, expenses (income statement accounts) and drawing. Closing entries are recorded in the general journal and posted to the general ledger to prepare the accounts for the next accounting period. **Note that not all accounts are closed. Real accounts**, also known as **permanent or balance sheet accounts** such as assets, liabilities and capital accounts are not closed. The **balance of nominal accounts are not carried over to the next accounting period, that is why these accounts are closed at the end of the accounting period.** The balance of permanent accounts is carried over to the next accounting period. Nominal accounts with debit balance are closed by crediting each account for the balance amount and debiting Income and Expense Summary for the total of the credited amounts. Nominal accounts with credit balance are closed by debiting each account for the balance amount and crediting Income and Expense Summary for the total of the debited amounts. After the nominal accounts are closed, the remaining balance of Income and Expense Summary is closed to Capital. Finally, the balance of drawing account is closed to Capital.

During the closing process, Income and Expense Summary, a new temporary account is introduced. The balance of Income and Expense Summary is also closed during the closing process.

The four closing entries are shown below:

PURPOSE	CLOSING ENTRY
1. Close credit balance accounts to Income and Expense Summary	Debit *each* credit balance account Credit the sum of all credit balance accounts to Income and Expense Summary
2. Close debit balance accounts to Income and Expense Summary	Debit the sum of all debit balance accounts to Income and Expense Summary Credit *each* debit balance account

3. Close Income and Expense Summary to Capital	If the resulting balance of Income and Expense Summary from 1 and 2 above is *debit* *(total debit per item 2 is greater than total credit per item 1), the business operation resulted in net loss*
	Debit Capital Credit Income and Expense Summary
	If the resulting balance of Income and Expense Summary from 1 and 2 above is *credit* *(total credit per item 1 is greater than total debit per item 2), the business operation resulted in net income*
	Debit Income and Expense Summary Credit Capital
4. Close Drawing to Capital	Debit Capital Credit Drawing

The last step in the accounting process done for the current accounting period is the preparation of the post closing trial balance, also called the after closing trial balance. As the name suggests, it is prepared after the recording of the closing entries in the general journal and posting them in the general ledger. Since the balances of temporary or nominal accounts are zeroed out during the closing process, only the real or permanent accounts are shown in the post closing trial balance. Therefore, only the balance sheet accounts, namely, assets, liabilities and capital are carried over to the next accounting period. The post closing trial balance shows the account titles for asset, liability and capital with their corresponding balances. The amounts in the post closing trial balance will serve as the beginning balance for assets, liabilities and capital for the next accounting period. Just like the ordinary trial balance, the total debit must equal the total credit.

CHAPTER 10   ACCOUNTING PROCESS: THE REVERSING ENTRIES

Reversing entries are accounting entries recorded in the general journal on the **first day of the next accounting period before any transactions for the next accounting period are recorded** in order to **reverse adjustments or adjusting entries** that increase assets or liabilities. Not all adjusting entries are reversed. To reverse an entry simply means to debit the account credited and credit the account debited in the original adjusting entry. In other words, do the opposite of what was done in the original adjusting entry. Reversing entries are prepared to simplify the recording of transactions and to adhere to the accounting principle of consistency.

The following adjusting entries are reversed:

1. prepaid expenses using the expense method

2. unearned revenues using the revenue method

3. accrual of revenues and receivables

4. accrual of expenses and payables

Upon pre-payment of the expense, a journal entry is prepared to debit the expense account and credit cash. At the end of the accounting period, an adjusting entry is prepared debiting an asset for the unexpired or unused portion of the expense and crediting the expense account, to recognize the asset for the unused or unexpired portion. After posting the adjusting entry to the expense account, the balance of the expense account is the used or expired portion. At the beginning of the next accounting period, the adjusting entry is reversed, by simply debiting the expense account and crediting the asset account in the adjusting entry. The reversing entry makes the balance of the prepaid expense equal to zero and establishes the balance of the expense account equal to the unused or unexpired portion.

Upon the advanced collection of the revenues, a general journal entry is made to debit cash and credit the revenues account (for example subscriptions revenues, ticket sales revenues, rent revenues, etc.). At the end of the accounting period, the unearned portion of the revenues account is recognized as a liability by crediting the unearned portion and debiting the revenues account for the same amount. After posting the adjusting entry, the balance of the revenues account is the portion already earned and this amount is closed to Income and Expense Summary during the closing process. At the start of the next accounting period, a reversing entry is made debiting the unearned revenue account and crediting the revenues account. The reversing entry will zero out unearned revenues.

Accrued revenues are revenues already earned but not yet collected as of the end of the accounting period. Since these are already earned but remains uncollected, the business must record an asset to recognize that it has a right to collect from its customers/debtors. At the end of the accounting period, an adjusting entry is made debiting a receivable account and crediting the revenues account Typical example of accrued revenues are interest revenues due on notes receivable, rental revenues for landlords, retainer fees of professionals such as lawyer's, etc. At the start of the next accounting period, the adjusting entry is reversed by debiting the revenues account and crediting the receivable account.

Accrued expenses are expenses that are already incurred but remain unpaid as at the end of the accounting period. Since these are already incurred even though still unpaid, the business must record a liability to recognize that it has an obligation to pay its creditors. At the end of the accounting period, an adjusting entry is made debiting an expense account and crediting a liability account Typical example of accrued expenses are accrued wages, accrued interest notes payable, accrued rent, accrued income tax payable, etc. At the start of the next accounting period, the adjusting entry is reversed by debiting the liability account and crediting the expense account.

CHAPTER 11   FINANCIAL STATEMENTS ANALYSIS

Businesses prepare financial statements in order to satisfy the information needs of various users of financial information. The usefulness of financial statements is served only when they are analyzed. Without analysis, the financial information in financial statements is simply a list of account titles and their corresponding balances. In assessing company performance, the decision maker must make qualitative and quantitative evaluation. The decision maker must be well informed not only about the specific company but also about so many other considerations about the business world in general.

Qualitative evaluation pertains to matters that are not strictly financial in nature such as assessing the company environment by ascertaining its strengths, weaknesses, opportunities and threats. Qualitative evaluation includes looking at the relative presence of the company in the market, its market share, whether its actions influence the direction of the industry, the strength of its brand name, its reputation, goodwill, integrity in the business community, its business ethics practices, its corporate responsibility projects. The industry where the company belongs is also a factor in assessing future direction and financial performance. In addition to assessing the overall business environment, decision makers now scrutinize the business ethics practices of companies.

Business ethics refers to the standards of moral conduct in business; doing what is right under the circumstances. Corporations practicing ethical standards of conduct are preferred over those that have reputations of being unethical. Corporate responsibility is also a major consideration in assessing company performance.

Corporate responsibility pertains to how businesses give back to the community. It involves corporate philanthropy or corporate giving. Many big corporations are always ready to donate funds and resources where their help is needed.

Quantitative evaluation involves the analysis and relationships of the financial information and disclosures reflected in the financial statements. Financial statements are meaningless, without an analysis of its components.

There are several methods used in analyzing financial statements. Trend analysis, vertical and horizontal analysis, industry bench marks and financial ratios are used in quantitative evaluation of financial statements.

In evaluating companies, information is obtained from internal and external sources. Information from internal sources are those originating from the company being evaluated while external sources of information are provided by outside parties.

With the advancement in information technology, it is now a lot easier to research anything; companies' profiles, historical financial information, products and services, business plans, etc are all available in websites accessible through the internet. The annual report of companies issued during the annual stockholders' meeting provides a lot of useful financial and non-financial information. The management report section of the annual report explains management decisions and actions, opportunities, challenges and other significant aspects of the company operations. Disclosures in the financial statements are additional information that can be used in the financial evaluation of the company. In addition to the annual report, companies make periodic announcements to the print and broadcast media concerning their financial and operational performance. External information can be obtained from news articles about the company, usually covered by business magazines, newspapers, bulletins from financial services firms such as the Dun and Bradstreet and Morningstar that rates the stock market performance of various company stocks. Business magazines such as the Business Week, Fortune and Forbes publish an annual report on the rankings of corporations based on certain financial criteria, such as sales, net income, total assets, etc. A word of caution in obtaining company information is advised; insider trading, getting information from sources not available to other prudent investors is illegal and punishable by law. Many financial advisers, stock brokers and even investors were prosecuted, fined and jailed for engaging in insider trading.

Trend analysis involves using past and current financial information in predicting probable future outcomes. If conditions remain relatively stable, past performance is an effective means of forecasting future performance.

Vertical analysis involves analyzing the financial information pertaining to one accounting period and evaluating one item relative to another item in the same financial statement. In making the income statement evaluation, all items in the income statement are related to net sales, which is given a percentage equivalent of 100% and in the computation of the item percentage, the numerator is the item being evaluated and the denominator is always the net sales amount. The result is multiplied by 100 to convert it to per cent. For the balance sheet vertical analysis, total assets is given the percentage equivalent of 100% and in the computation of the item percentage, the numerator is the item being evaluated and the denominator is the total assets amount. The result is multiplied by 100 to convert it to per cent.

Horizontal analysis involves analyzing the same financial information pertaining to several accounting periods to establish the growth trends of that specific financial information. The earliest year is used as the starting point in establishing the base year. Horizontal analysis requires comparative financial statements. **Comparative financial statements** are financial statements that present financial information covering more than one accounting period; at least two accounting periods' financial information are presented in the financial statements.

Component percentages analysis is used when financial statement information are presented in percentages, to help in comparing the same company's financial performance from one period to another. Component percentages analysis is also used to facilitate the comparison of companies of different sizes. The financial statements that show component percentages, instead of absolute dollar amounts are known as **common-size financial statements.** For the income statement, net sales is assigned the equivalent of 100% and the component percentage of each income statement item is computed by dividing the dollar amount of the specific item by the net sales amount and the result is multiplied by 100 to convert it to per cent. For the balance sheet, total assets is assigned the equivalent of 100% and the component percentage of each balance sheet item is computed by dividing the dollar amount of the specific item by the total assets amount and the result is multiplied by 100 to convert it to per cent.

Financial ratios are essential yardsticks used in financial statement analysis. Financial ratios measure the **short term liquidity, long-term solvency and profitability** of businesses. Among the various users of financial information, the owners/equity investors and the creditors are the user groups who rely heavily on financial ratios before rendering financial decisions. Although creditors and owners/equity investors both intend to preserve their investments in the business, their financial interests in the company vary. Creditors want to be assured that they will be paid when it is time to collect maturing liabilities of their debtors. Creditors are interested in the short term liquidity and long term solvency of their debtors. On the other hand, owners/equity investors are more interested in the profitability as well as long-term solvency of the business. Owners/equity investors expect income returns as well as value growth from their investments. Owners/equity investors want to make sure that they are investing in profitable ventures that will provide them with their income expectations through dividends and that if they decide to sell their investments they will be able to make a profit by selling their investments at a higher price than what they originally paid. Business profitability builds the value of the business and a company that continuously makes profit sustains its long term existence.

Short term liquidity is the short term staying power of the business; it is the ability of the business to pay currently maturing obligations; those that are due within one year from balance sheet date. A company may have so much asset to cover all its liabilities but if the assets are considered as non-liquid assets, the interests of short term creditors are prejudiced if cash is unavailable when the short term liabilities become due. Prudent financial managers must always make sure that maturing obligations are paid on time. Creditors are not willing to extend loans to non-paying or late paying customers. Once a business entity mismanages its cash, its credit rating suffers and it encounters difficulties in raising capital. If this happens, it becomes a high credit risk and if creditors extend credit to the business, it is at a much higher interest rate. Financing costs become more expensive. Short term liquidity ratios reflect that there are enough current assets to cover maturing short term liabilities at maturity date. **Working capital** is the difference between current assets and current liabilities. It is the amount available to fund the operations of the business after current liabilities are paid; it is the amount earmarked to pay for purchases of merchandise inventory for a merchandising business and raw materials for a manufacturing business and pay for all the expenses of the business. **Current ratio** is the most popular short term liquidity ratio. Current ratio is the relationship of current assets to current liabilities and it is computed by dividing total current assets by total current liabilities. In actual business practice, it is common to set a bench mark of 2:1 ($2 current assets for every $1 current liabilities). However, this bench mark may not be applicable to all industries. The higher the current ratio, the more favorable it is for short term creditors. **Quick ratio** or **acid test ratio** is a more stringent measurement of short term liquidity. The numerator includes only cash, marketable securities and accounts receivable. These are assets that are very easily convertible into cash. Merchandise inventory and prepaid expenses are excluded from the numerator. The numerator is divided by the total current liabilities to arrive at the quick ratio. Liquidity is also affected by how fast accounts receivables are collected and how fast merchandise inventories are sold. Companies want to collect credit sales and convert accounts receivable to cash as soon as possible. The efficiency of the collection department is measured by the accounts receivable turnover ratio and the number of days sales in receivables. **Accounts receivable turnover ratio** is computed by dividing net credit sales by the average accounts receivable. Average accounts receivable is equal to the sum of accounts receivable at the beginning and accounts receivable at the end of the period, divided by 2 ((accounts receivable, beginning + accounts receivable, end) / 2). The accounts receivable turnover ratio indicates the number of times during the period the company was able to roll over its accounts receivable and convert them back to credit sales. Number of days sales in receivable reflects how long the receivables remain uncollected and outstanding; it is also called average collection period in days. **Days sales in receivable** is computed by dividing 365 days by the accounts receivable turnover ratio. Companies want to have their accounts receivable at the lowest possible level; **the higher the accounts receivable turnover ratio the better it is**. The number of days sales in receivable is indirectly related to accounts receivable turnover. A lower accounts receivable turnover ratio results in higher days sales in receivable and vice-versa. Companies want to sell their merchandise as fast as they can. The efficiency of the sales department is measured by computing the merchandise inventory turnover ratio and the days sales in inventory. The inventory turnover ratio indicates the number of times during the period that the company was able to roll over its inventory and convert it back to cost of goods sold. The days sales in inventory shows the average number of days it takes to convert merchandise inventory to cost of goods sold, effectively, the average number of days it takes to sell merchandise inventory. **Inventory turnover ratio** is equal to cost of goods sold divided by average merchandise inventory. Average merchandise inventory is equal to the sum of merchandise inventory at the beginning and merchandise inventory at the end, divided by 2 ((merchandise inventory, beginning + merchandise inventory, end) / 2). **Days sales in inventory** is equal to 365 days divided by the inventory turnover ratio. **A high inventory turnover ratio** indicates good sales performance, meaning merchandise inventory are converted to cost of goods sold, effectively to sales at a fast pace. The inventory turnover ratio is indirectly related to days sales in inventory. A higher inventory turnover ratio results in lower days sales in inventory and vice-versa. **Cash-to-cash operating cycle** reflects the number of days it takes for the business to convert cash back to cash and it is the sum of days sales in receivable and days sales in inventory.

Solvency is the long-term staying power of the business; it is the ability of the business to obtain sufficient cash to pay long-term debts at maturity date. Long-term debts are obligations that mature beyond one year from balance sheet date. Owners/equity investors and creditors are both concerned about the solvency of the business. They are interested in ascertaining the degree of insolvency risk and profit stability. A business that becomes insolvent will not be able to pay its maturing obligations to the creditors and fail to pay income returns and provide investment growth to it owners/equity investors. Businesses that have proportionately higher liabilities in relation to owners' equity have a lot of pressure to pay interests and therefore have greater chances of suffering losses. **Total debts to total assets ratio** show the share of the creditors to the total assets of the business. Owners must have more stake than creditors in the assets of the business. If creditors have greater claim on the assets, it is a sign of poor financial health on the part of the business. Total debts to total assets ratio is computed by dividing total liabilities to total assets. It is the goal of businesses to have low total debts to total assets ratio; it means that the owners have more claims to the assets of the business than creditors. **Total debts to total equity ratio** shows the relationship between the claim of the creditors to the claim of the owners/equity investors in the business; it is computed by dividing total liabilities by total owners' equity. **Interest coverage ratio** is a measurement of how many times interest expenses will be covered sufficiently by operating income (net income before interest and taxes). Many companies establish interest coverage ratio of 5 times; but again bench marks do not apply uniformly to all companies. Interest coverage ratio is equal to net income before interest and taxes divided by interest expense.

Profitability is the ability of the business to make profits continuously. Owners/equity investors are focused on a company's profitability. If a business continuously suffers losses there is a high risk that it will not be able to operate over time because its working capital will eventually dry up. In due time it will close down and owners/equity investors will also lose their investments. **Gross profit ratio or gross profit margin** is the relationship between gross profit and net sales and it reflects what part of net sales is allocated to gross profit. Gross profit ratio is equal to gross profit divided by net sales. **ROE or Return on equity (stockholders' equity for corporations)** is the relationship between net income and owner's equity and it shows the amount of owners' equity needed to generate net income. ROE is equal to net income divided by average owners' equity. Average owners' equity is equal to (owners' equity, beginning + owners' equity, end) / 2. A high ROE is a good indicator of profitability. **Return on sales (ROS) or net profit margin ratio** is the relationship between net income and net sales and it shows the portion of net sales that goes to net income. ROS is equal to net income divided by net sales. **Return on assets (ROA)** is the relationship between net income and total assets and it shows the level of total assets needed to generate net income. ROA is equal to net income divided by average total assets. Average total assets is equal to (total assets, beginning + total assets, end) / 2. **Asset turnover ratio** is the relationship between net sales and total assets and it shows the level of total assets needed to generate sales for the period. Asset turnover ratio is equal to net sales divided by average total assets.

In order to evaluate the significance of calculated financial ratios they must be related or compared to other ratios. The calculated ratios can be compared to (1) the company's own historical ratios over a specific period of time; (2) rules of thumb established by the accounting profession or the business community and (3) ratios of other companies belonging to the same industry. The calculated ratios are merely numbers and without comparing them with other ratios, they are meaningless.

INDEX LIST

A
accountants 2
account codes 88, 89, 364
account form balance sheet 254, 260, 267, 270, 377
accounting 2, 359
accounting cycle 112, 365
accounting elements 19, 21, 361
accounting entries 119, 366
accounting period 112, 365
accounting principles 3, 6, 7, 8, 9
Accounting Principles Board 3
accounting process 84, 112, 365
accounting profession 2
accounting reports 252
accounting year 112, 365
accounts payable 20
accounts receivable 19, 21, 193
accounts receivable turnover ratio 334, 337, 383
account titles 88
accrual basis of accounting 167, 371
accrual of expenses and payables 173-178, 313-314, 371, 380
accrual of revenues and receivables 179, 311-312, 371, 380
accrued income tax 177-178
accrued interest 174-175
accrued rent 176-177
accrued salaries/accrued wages 175-176
accumulated depreciation 190, 373
acid test ratio 333, 337, 383
acquisition cost 190, 373
adjusted trial balance 152, 224, 369, 375
adjusting entries 119, 166-195, 367, 370, 375
adjustments 166, 224, 367, 370, 375
after closing trial balance 152, 369, 379
AICPA American Institute of Certified Public Accountants 3, 10
allowance for depreciation 190, 373
allowance method 193-194
analyzing transactions 21, 22, 84, 361
asset method 168, 371

assets 19, 86, 360, 362
asset turnover ratio 335, 337, 385
audited financial statements 3, 10
auditing 4, 359
auditor 4
auditor's report 10

B
bad debts expense 193
balance of account 122
balance sheet 119, 224, 258, 267, 367, 377
balance sheet accounts 282, 375, 378
balancing 95, 365
basic accounting elements 19, 360
basic accounting equation 19, 360
board of directors 6
bookkeeper 4
bookkeeping 4, 359
books of accounts 113
book value 190, 373
budget accountants 9
business ethics 329, 381
business transaction 84, 85, 361

C
calendar year 112, 365
capital 19, 21, 86, 361, 362
career opportunities 9
cash 19, 262
cash basis of accounting 167, 371
cash inflows 262, 377
cash outflows 262, 377
cash-to-cash operating cycle 334, 337, 384
certified information systems auditor (CISA) 10
certified internal auditor (CIA) 10
certified management accountant (CMA) 9
certified public accountant (CPA) 2, 3, 4, 10, 359
chart of accounts 88, 364
chief financial officer (CFO) 9
classified balance sheet 258
classifying 120, 368
closing entries 119, 282, 286, 367, 378

closing process 21
common-size financial statements 332, 382
comparative financial statements 332, 382
component percentage analysis 332, 346-348, 382
compound entry 113, 120, 366, 367
conservatism 6, 193
consistency 7, 359
corporate responsibility 330, 381
correcting entries 119, 367
cost 119, 367, 373
cost accountants 9
cost recovery principle 166, 370
credit 86, 362
credit balance 122, 363
credit footing 88, 364
creditors 5, 21
cross referencing 122, 369
current assets 19, 259, 360
current liabilities 259, 360
current ratio 333, 337, 383

D
days sales in inventory 334, 337, 384
days sales in receivable 334, 337, 384
debit 86, 362
debit balance 122, 363
debit footing 95, 365
decision makers 4
deferred revenues 181
depreciable cost 191, 374
depreciation 190, 373
depreciation expense 191
depreciation rate 190, 374
direct write off – cash flow statement 263-265, 378
direct write off method 193
disposal value 190, 374
dividends 21, 86
document reference 114
double entry accounting system 88, 363
drawing 19, 21, 86, 362, 367
dual entry accounting system 88, 363

E
employees 5
expanded accounting equation 19, 86, 360
expanded accounting equation chart 25
expense method 168, 372, 379-380
expenses 19, 21, 86, 119, 361-362, 367
explicit transactions 166, 370
expressed transactions 166, 370
equity statement 119, 257, 367, 376
external auditor 10
external users of financial information 4

F
FASB 3, 6, 262, 359
financial planning and forecasting 9
financial ratios 333, 350, 383
financial statements 2, 119, 252, 266, 367, 375-378
financial statements analysis 329-350, 381-385
financing activities 262, 377
fiscal year 112, 365
fixed assets 20, 360, 373
footing 95, 364
forensic accountants 10
four-column general ledger 121
full disclosure 7, 359

G
GAAPs 2, 6, 359
GASB 3
general accountants 9
general journal 113, 114, 366
general journal entry 113, 119, 366, 367
general ledger 113, 120, 366, 368
general public 5
going concern 6, 359
gross profit 335, 337, 385
gross profit margin 335, 337, 385
government accounting 3

H
horizontal analysis 332, 343-345, 382

I
implicit transaction 167, 370
implied transaction 167, 370
income and expense summary 282-283, 378-379
income statement 119, 224, 252, 266, 367, 375, 376
indirect method – cash flow statement 263, 378
Information Systems Audit and Control Association 10
Institute of Internal Auditor 10
Institute of Management Accountants 9
intangible assets 20, 190
interest coverage ratio 335, 337, 384
interest payable 20
internal auditor 10
internal users of financial information 4, 5
International Accounting Standards Committee 4
inventory turnover ratio 334, 337, 384
investing activities 263, 378
investors 5

J
journalizing 113, 366

L
labor unions 5
language of business 2
liabilities 19, 20, 86, 360, 362
liability method 181, 182, 184-185, 187-188, 373
liquidity 333, 337, 383
long-lived assets 20, 360, 373
long term assets 20, 360, 373
long term liabilities 20, 259, 360

M
management 5
management accountants 9
management advisory services 9
manufacturing business 253, 258
matching of costs and revenues 8, 166, 193, 360, 370
materiality 7, 359

memorandum entries 119, 367
merchandise inventory 19
merchandising business 253, 258
monetary measurement 8, 360
mortgage payable 20
multi-step income statement 253-256, 266-267

N
natural resources 20, 190
net profit margin ratio 335
nominal accounts 119, 282, 367, 378
normal balance of accounts 88, 363
notes receivable 21
notes payable 20

O
objectivity 8
operating activities 262, 377
operating cycle 258
operating income 335
outside directors 6
owner's equity 19, 21, 361

P
percentage of receivables 194
percentage of sales 194
periodic inventory system 282
permanent accounts 282, 283, 378
plant assets 20, 360, 373
post closing trial balance 152, 283, 287, 369, 379
posting 120, 368
posting reference 115, 116, 131, 369
prepaid expenses 19-20, 168-173, 308-310, 371, 379-380
profitability 333, 335, 337, 383, 385
property, plant and equipment 20, 360, 373
public accounting 359

Q
qualitative evaluation 329, 381
quantitative evaluation 329, 331, 381-385
quick ratio 333, 337, 383

R

real accounts 282, 283, 378
realization principle 9, 360
report form balance sheet 254, 261, 267, 269, 377
reporting period 112, 365
residual value 190
return on assets (ROA) 335, 337, 385
return on equity (ROE) 335, 337, 385
return on sales (ROS) 335, 337, 385
revenue method 181,183, 185, 188-189, 373
revenues 19, 21, 86, 119, 361, 362, 367
reversing entries 120, 307-314, 367, 379-380
rules of debit and credit 21, 22, 86, 87, 122, 361

S

sales journal 118
salvage value 190, 374
Sarbanes-Oxley Act 10, 330
scrap value 190, 374
Securities and Exchange Commission 10
separate business entity 7, 84, 359, 362
service business 253, 258
simple entry 113, 120, 366, 367
single-step income statement 253, 266, 268
solvency 333, 334, 337, 383, 384
source documents 112, 113, 120, 366, 367
sources of financial information 331
special combination journals 118
stable currency 8
statement of cash flows 252, 262-265, 367, 377
statement of owner's equity 119, 257-258, 266, 268, 367, 376
statement of partners' equity 119, 257, 367, 376
statement of stockholders' equity 119, 257, 367, 376
straight line depreciation method 190, 374
subsidiary ledger accountants 9
summarizing 151, 369

T

T account 91, 94, 95, 364, 369
tangible assets 20, 190, 373
tax accountants 9
temporary accounts 119, 282, 367, 378
three-column general ledger 121
total debts to total assets ratio 335, 337, 384
total debts to total equity ratio 335, 337, 384
transaction analysis chart 91, 93, 364
trend analysis 331, 382
trial balance 151, 369, 374

U

uncollectible accounts 193
undepreciated cost 373
unearned revenues 21, 181-189, 310-311, 372, 380
useful life 190, 373
users of financial ratios 4

V

vertical analysis 332, 340-342, 382

W

wages payable 20
wasting assets 20, 190
working capital 333, 337, 383
worksheet 224-226, 374-375

Printed in the United States
111652LV00006B/85/A